OXFORD MONOGRAPHS IN INTERNATIONAL LAW

The aim of this series is to publish important and original pieces of research on all aspects of international law. Topics that are given particular prominence are those which, while of interest to the academic lawyer, also have important bearing on issues which touch the actual conduct of international relations. Nonetheless the series is wide in scope and includes monographs on the history and philosophical foundations of international law.

RECENT TITLES IN THE SERIES

Institutionalizing State Responsibility
Global Security and UN Organs
Vincent-Joël Proulx

The Power of Process
The Value of Due Process in Security Council Sanctions Decision-Making
Devika Hovell

Jurisdiction in International Law
2nd Edition
Cedric Ryngaert

OXFORD MONOGRAPHS
IN INTERNATIONAL LAW

Irresolvable Norm Conflicts in International Law

Irresolvable Norm Conflicts in International Law

The Concept of a Legal Dilemma

VALENTIN JEUTNER

OXFORD
UNIVERSITY PRESS

OXFORD
UNIVERSITY PRESS

Great Clarendon Street, Oxford, OX2 6DP,
United Kingdom

Oxford University Press is a department of the University of Oxford.
It furthers the University's objective of excellence in research, scholarship,
and education by publishing worldwide. Oxford is a registered trade mark of
Oxford University Press in the UK and in certain other countries

First Edition published in 2017

British Library Cataloguing in Publication Data
Data available

Library of Congress Control Number: 2017944152

ISBN 978–0–19–880837–4

Meiner Großmutter

Preface

This book is based upon my doctoral thesis that I submitted to the Law Faculty of the University of Cambridge in the late summer of 2015. It is with great gratitude that I acknowledge the academic guidance and personal encouragement of my two supervisors, Julie Dickson and Roger O'Keefe. Julie's extremely detailed comments (always returned within a maximum of 36h!) and her jurisprudential expertise were instrumental in ensuring that I could realize and develop the theoretical aspects of the thesis and the book. I thank Julie for her kindness and for her words of wisdom whenever I found myself in times of trouble. Roger, in turn, ensured that I did not lose myself entirely in the jurisprudential ether and he did his very best to keep my feet on the firm ground of public international law. Roger's extraordinary sense of humour brought much light-heartedness to the otherwise rather gloomy world of irresolvable norm conflicts.

I also wish to thank the two examiners of my thesis, Maksymilian Del Mar and Michael Waibel, for a most instructive viva and for their various suggestions that helped me improve the manuscript significantly. At Oxford University Press, I thank three anonymous reviewers for their manifold observations and for the time they invested in reading and critiquing my work. Merel Alstein and Emma Endean-Mills guided me most helpfully through the entire publication process.

Without the generous financial support of various institutions and persons I would not have been able to carry out my studies and research. In this regard, I thank Gonville and Caius College in Cambridge for awarding me the WM Tapp Studentship, Harry Grundmann and Dirk Thelemann of the Hans Rudolf Foundation in Munich, Peter Carpenter of the Kurt Hahn Trust in Cambridge, Gunter Mengers of the Anglo German Club in Hamburg, the Ragnar Söderberg Foundation in Stockholm, the Friedrich Ebert Foundation in Bonn, Susanne Bostelmann and Stefan Kahle in Hamburg, and Eduard Berger in Dresden.

Throughout my doctoral studies, I benefitted greatly from uncountable conversations with colleagues and friends in Cambridge, Oxford, and beyond. In Cambridge, where my doctoral studies commenced, I would like to thank Pippa Rogerson and Jens Scherpe for their College guardianship and for curating the colourful community of lawyers at Caius. Daniel Clarry, Daniel Peat, and Matthew Windsor were illustrious members of that community and I thank them for their friendship and support. Tatyana Eatwell, Naomi Hart, and Odette Murray of the Reading Group provided most valuable feedback, especially at the early stages of the project. I also wish to thank Berk Demirkol, the PhD room's happiest inhabitant and my regular lunch companion.

In Oxford, where I completed the manuscript, I gratefully acknowledge Rebecca Williams and Ariel Ezrachi who welcomed me back to Pembroke College. Exactly nine years ago, it was in Pembroke that Rebecca and Ariel introduced me to the fabulous world of law and both of them have remained a source of good advice and encouragement. I thank Stefan Talmon for stimulating my interest in public international law and for having become a very trusted adviser on anything related (and on many things unrelated) to international law. Hannah Glover was a most agreeable office companion who made the intolerably high temperatures in our office (located above the College's boiler room) slightly easier to bear. For numerous jurisprudential exchanges, I also wish to thank Mikołaj Barczentewicz, Andrea Dolcetti, James Manwaring, Robert Mullins, and Leah Trueblood of the Jurisprudence Discussion Group. I thank Ryan Goss and Jeremias Prassl for frequently sharing their experience and expertise with me throughout the last few years.

The final stages of transforming the thesis into a book occurred in Lund where I was warmly received by new colleagues and friends. Ulf Linderfalk welcomed me to the proportionality research group and helped me navigate the early phase of postdoc life. Eduardo Gill-Pedro, Markus Gunneflo, Letizia Lo Giacco, Gregor Noll, and Anne Orford engaged most helpfully with various parts of my work. For the daily encounters and inspirations, I also wish to thank the residents of my corridor, Eduardo and Markus, Hans Liepack, Teresa O'Neill, Elin Osbeck, Amin Parsa, and Niklas Selberg.

I am particularly grateful to Nabila Abdel Aziz, Bart Smit Duijzentkunst, Benjamin Spagnolo, and to my brother Jonathan Jeutner. They carefully read the full manuscript in a most diligent and dedicated manner. Their comments, suggestions, and observations helped refine my arguments significantly. Christian Neumeier also read the manuscript in full. Not once or twice, but on a regular basis for about three years. I am extremely grateful for his patience and for his honest, perceptive, and constructive observations. It would have been difficult to complete the thesis and the book without Christian's continuous wise counsel and encouragement.

For cheering me up along the way, I thank my extraordinary siblings Anemone, Benedikt, and Jonathan. For being an inexhaustible source of stability and for raising me in a manner that allowed for dilemmatic thinking, I thank my parents Marie Anne and Thomas.

Finally, I thank my late grandmother Helga Subklew (1925–2009) for teaching me all of life's essential skills: reading, writing, swimming, and knitting. I dedicate the book to her memory.

Valentin Jeutner

Berlin
14 February 2017

Contents

Table of Figures and Table

Figures

Table

Table of Cases

PERMANENT COURT OF INTERNATIONAL JUSTICE

INTERNATIONAL COURT OF JUSTICE

COURT OF JUSTICE OF THE EUROPEAN UNION

OTHER INTERNATIONAL CASES

DOMESTIC CASES

Table of Treaties and Documents

TREATIES

UN DOCUMENTS

OFFICIAL DOCUMENTS

DOMESTIC STATUTES

Table of Abbreviations

ACHR	American Convention on Human Rights
AJIL	American Journal of International Law
ARSIWA	Articles on the Responsibility of States for Internationally Wrongful Acts
ASIL	American Society of International Law
BIT	Bilateral Investment Treaty
BVerfGe	Bundesverfassungsgericht
BYIL	British Yearbook of International Law
CJEU	Court of Justice of the European Union
CTS	Consolidated Treaty Series
CUP	Cambridge University Press
EC	European Communities
ECHR	Convention for the Protection of Human Rights and Fundamental Freedoms
ECtHR	European Court of Human Rights
EHRR	European Human Rights Reports
EJIL	European Journal of International Law
EU	European Union
EWCA	England and Wales Court of Appeal
IACtHR	Inter-American Court of Human Rights
ICC	International Criminal Court
ICCPR	International Covenant on Civil and Political Rights
ICESCR	International Covenant on Economic, Social and Cultural Rights
ICJ	International Court of Justice
ICJ Rep	Reports of the International Court of Justice
ICLQ	International & Comparative Law Quarterly
ICSID	International Centre for Settlement of Investment Disputes
ICTY	International Criminal Tribunal for the former Yugoslavia
ILC	International Law Commission
ILC Ybk	Yearbook of the International Law Commission
ILM	International Legal Materials
ILR	International Law Reports
ITLOS	International Tribunal for the Law of the Sea
ITLOS Rep	Reports of the International Tribunal for the Law of the Sea
LNTS	League of Nations Treaty Series
MLR	Modern Law Review
NATO	North Atlantic Treaty Organization
OED	Oxford English Dictionary
OJ	Official Journal of the European Union
OSPAR Convention	Convention for the Protection of the Marine Environment of the North East Atlantic
OUP	Oxford University Press
PCA	Permanent Court of Arbitration

PCIJ	Permanent Court of International Justice
RIAA	Reports of International Arbitral Awards
SOLAS	International Convention for the Safety of Life at Sea
TEU	Treaty on European Union
TFEU	Treaty on the Functioning of the European Union
UK	United Kingdom
UKSC	United Kingdom Supreme Court
UKTS	United Kingdom Treaty Series
UN	United Nations
UN Charter	Charter of the United Nations
UNGA	General Assembly of the United Nations
UNGA Res	Resolution of the General Assembly of the United Nations
UNHRC	United Nations Human Rights Council
UNSC	Security Council of the United Nations
UNSC Res	Resolutions of the Security Council of the United Nations
UNTS	United Nations Treaty Series
UNWC	United Nations Convention on the Law of the Non-Navigational Uses of International Watercourses
UP	University Press
US	United States of America
VCLT	Vienna Convention on the Law of Treaties
WLR	Weekly Law Reports
WTO	World Trade Organization
WTO DSU	WTO Understanding on Rules and Procedures Governing the Settlement of Disputes

Introduction

It was 09.23 on a wintry Wednesday morning when a rapidly approaching rocket appeared on Russian military radars. The Russian Missile Attack Warning System immediately activated the Russian president's nuclear briefcase.[1] The briefcase's screen indicated that the missile originated from the Norwegian Sea. It could be a surprise attack by NATO or the United States. Judging from the missile's trajectory Moscow was within its range.[2] All relevant command posts were put on alert. Four minutes after Russian radar operators first spotted the suspicious high-velocity object on their monitors, 4,700 Russian nuclear warheads were ready to launch at the president's command.[3] It was 09.27 on 25 January 1995.

Before any further action was required, it became clear that the rocket was not flying towards Russia. At 09.48, the missile, a Norwegian meteorological rocket, went down near the Norwegian island of Spitsbergen.[4] Exactly seven days later, on Wednesday, 1 February 1995, the International Court of Justice ('ICJ') fixed the time limits[5] in connection with the proceedings concerning the *Legality of the Threat or Use of Nuclear Weapons* ('*Nuclear Weapons Advisory Opinion*').[6] The UN General Assembly's request for an advisory opinion asked the ICJ whether 'the threat or use of nuclear weapons [is] in any circumstance permitted under international law'.[7] Although relations between NATO States[8] and Russia were strained at the time, few would have guessed just how current the question

[1] According to President Boris Yeltsin, this was the first time his briefcase was activated. See Vasiliy Kononenko, 'Yeltsin Leaves Chechnya Behind in Lipetsk, but Takes the "Black Attache Case" with Him' *Moscow Izvestiya* (Moscow, 27 January 1995) 1.

[2] Oleg Falichev, '"Iron Cucumbers" in Dangerous Orbits. Necessary Postscript to Norwegian Missile Incident (Interview with Lieutenant General Anatoliy Sokolov)' *Krasnaya Zvezda* (Moscow, 7 February 1995) 2.

[3] Peter Vincent Pry, *War Scare: Russia and America on the Nuclear Brink* (Greenwood Publishing Group 1999) 227.

[4] For an overview of the day's events, see this account by one of the chief designers of the Russian nuclear briefcase: Nikolay Devyanin, 'All that Has Happened, Alas, Had to Happen' *Moskovskiye Novosti* (Moscow, 31 January 1995) 1, 12.

[5] *Legality of the Threat or Use of Nuclear Weapons (Advisory Opinion)* (Time Limits) [1995] ICJ Rep 3.

[6] *Legality of the Threat or Use of Nuclear Weapons (Advisory Opinion)* [1996] ICJ Rep 226 ('*Nuclear Weapons Advisory Opinion*').

[7] United Nations General Assembly Resolution 49/75 K (15 December 1994) UN Doc A/RES/49/75 K [11].

[8] The term 'State' is capitalized throughout this book when reference is made to the legal and political entity to avoid confusion with other states (eg dilemmatic states).

was when the UN General Assembly had requested the advisory opinion on 15 December 1994.[9]

On Monday, 8 July 1996,[10] the ICJ rendered its advisory opinion.[11] The ICJ observed that it was uncertain which conclusions were to be drawn from the relevant legal principles, State practice, and the various conventions regulating nuclear weapons. Although the ICJ noted that the use of nuclear weapons was 'scarcely reconcilable'[12] with international humanitarian law, the ICJ also held that it could not 'lose sight of the fundamental right of every State to survival, and thus its right to resort to self-defence ... when its survival is at stake'.[13] Hence, a divided[14] ICJ concluded in paragraph 105(2)(E) of the advisory opinion that, while 'the threat or use of nuclear weapons would generally be contrary to the rules of international law', it

> [could] not conclude definitively whether the threat or use of nuclear weapons would be lawful or unlawful in an extreme circumstance of self-defence, in which the very survival of a State would be at stake.[15]

The exact meaning and implications of the *Nuclear Weapons Advisory Opinion*'s paragraph 105(2)(E) were a matter of dispute even among the different ICJ judges. For some,[16] the paragraph acknowledged that the threat or use of nuclear weapons

[9] Fewer still might have guessed that all nuclear weapon States are currently modernizing their arsenals (Stockholm International Peace Research Institute, *SIPRI Yearbook 2016: Armaments, Disarmament and International Security* (SIPRI Yearbook Series, OUP 2016) ch 16) and that, after a period of more amicable relations between NATO States and Russia, open nuclear threats would reappear on the agenda. Regarding a recent threat by Russia to Denmark, see Lars From, 'Ambassadør Advarer: Missilskjold Vil Koste Dyrt Og Give Mindre Sikkerhed' *Jyllands-Posten* (Viby, 20 March 2015).

[10] The advisory opinion was rendered almost exactly fifty-one years after the first explosion of a nuclear weapon (the 'Trinity Test') on 16 July 1945 at the White Sands Proving Ground, a United States Army nuclear testing site in New Mexico.

[11] *Nuclear Weapons Advisory Opinion* (n 6).

[12] *Nuclear Weapons Advisory Opinion* (n 6) [95].

[13] *Nuclear Weapons Advisory Opinion* (n 6) [96].

[14] President Bedjaoui and Judges Ranjeva, Herczegh, Shi, Fleischhauer, Vereshchetin, and Ferrari Bravo voted in favour of the paragraph. Vice-President Schwebel and Judges Oda, Guilleaume, Shahabuddeen, Weeramantry, Koroma, and Higgins dissented. Judge Andrés Aguilar Mawdsley died six days before the hearings of the case commenced.

[15] *Nuclear Weapons Advisory Opinion* (n 6) [105(2)E], [97]. With respect to the remaining operative paragraphs, there was little to no disagreement. Complying with the request for an advisory opinion (*Nuclear Weapons Advisory Opinion* (n 6) [105(1)]), the ICJ held (a) that neither customary nor conventional international law specifically authorized the threat or use of nuclear weapons (*Nuclear Weapons Advisory Opinion* (n 6) [105(2)A]); (b) that neither customary nor conventional international law contained a comprehensive and universal prohibition of the threat or use of nuclear weapons (*Nuclear Weapons Advisory Opinion* (n 6) [105(2)B]); (c) that a threat or use of nuclear weapons contrary to Article 2(4) of the Charter of the United Nations (Charter of the United Nations (adopted 26 June 1945, entered into force 25 October 1945) 1 UNTS XVI ('UN Charter')) and not falling within the provisions of the UN Charter's Article 51, relating to self-defence, is unlawful (*Nuclear Weapons Advisory Opinion* (n 6) [105(2)C]); (d) that a threat or use of nuclear weapons must comply with the international law applicable in armed conflict and specifically with the rules of international humanitarian law, and with the provisions of those treaties that specifically address nuclear weapons (*Nuclear Weapons Advisory Opinion* (n 6) [105(2)D]); (e) that there is an obligation to conclude negotiations leading to general nuclear disarmament (*Nuclear Weapons Advisory Opinion* (n 6) [105(2)F]).

[16] *Nuclear Weapons Advisory Opinion* (n 6), Separate Opinion of Judge Guillaume [9]; *Nuclear Weapons Advisory Opinion* (n 6), Dissenting Opinion of Judge Koroma, 558, 581; *Nuclear Weapons Advisory Opinion* (n 6), Separate Opinion of Judge Fleischhauer [6]. Less explicitly, *Nuclear Weapons*

could be internationally lawful 'in an extreme circumstance of self-defence, in which the very survival of a State would be at stake'.[17] In a hypothetical Cartesian coordinate system of law (see Figure IN.1),[18] these judges would have located the threat or use of nuclear weapons in such circumstances in the 'legality' quadrant.[19] Others considered paragraph 105(2)(E) to rule out the international lawfulness of any threat or use of nuclear weapons.[20] They would have placed the threat or use of nuclear weapons even in the extreme circumstances cited, in the 'illegality' quadrant. A third group, observing that paragraph 105(2)(E) did not 'give a signal either way',[21] neither prohibiting nor permitting the threat or use of nuclear weapons in the circumstances cited, would seemingly have placed such threat or use in the 'a-legality' quadrant.[22]

In contradistinction to each of these three views, this book argues that certain legal scenarios, including but not limited to[23] the threat or use of nuclear weapons, are best[24] described as being internationally legal and illegal at the same time. In other words, that they represent a state of 'legal superposition'[25] and should be located in the fourth quadrant of Figure IN.1. The position taken here is that such superimposed legal states result from irresolvable norm conflicts and give rise to legal dilemmas.[26]

Advisory Opinion (n 6), Declaration of Judge Ferrari Bravo, 283; *Nuclear Weapons Advisory Opinion* (n 6), Declaration of Judge Herczegh, 275; *Nuclear Weapons Advisory Opinion* (n 6), Dissenting Opinion of Judge Higgins [26], [29].

17 *Nuclear Weapons Advisory Opinion* (n 6) [105(2)E].

18 It would unquestionably be unduly formalistic to insist that all legal states could be represented by a Cartesian coordinate system. Many actions might defy classification altogether or will be situated in the borderlands between the different quadrants. The figure here merely aims to map the different positions of the judges in the *Nuclear Weapons Advisory Opinion* and to illustrate the fundamental difference between the states of a-legality and dilemmatic superposition.

19 See Figure IN.1. Priest utilizes a similar figure to illustrate the non-exclusivity and non-exhaustiveness of truth and falsity in paraconsistent logic. See Graham Priest, 'What's So Bad about Contradictions?' in Graham Priest, JC Beall, and Bradley Armour-Garb (eds), *The Law of Non-Contradiction* (OUP 2004) 26–7.

20 *Nuclear Weapons Advisory Opinion* (n 6), Dissenting Opinion of Judge Shahabuddeen, 376–7, 390–7; *Nuclear Weapons Advisory Opinion* (n 6), Dissenting Opinion of Judge Schwebel, 323–8.

21 *Nuclear Weapons Advisory Opinion* (n 6), Declaration of President Bedjaoui [14]. See also *Nuclear Weapons Advisory Opinion* (n 6), Separate Opinion of Judge Ranjeva, 303–4; *Nuclear Weapons Advisory Opinion* (n 6), Dissenting Opinion of Judge Weeramantry, 440, 495–6.

22 See also Vladen Vereshchetin, 'Is "Deceptive Clarity" Better than "Apparent Indecision" in an Advisory Opinion?' in Emile Yakpo and Tahar Boumedra (eds), *Liber Amicorum—Mohammed Bedjaoui* (Kluwer Law International 1999) 542.

23 See section B.1–5 of the Introduction for further examples of potentially dilemmatic norm conflicts.

24 See Part III for arguments defending the desirability of legal dilemmas.

25 The term 'superposition' is borrowed from quantum physics where it is used to describe a particle (eg an electron) whose state is suspended between two physical attributes. Schrödinger devised the most famous illustration of such a superposition state, involving a cat that is either dead or alive. See Erwin Schrödinger, 'Die gegenwärtige Situation in der Quantenmechanik' (1935) 23 Die Naturwissenschaften 807, 812. See also Serge Haroche and Jean-Michel Raimond, *Exploring the Quantum: Atoms, Cavities, and Photons* (OUP 2006) 19, 27, 70–1, 82.

26 Part I.A.1 considers the merits of describing such states as dilemmas compared to the utilization of the more technical term 'irresolvable norm conflicts'.

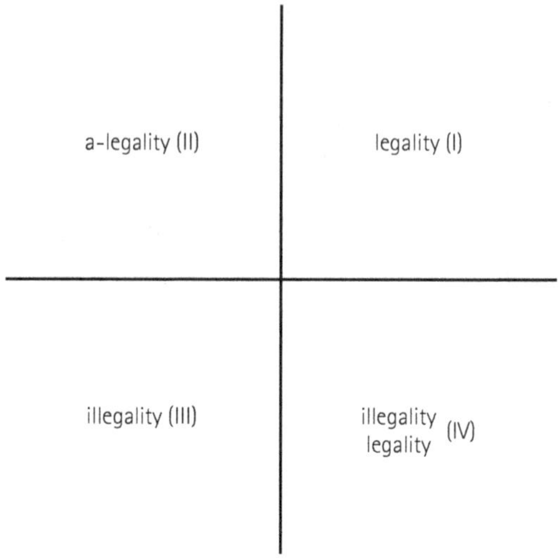

Figure IN.1: Legal states may be represented by a hypothetical Cartesian coordinate system making particularly apparent the distinctions between a-legality (the absence of law, Quadrant II) and illegality legality (a state of 'legal superposition', Quadrant IV) on which this book focuses.

A. Objectives

This book aims to identify the character and consequences of legal dilemmas, to distil their legal function within the sphere of international law, and to engender and contribute to serious theoretical and practical investigations into the conditions that lead to a legal dilemma. A legal dilemma, as conceived of in this book, exists when a legal actor confronts an irresolvable conflict between legal norms so that the application of one norm necessarily impairs the other.[27] Beyond this definition, the basic elements of a dilemmatic understanding of irresolvable norm conflicts include the acceptance of the inescapability of legal wrongdoing (irrespective of which response to the dilemma is adopted), the delegation of the competence to decide a dilemma to sovereign actors, and the acknowledgement of international law's limited ability to answer every legal question unequivocally. As Figure IN.1 illustrates, a legal dilemma thus conceptualized introduces a fourth legal quadrant into international law's coordinate system, making room for the existence of overlapping or 'superimposed' legal states. This book aims to show that an acknowledgement of the existence of such superimposed or 'dilemmatic' legal states and a thorough and nuanced understanding of their character in accordance with the book's proposal can

[27] This is an abbreviated version of the more nuanced definition introduced in Part I.A.2.

enhance international law's conceptual accuracy, and can lead to better substantive and more legitimate decisions.[28]

The proposed concept of a legal dilemma, crafted in pursuit of the aims of this book, is novel. Neither international nor domestic law has featured perspicacious and nuanced discussions of legal dilemmas that could compare with, for example, the voluminous and varied debates that the concept of a dilemma has triggered *inter alia* in theology,[29] moral philosophy,[30] or physics.[31] For sure, the debates surrounding (irresolvable) norm conflicts,[32] the question of international law's completeness and *non liquet* declarations,[33] or the 'political decision principle'[34] all relate to aspects of the concept of a legal dilemma. There is also an extensive amount of literature that discusses questions concerning, for example, law's indeterminacy, its inherent contradictoriness, law's vagueness, and normative disagreements. However, related though these issues are, they address questions that differ from those engaged by the concept of a legal dilemma.[35] In particular, compared

[28] See Part III.

[29] For an overview, see MV Dougherty, *Moral Dilemmas in Medieval Thought: From Gratian to Aquinas* (CUP 2011).

[30] For an overview, see Walter Sinnott-Armstrong, *Moral Dilemmas* (Blackwell 1988).

[31] The controversy concerning (in)deterministic understandings of the natural sciences championed initially by Pierre-Simon Laplace in the early nineteenth century and the later exchange between Einstein and Bohr on the (in)determinacy of quantum physics in many ways resemble the debates of the theologians and moral philosophers. See Pierre-Simon Laplace, *A Philosophical Essay on Probabilities* (Frederick Wilson Truscott and Frederick Lincoln Emory trs, Chapman & Hall 1902) 4; Albert Einstein, Boris Podolsky, and Nathan Rosen, 'Can Quantum-Mechanical Description of Physical Reality Be Considered Complete?' (1935) 47 Physical Review 777, 780; Albert Einstein, 'Physik und Realität' (1936) 221 Journal of the Franklin Institute 313, 342–3; Albert Einstein, Max Born, and Hedwig Born, *Briefwechsel 1916-1955* (Rowohlt 1972) 98; Niels Bohr, *Atomic Theory and the Description of Nature* (CUP 1934) 109; Niels Bohr, 'Discussion With Einstein on Epistemological Problems in Atomic Physics' in J Kalckar (ed), *Foundations of Quantum Physics II (1933-1958)* (Elsevier 1969); Stephen Hawking, 'Does God Play Dice?' <http://www.hawking.org.uk/does-god-play-dice.html> accessed 25 January 2017.

[32] See, eg, Joost Pauwelyn, *Conflict of Norms in Public International Law* (CUP 2003) 418 ff; Marko Milanovic, 'The Lost Origins of *Lex Specialis*: Rethinking the Relationship between Human Rights and International Humanitarian Law' in Jens David Ohlin (ed), *Theoretical Boundaries of Armed Conflict and Human Rights* (CUP 2016) 110.

[33] For the opinions of the chief protagonists of the debate, see Julius Stone, 'Non Liquet and the Function of Law in the International Community' (1959) 35 BYIL 124; Julius Stone, 'Non Liquet and the International Judicial Function' in Chaim Perelman (ed), *Le problème des lacunes en droit* (Bruylant 1968); Gerald Fitzmaurice, 'The Problem of Non-Liquet: Prolegomena To a Restatement', *Mélanges offerts à Charles Rousseau: la communauté internationale* (A Pedone 1974); Hersch Lauterpacht, 'Some Observations on the Prohibition of "Non Liquet" and the Completeness of the Law' in Elihu Lauterpacht (ed), *International Law—Collected Papers*, vol 2 (CUP 1975). This book argues that *non liquet* declarations relate to the a-legality quadrant of international law's coordinate system illustrated by Figure IN.1, and thus that they raise questions that differ from those raised by legal dilemmas. See Part I.A.3.d and Part II.C.

[34] Manfred Zuleeg, 'Vertragskonkurrenz im Völkerrecht. Teil I: Verträge zwischen souveränen Staaten' (1977) 20 German Yearbook of International Law 246, 267.

[35] See Part I.A.3. A notable exception is Leibniz's 1666 dissertation on 'Perplexing Cases in Law'. However, in accordance with the Zeitgeist of his epoch, Leibniz unequivocally concluded that irresolvable norm conflicts could not exist. See Gottfried Wilhelm Leibniz, 'Inaugural Dissertation on Perplexing Cases in the Law' in Alberto Artosi, Bernardo Pieri, and Giovanni Sartor (eds), *Leibniz: Logico-Philosophical Puzzles in the Law* (Springer 2013). More recently, Christófolo considered conflicts between *ius cogens* norms but, stopping short of accepting their irresolvability,

to recent studies of norm conflicts,[36] the book considers a more fundamental question concerning the relationship between a legal subject and a legal order[37] that crystallizes in situations when a legal order confronts legal subjects with seemingly impossible expectations.

It is difficult to establish the cause of international law's lack of interest in dilemmas with certainty. One reason might be that the concept of a legal dilemma, as examined in this book, challenges three fundamental assumptions about the function and operation of international law. In order to contextualize the forthcoming debates, it may be helpful to acknowledge these challenges here briefly.

First, legal dilemmas may appear to challenge the consistency, coherence, and completeness of the architecture of international law, by assuming that there can be contrary and contradictory[38] legal states that legal methods cannot resolve.[39] In this regard, the concept of a legal dilemma questions the '[assumption] that the history of international law is a progress narrative in which the trend is toward a more complete, coherent, and comprehensive system'.[40]

The first challenge implies a second directed at the competence of the architects who built and maintain the international legal order. The most important members of this group are judicial and sovereign actors.[41] If international law contains legal dilemmas, one might think that its guardians are either unable or unwilling to create an order free of dilemmas, or at least to rectify those dilemmas that are found to exist. This observation explains why dilemmas have been particularly controversial

concludes such conflicts could be solved by means of 'weighing and balancing'. See João Ernesto Christófolo, *Solving Antinomies between Peremptory Norms in Public International Law* (Schulthess 2016) 46–57, 324–8.

[36] See, eg, Pauwelyn (n 32); Dirk Pulkowski, *The Law and Politics of International Regime Conflict* (OUP 2014); Surabhi Ranganathan, *Strategically Created Treaty Conflicts and the Politics of International Law* (CUP 2014).

[37] This difference in emphasis is particularly apparent with respect to Ranganathan's recent study (Ranganathan (n 36)), since strategic treaty conflicts are instances where legal actors intentionally manipulate the legal system in the legal actors' interests. They are, in a sense, non-tragic, non-dilemmatic irresolvable norm conflicts since legal actors are entirely aware of what they are dealing with *ab initio*. Thus, strategic treaty conflicts lack the uncertainty concerning the retrospective assessment of their actions that makes a particular situation tragic. See also Søren Kierkegaard, *Fear and Trembling/Repetition* (Howard Vincent Hong and Edna Hatlestad Hong trs, Princeton UP 1983) 63.

[38] On the distinction between contrary and contradictory conflicts, see Part I.A.2.d.

[39] See Part III.

[40] David J Bederman, *The Spirit of International Law* (University of Georgia Press 2002) 100. Indeed, the modern idea of turning the study of (international) law into a science was arguably motivated by the desire to establish a harmonious order of consistent and coherent norms. See Mireille Delmas-Marty, *Global Law: A Triple Challenge* (Transnational Publishers 2003) 50; Antony Anghie, *Imperialism, Sovereignty and the Making of International Law* (CUP 2007) 49–51. See generally, David Sugarman, 'A Hatred of Disorder: Legal Science, Liberalism and Imperialism' in Peter Fitzpatrick (ed), *Dangerous Supplements: Resistance and Renewal in Jurisprudence* (Pluto Press 1991); Carlos Eduardo Alchurrón, 'On Law and Logic' (1996) 9 Ratio Juris 331, 348.

[41] In an attempt to explain why judicial actors generally refrain from *non liquet* declarations, Weil argues, eg, that '[l]awyers are quite understandably reluctant to admit that their discipline is imperfect. Judges, especially, are reluctant to find that they have no solution to the problem before them.' See Prosper Weil, '"The Court Cannot Conclude Definitively …" *Non Liquet* Revisited' (1998) 36 Columbia Journal of Transnational Law 109, 114. Similarly, Bedermann observes: 'International lawyers tend to abhor a juridical vacuum', Bedermann (n 40) 100.

in theological contexts, where they raise the question why God should create a system of norms with which, in at least some instances, humans cannot comply such that sin appears to be inevitable.[42]

In the contemporary legal world, which aims to disentangle morality, religion, and law to the greatest possible extent,[43] legal dilemmas might be even more problematic. Since human lawmakers are in principle competent to create and modify law, legal dilemmas are at once easier to avoid and more difficult to justify. Compared to theology or physics, for example, human legal thought creates, constitutes, and conditions the legal reality with which it subsequently engages. This means that potential systemic imperfections that one may tolerate as 'necessary' or 'God-given' in other contexts call for specific justifications in the realm of positive law. Many believers may find it difficult enough to accept the argument that God created a world in which sin is inevitable.[44] But few, if any, might agree that laws created by humans that make unlawful behaviour unavoidable could ever be desirable.

The third challenge concerns the practical consequences of legal dilemmas. Conceptual difficulties aside, one might argue that legal dilemmas are in practice unsatisfactory to the extent that 'dilemmatic declarations'[45] could impair law's dispute resolution function.[46] Further, legal dilemmas could supposedly lead to a 'denial of justice'[47] to subjects affected by a dilemmatic dispute. Confronted with a legal dilemma courts might, for example, withhold a definitive resolution of a legal dispute or issue dilemmatic decisions that may make it difficult for legal subjects 'to predict the reaction of official institutions to their behaviour and to plan their activity accordingly'.[48] Additionally, one might be concerned that the proposed[49] delegation of the decision-making competence to sovereigns could lead to unfettered decisionism,[50] which undermines the authority of law, and could entail otherwise undesirable consequences.

[42] Although the prospect of concluding that God created a world where sin was inevitable did prevent many Christian theologians from accepting the existence of genuine dilemmas, there are significant exceptions, such as Raymond Lull. See Dougherty (n 29) 108ff. Note also Bonhoeffer's approach to the concept of the '*Staatsnotwendigkeit*' discussed in his *Ethik*. See Dietrich Bonhoeffer, *Ethik* (Eberhard Bethge ed, 2nd edn, Christian Kaiser Verlag 1953). See also Part III.C.2.

[43] Martti Koskenniemi, *From Apology to Utopia: The Structure of International Legal Argument* (CUP 2005) 98–9.

[44] Dougherty (n 29) 27–8.

[45] The book uses the term 'dilemmatic declaration' as a term of art to refer to a court's declaration that a dilemma exists and that sovereigns are responsible for deciding it. See Part III.A.1.

[46] See Part III.B.3.

[47] In the domestic context, Luhmann observes, eg, that 'courts have to decide every case submitted to them. The corresponding norm is called … the prohibition of the denial of justice.' See Niklas Luhmann, *Law as a Social System* (Fatima Kastner and others eds, Klaus A Ziegert tr, OUP 2004) 284. See also, Christófolo (n 35) 7–8. For a discussion of the potential unfairness of legal dilemmas, see Part III.C.3.

[48] ILC, Report of the Study Group of the International Law Commission finalized by Martti Koskenniemi, *Fragmentation of International Law: Difficulties Arising from the Diversification and Expansion of International Law*, UN Doc A/CN.4/L.682 (13 April 2006) ('*Fragmentation Report*') para 52.

[49] See Part III.A.2.

[50] See Part III.C.2.

The book acknowledges that these challenges exist and that they are at least in some respects not insignificant. These and additional concerns relating to the desirability of the concept of a legal dilemma are addressed throughout and, in particular, in the final part.[51] These objections notwithstanding and in light of the extensive and continuing debates concerning dilemmas in other disciplines, this book's objective is to introduce the concept of a dilemma as a figure of thought and to discern to which extent this concept can reveal novel dimensions of legal reasoning that may help to reframe some of international law's most protracted and perplexing questions.

B. Overview

The book consists of three parts. Each part aims to answer one question in the pursuit of meeting the objectives defined above. The first question asks 'What is a legal dilemma?'. Thus, the first part provides a detailed definition of the concept of a legal dilemma in international law. By distinguishing the concept from related notions such as moral dilemmas, hard cases, legal gaps, or legal disagreement, the first part also demarcates the boundaries of the present enquiry. In particular, it emerges that the book considers the concept of a legal dilemma mainly within the realm of contemporary public international law. In principle, however, legal dilemmas can also arise in domestic law or, indeed, in any other normative system, like morality or divine law.[52] While a detailed consideration of legal dilemmas in other legal contexts is beyond the scope of the book, references will at times be made to domestic legal cases and scenarios to illustrate the potential relevance of specific arguments in that realm. Beyond these definitional aspects, the first part also considers particular factors, including fragmentation and imperfect drafting, that facilitate the emergence of legal dilemmas within the international legal order. Finally, this first part introduces a distinction between legal dilemmas responding to epistemological and metaphysical uncertainty and explains why this distinction matters.

The second part addresses the second question. Namely, 'Can legal dilemmas exist in contemporary international law?' In response to this question, the second part aims to identify the functional and teleological limits of contemporary legal means to resolve norm conflicts by establishing a compromise or priority between conflicting norms. These include the various traditional norm conflict resolution principles (*lex specialis, lex posterior*, and *lex superior*), proportionality tests, or conflict-of-laws approaches. Attempting to refine the contours of the concept of a legal dilemma further, the second part also considers the merits and

[51] See Part III.B–C.

[52] A key difference between international and domestic legal dilemmas is, however, that the sovereign subjects of international law are the architects of the legal order to which they belong. Thus, while international legal dilemmas are always also an invitation for States to reconsider the state of international law, the same does not apply in the domestic or moral sphere, where individual legal subjects or moral agents cannot as easily, if at all, modify the normative order to which they belong.

shortcomings of default rules and *non liquet* declarations, and of the norm conflict accommodation mechanisms provided for by the Vienna Convention on the Law of Treaties ('VCLT')[53] or by the International Law Commission's ('ILC') Articles on Responsibility of States for Internationally Wrongful Acts ('ARSIWA').[54] In the course of establishing the various limitations of international law's conventional devices to address norm conflicts, the book assumes an inherently deontological approach to international law, as traditionally understood. That means that the validity of legal norms and statements is generally established with reference to the ordinary standards of international law including the sources listed in the Statute of the ICJ[55] or the VCLT. It also means, and this is of particular importance in the context of any study of dilemmas, that consequentialist arguments are in principle denied any legal relevance.[56] For example, the quantity of potential victims of a nuclear attack is irrelevant for the purposes of establishing whether a norm conflict exists between a State's right to self-defence and the prohibition of nuclear weapons. Nor could other particular consequences of a nuclear attack be invoked in support of a legal recommendation to comply with either one of two otherwise irreconcilably conflicting norms.

Further, the second part does not seek to, and it would in any event be unable to, establish that legal dilemmas are a necessary legal phenomenon. In accordance with a particular world view, which might reject deontological approaches, or a world view based on particular assumptions concerning the function of law, it is perfectly possible to construct legal systems that are complete, closed, and systematically preclude the possibility of dilemmas. Since legal systems are artificial constructs, the architects of each normative system can of course opt to construe norm conflicts differently or simply forbid the possibility of their manifestation just like certain systems of logic simply prohibit true contradictions.[57] In contradistinction to such views, the book argues, however, that particular constellations of contemporary international legal norms are best understood as giving rise to dilemmatic

[53] Vienna Convention on the Law of Treaties (opened for signature 23 May 1969, entered into force 27 January 1980) 1155 UNTS 331.

[54] ILC, 'Articles on the Responsibility of States for Internationally Wrongful Acts' annexed to UNGA Res 56/83 (12 December 2001) UN Doc A/Res/56/83 ('ARSIWA') Arts 25(2)b, 24(2)a, 23(2)a. See also Sandra Szurek, 'The Notion of Circumstances Precluding Wrongfulness' in James Crawford and others (eds), *The Law of International Responsibility* (OUP 2010) 436.

[55] Statute of the International Court of Justice (adopted 26 June 1945, entered into force 24 October 1945) 1946 UKTS 67 Art 38(1).

[56] Nonetheless, it could be argued that the book's conceptualization of legal dilemmas and their consequences is *de facto* quite similar to a threshold understanding of deontology, which allows for a limited validity of consequentialist considerations, to the extent that the concept of a legal dilemma acknowledges that unlawful behaviour could be inevitable in certain situations.

[57] See Part III.B.1. With respect to the possibility of precluding the exception, Schmitt similarly observes that '[w]hether one has confidence and hope that [the exception] can be eliminated depends on philosophical, especially on philosophical-historical or metaphysical, convictions'. See Carl Schmitt, *Political Theology: Four Chapters on the Concept of Sovereignty* (University of Chicago Press 1985) 7. With respect to the possibility of eradicating moral dilemmas and incommensurable values, see Alasdair MacIntyre, 'Moral Dilemmas' (1990) 50 Philosophy and Phenomenological Research 367, 382; John Gray, *Isaiah Berlin* (Princeton UP 1996) 63.

circumstances. The book argues that a view which allows the architects and guardians of the international legal system to recognize legal dilemmas is preferable for the various reasons considered in the book's final part.

The final question, 'By whom and how should a legal dilemma be decided?' remains to be answered by the third part. Against the background of the shortcomings of contemporary strategies to deal with irresolvable norm conflicts established in the second part, the third part commences by introducing the book's central proposal for dealing with legal dilemmas. The proposal is formed of three elements consisting of a 'dilemmatic declaration' issued by judicial actors in response to the judicial identification of a legal dilemma, a sovereign decision, and the subsequent enforcement of any violated norm. Having set out the book's proposal, the third part proceeds to consider potential objections the proposal might attract both based on theoretical and practical grounds. By considering, qualifying or rejecting the objections that challenge the merits of a dilemmatic approach to irresolvable norm conflicts, the third part also seeks to show that legal dilemmas can play a beneficial and important role in the contemporary international legal order.

It should be remembered at this stage that the book's main focus is on the identification and elucidation of the key parameters of the concept of a legal dilemma. Thus, the book's third part concentrates on identifying the general principles that should guide the approach to legal dilemmas. It does not seek to offer recommendations regarding the resolution of particular disputes and it addresses only marginally the various specific rules of procedure of specific substantive regimes which legal dilemmas may engage. The decision to focus on an analysis of the metaphysical core elements of a legal dilemma is not informed by the view that the issues thus omitted from the scope of the book are not worthy of attention. Ultimately, there is no doubt that, if the concept of a legal dilemma is to have any subsequent practical relevance, these issues need to be addressed. However, for the purposes of triggering an initial debate concerning the principle desirability of legal dilemmas and the most suitable method of dealing with them, it is believed that something can be learned about the function of legal dilemmas and international law by postponing an engagement with the practical issues for a moment.

All parts refer at times to various examples and cases to highlight particular aspects of the concept of a legal dilemma and to illustrate the more abstract claims of this book. Five of the most frequently used scenarios will be introduced here for subsequent ease of reference.

1. Nuclear weapons

The book's prime example concerns the aforementioned regulation of the use of nuclear weapons in extreme circumstances of self-defence. According to customary international law[58] and Article 51 of the Charter of the United Nations ('UN

[58] *Military and Paramilitary Activities in and against Nicaragua (Nicaragua v United States)* (Merits) [1986] ICJ Rep 14 [176]; Robert Yewdall Jennings and Arthur Watts, *Oppenheim's International Law*, vol 1 (9th edn, Longman 1992) para 127.

Charter'),[59] States possess an 'inherent right' to self-defence. At the same time, 'intransgressible principles of international customary law'[60] stipulate that any use of force must not occur by means of weapons incapable of distinguishing between combatants and non-combatants. Support for these principles can also be found, *inter alia*, in Articles 48, 51(2), and 52(2) of the 1977 Additional Protocol to the Geneva Conventions.[61] Further, Article 23(3) of the 1907 Hague Regulations Concerning the Laws and Customs of War on Land[62] provides, *inter alia*, that any use of force must not 'cause unnecessary suffering to combatants'.[63]

In principle, this set of norms may appear to be unproblematic. However, a norm conflict can arise in an extreme circumstance of self-defence when a State cannot utilize its 'inherent' right to self-defence without, at the same time, utilizing weapons that cause unnecessary suffering or that are incapable of distinguishing between combatants and non-combatants. While the ICJ wisely refrained from speculating about the factual specifics of such a situation, one of the judges suggested extreme circumstances of self-defence could exist if a State faced 'untold suffering or the obliteration of a State or peoples'.[64] In a situation of this kind a State would need to choose between exercising its right to self-defence (thereby violating international humanitarian law), or honouring its obligations under international humanitarian law (thereby forgoing its right to self-defence and accepting any consequences this entails).[65]

2. Submarine warfare

The second example concerns the provisions of the 1922 Treaty relating to the Use of Submarines and Noxious Gases in Warfare ('1922 Submarine Treaty').[66] The 1922 Submarine Treaty had been negotiated to regulate the use of submarine warfare which had reached unprecedented levels during the recently concluded First World War. According to Article 1(1) of the 1922 Submarine Treaty, a submarine may destroy a merchant vessel if the merchant vessel 'refuses to submit to visit and search ..., or [if the vessel refuses] to proceed as directed after seizure'.[67] Further, a submarine may destroy a merchant vessel if the merchant

[59] UN Charter (n 15). [60] *Nuclear Weapons Advisory Opinion* (n 6) [79].

[61] Protocol Additional to the Geneva Conventions of 12 August 1949, and relating to the Protection of Victims of International Armed Conflicts (adopted 8 June 1977, entered into force 7 December 1978) 1125 UNTS 3 ('Geneva Conventions Protocol I'). See also Hague Convention (IV) respecting the Laws and Customs of War on Land and its Annex: Regulations concerning the Laws and Customs of War on Land (adopted 18 October 1907, entered into force 26 January 1910) (1907) 3 Martens (3d) 504 ('Hague Convention IV') Art 25.

[62] Hague Convention IV (n 61). See also Geneva Conventions Protocol I (n 61) Art 35(2).

[63] *Nuclear Weapons Advisory Opinion* (n 6) [78].

[64] *Nuclear Weapons Advisory Opinion* (n 6), Dissenting Opinion of Judge Higgins [18].

[65] For a discussion of conflicts between permissive and prescriptive norms, see Part I.A.2.d.

[66] Treaty relating to the Use of Submarines and Noxious Gases in Warfare (signed 6 February 1922) 25 LNTS 202 ('1922 Submarine Treaty'). Although all five contracting powers (France, Italy, Japan, the United Kingdom ('UK'), and the US) signed the 1922 Treaty, it never entered into force since France failed to ratify it.

[67] 1922 Submarine Treaty (n 66) Art 1(1).

vessel's 'crew and passengers have been first placed in safety'.[68] However, according to the Submarine Treaty's Article 1(2), submarines must 'desist from attack and from seizure and [must] permit the merchant vessel to proceed unmolested' if the submarine 'cannot capture a merchant vessel'.[69] Moreover, Article 4 of the 1922 Submarine Treaty notes the 'impossibility of using submarines as commerce destroyers without violating'[70] international law and imposes an express and unqualified 'prohibition of the use of submarines as commerce destroyers'.[71]

The result is an intentionally created legal framework that confronts submarine commanders and, by extension, those States to which a particular commander's acts are attributable,[72] with two conflicting norms: on the one hand, Article 1(1) authorizes the destruction of a merchant vessel under specific circumstances, namely when a merchant vessel refuses to cooperate and when the lives of the merchant vessel's crew and passengers have been placed in safety. On the other hand, Articles 1(2) and 4 outlaw the destruction of merchant vessels outright.[73] In a situation where a submarine has destroyed a merchant vessel that refused to cooperate and where the lives of crew and passengers were saved,[74] Articles 3 and 4 of the Submarine Treaty would bestow upon a State whose merchant vessel the submarine destroyed 'every right'[75] to try the submarine's captain as a pirate. Simultaneously, however, the State to whom the captain's actions are attributable would have the 'perfect right to claim immunity for [its] captain as acting under the rules of Article I ... in a perfectly legal ... manner'.[76] At least from a submarine commander's point of view, this norm conflict is of significant import, given that the violation of the treaty entailed the commander's punishment commensurate with that of a pirate: hanging.[77]

3. Military alliances

The third example relates to Egypt's conclusion of the 1950 Joint Defence Treaty ('1950 Treaty')[78] with members of the Arab League and Egypt's subsequent

[68] The original provisions of the 1922 Submarine Treaty are worded negatively ('must not be attacked unless' and 'must not be destroyed unless'), but the positive wording is chosen here to make the contradiction more apparent. See 1922 Submarine Treaty (n 66) Art 1(1).

[69] 1922 Submarine Treaty (n 66) Art 1(2).

[70] 1922 Submarine Treaty (n 66) Art 4.

[71] 1922 Submarine Treaty (n 66) Art 4.

[72] ILC, *ARSIWA* (n 54) Art 4.

[73] Holwitt observes in this regard: 'While the first article laid out rules that would allow submarines to capture or sink commerce, the fourth article would have prohibited submarines to sink any commerce at any time.' See Joel Ira Holwitt, *'Execute against Japan': The U.S. Decision to Conduct Unrestricted Submarine Warfare* (Texas A&M UP 2009) 33–4.

[74] For various hypothetical examples of situations of this kind, see Department of the Navy, 'An Attempt to Interpret the Treaty Entered into to Make More Effective the Rules Adopted by Civilized Nations for the Protection of the Lives of Neutrals and Noncombatants at Sea in Time of War' (General Records of the Department of the Navy 1900–1947, General Board 438, Box: 168, Entry 281 A-1, 13 February 1922) 11–14.

[75] Department of the Navy (n 74) 11.

[76] Department of the Navy (n 74) 11–12.

[77] 1922 Submarine Treaty (n 66) Art 3. See also Holwitt (n 73) 37.

[78] Joint Defence and Economic Co-operation Treaty Between the States of the Arab League (signed 13 April 1950, entered into force 22 August 1952) (1955) 49 AJIL Supplement 51.

conclusion of the 1979 Peace Treaty ('1979 Treaty')[79] with Israel. According to Article 2 of the 1950 Treaty, Egypt is obliged to 'go without delay to the aid of [Arab League Member States] against which ... an act of aggression is made, and immediately to take, individually and collectively, all steps available, including the use of armed force, to repel the aggression'. In its 1979 Peace Treaty with Israel, Egypt in turn undertakes to 'refrain from the threat or use of force, directly or indirectly, against [Israel, and to] settle all disputes between them by peaceful means'.[80]

If Israel attacks an Arab League member State, Egypt may thus find itself confronted with two potentially conflicting treaty obligations: an obligation to defend the members of the Arab League[81] against 'an act of aggression', including, if necessary, the obligation to use armed force pursuant to the 1950 Treaty, and an obligation not to use force 'directly or indirectly' against Israel, in accordance with the 1979 Treaty.[82] Egypt would need to decide whether to honour its obligation pursuant to the 1950 Treaty owed to the League members and to 'repel the aggression' by means of force, thereby violating Article 3(1)c of the 1979 Peace Treaty, or to prioritize its obligations to Israel under the 1979 Peace Treaty by refusing to come to the aid of the attacked League member State and thereby violating the 1950 Treaty.[83]

4. Canal treaties

A fourth example of a possible legal dilemma concerns Nicaragua's conclusion of the 1858 Cañas–Jerez Treaty[84] ('1858 Treaty') with Costa Rica and Nicaragua's subsequent conclusion of the 1914 Bryan-Chamorro Treaty ('1914 Treaty')[85] with the United States of America ('US'). Both treaties relate to the San Juan River, a border river between Costa Rica and Nicaragua that continues to invite controversy between the two States until today.[86] Article 8 of the 1858 Treaty provides that Nicaragua 'engages not to conclude any other contract on [canalization or transit of the San Juan River] without first hearing the opinion of the

[79] Peace Treaty Between the State of Israel and the Arab Republic of Egypt (signed 26 March 1979, entered into force 25 April 1979) 18 ILM 362 ('1979 Peace Treaty').

[80] 1979 Peace Treaty (n 79) Art 3(1)(c).

[81] At the time, the members of the Arab League were Jordan, Syria, Iraq, Saudi Arabia, Lebanon, Egypt, and Yemen.

[82] Koskenniemi calls the problem of tripartite military alliances '[t]he school example discussed by classical lawyers (Gentili, Grotius, Vattel)'. See ILC, *Fragmentation Report* (n 48) para 234.

[83] See also Binder, who observes that it is 'fairly clear' that 'the outbreak of hostilities between Israel and Egypt's Arab League partners could place Egypt under conflicting obligations', Guyora Binder, 'The Dialectic of Duplicity: Treaty Conflict and Political Contradiction' (1985) 34 Buffalo Law Review 329, 349.

[84] Treaty of Territorial Limits (Costa Rica–Nicaragua) (signed 15 April 1858) (1858) 118 CTS 439 ('1858 Treaty').

[85] Convention on Interoceanic Canal (US–Nicaragua) (signed 5 August 1914, entered into force 22 June 1916) (1914) 10 Bevans 379 ('1914 Treaty').

[86] For the latest instalment of the border dispute between Costa Rica and Nicaragua related to the San Juan River, see the ICJ's judgment in *Certain Activities Carried out by Nicaragua in the Border Area (Costa Rica v Nicaragua)/Construction of a Road in Costa Rica along the San Juan River (Nicaragua v Costa Rica)* 16 December 2015, ICJ General List Nos 150 and 152.

Government of Costa Rica concerning the inconveniences it might occasion to both countries'. The 1888 Cleveland Award, which interpreted the 1858 Treaty, expressly confirmed the validity and meaning of Article 8 by observing that the 1858 Treaty 'bound [Nicaragua] not to make any grants for canal purposes across her territory without first asking the opinion of the Republic of Costa Rica'.[87] However, in 1914, disregarding its obligation to seek Costa Rica's opinion on any contract concerning the 'canalization or transit of the San Juan River',[88] Nicaragua signed a treaty with the US to facilitate the construction of a new interoceanic canal 'by way of the San Juan River'.[89] Specifically, Nicaragua granted to the US Government 'in perpetuity ... the exclusive proprietary rights necessary and convenient for the construction, operation and maintenance'[90] of such an interoceanic canal. Nicaragua's conclusion of the 1914 Treaty was not only problematic because it occurred without consulting Costa Rica but also, and especially, because the 'exclusive proprietary rights' granted to the US were of such a nature that they necessarily impaired Costa Rica's rights.[91]

Consequently, Nicaragua confronted two conflicting contractual obligations: one concerning the obligation to honour the grant of 'exclusive proprietary rights' to the US by virtue of the 1914 Treaty and one concerning the obligation to rectify Nicaragua's violation of Costa Rica's rights in accordance with the 1858 Treaty. While Nicaragua's violation of Costa Rica's rights would continue for as long as the 1914 Treaty remained unchanged,[92] withdrawing from the 1914 Treaty would violate the rights of the US.

5. Distress at sea

A final example concerns the obligation of a ship master to provide assistance to persons in distress at sea.[93] According to Regulation 33 of Chapter V of the

[87] *Award of the President of the United States in Regard to the Validity of the Treaty of Limits between Costa Rica and Nicaragua of 15 July 1858 (Costa Rica/Nicaragua)* (1888) 28 RIAA 189 [10].

[88] 1858 Treaty (n 84) Art 8.

[89] 1914 Treaty (n 85) Art 1.

[90] 1914 Treaty (n 85) Art 1.

[91] In 1916, the Central American Court of Justice confirmed that Nicaragua's conclusion of the 1914 Treaty violated not only Costa Rica's right to be heard but also Costa Rica's territorial integrity, since, *inter alia*, the route of the canal in question 'necessarily implies the occupation of the Costa Rican shore'. See *Costa Rica v Nicaragua* (1917) 11 AJIL 181, 223.

[92] The US, aware of the 1914 Treaty's potential conflict with Nicaragua's prior commitments to other States, noted that 'nothing in the said Convention is intended to affect any existing right of' Costa Rica et al. See 1914 Treaty (n 85) Art 1. See also Philip Marshall Brown, 'Costa Rica v. Nicaragua' (1917) 11 AJIL 156, 157. The Central American Court held, however, that although the 'intention here ... is most noble and of high importance ... it is without efficacy in so far as it deals with the legal relations between' Costa Rica and Nicaragua. See *Costa Rica v Nicaragua* (n 91) 226–7.

[93] This is a legal emanation of the often-cited moral dilemma of the mother who has to choose which of her two children should be rescued in *Sophie's Choice*. See William Styron, *Sophie's Choice* (Random House 1979). For a discussion of the story's moral aspects, see Patricia S Greenspan, 'Moral Dilemmas and Guilt' (1983) 43 Philosophical Studies 117, 118; Mary Mothersill, 'The Moral Dilemmas Debate' in HE Mason (ed), *Moral Dilemmas and Moral Theory* (OUP 1996) 75; Verena Weber, *Tugendethik und Kommunitarismus: Individualität, Universalisierung, moralische Dilemmata* (Königshausen & Neumann 2002) 123.

International Convention for the Safety of Life at Sea ('SOLAS'),[94] the master of a ship is bound 'to proceed with all speed' to the assistance of persons 'in distress at sea'. A dilemmatic norm conflict could arise when a ship master encounters multiple persons in distress (person A and person B), and when the ship master's decision to render assistance to person A entails the impossibility of rendering assistance to person B. This might be the case if different groups or persons in distress are geographically separated (for example, if two different ships are in distress at the same time), so that the ship master can assist only one of them; if the physical space on the master's ship is limited, such that there is not enough space for all people in distress to be rescued; or if the speed with which a sinking ship submerges simply does not allow for the rescue of both A and B. In such a situation, the ship master faces obligations which the master cannot honour simultaneously.

In addition to these international law scenarios, the book will refer to two domestic examples that are structurally very similar to the *Distress at Sea* scenario. The first case, the *Hijacked Airplane* scenario, relates to proceedings that arose before the Federal Constitutional Court of Germany in response to the German Government's attempt to pass a law that would empower the German Government to shoot down a civilian airplane hijacked by terrorists intent on crashing the plane into a full football stadium. By attempting[95] to authorize the destruction of the airplane, the provision in question, Article 14(3) of the German Aviation Security Act,[96] arguably created a conflict between the Government's obligation to safeguard the right to life of innocent civilians on board the aircraft and to protect the right to life of the civilians on the ground.

The second example relates to decision of the English Court of Appeal in *Re A (Conjoined Twins) 2000*.[97] The case concerned a pair of conjoined twins where the organs of one twin were sustaining both twins. Unless the dependent twin were separated from the stronger twin by means of a medical operation, the death of both twins was both imminent and unavoidable. Separating the twins would lead to the certain survival of the stronger twin and to the certain death of the weaker twin. Thus, the question arose whether it was permissible to prioritize the right to life of one twin over that of the other.[98]

[94] International Convention for the Safety of Life at Sea (concluded 1 November 1974, entered into force 25 May 1980) 1184 UNTS 278. Similar obligations are imposed by International Convention on Salvage (concluded 28 April 1989, entered into force 14 July 1996) 1953 UNTS 165 Art 10; United Nations Convention on the Law of the Sea (opened for signature 10 December 1982, entered into force 16 November 1994) 1833 UNTS 3 Art 98; International Convention on Maritime Search and Rescue (concluded 27 April 1979, entered into force 22 June 1985) 1405 UNTS 119 ch 2.1.9–2.1.10.

[95] The attempt failed since a controversial decision of the Federal Constitutional Court of Germany declared the provision unconstitutional. See *Case Concerning the Aviation Security Act* (2005) Case No 1 BvR 357/05, BVerfGE 115, 118, [84ff] (German Federal Constitutional Court). See also Manuel Ladiges, *Die Bekämpfung nicht-staatlicher Angreifer im Luftraum: Unter besonderer Berücksichtigung des § 14 Abs. 3 LuftSiG und der strafrechtlichen Beurteilung der Tötung von Unbeteiligten* (Duncker & Humblot 2013).

[96] Aviation Security Act 2005 (Germany).

[97] *Re A (Children) (Conjoined Twins: Surgical Separation)* [2000] EWCA Civ 254, [2001] 2 WLR 480 (Court of Appeal of England and Wales).

[98] For commentary on the decision see, eg, Michael Bohlander, 'Of Shipwrecked Sailors, Unborn Children, Conjoined Twins and Hijacked Airplanes—Taking Human Life and the Defence of

The book will frequently return to and develop these examples as the book's argument unfolds. However, it should be noted that the examples are not meant to serve any evidentiary or precedential function. This means that the critique of a given example should not, without more, be accepted as a valid criticism of the core argument that the examples are meant to illustrate. For example, whether or not the regulation of nuclear weapons does constitute a legal dilemma in a particular case, in accordance with the meaning this book attributes to that term, would require a comprehensive analysis of the particular facts of a specific situation[99] that is beyond the scope of this book. Acknowledging the limitations of this and all the other examples, the book does not claim to establish the existence of any particular legal dilemma with certainty. Instead, and given that the book's main goal is to sketch the conceptual contours of legal dilemmas, certain factual situations will only be identified as being potentially dilemmatic. Definitive conclusions concerning specific norm conflicts would need to be worked out by future research.

Necessity' (2006) 70 The Journal of Criminal Law 147; Raanan Gillon, 'Jodie and Mary, Conjoined Twins: A Case of Judicial Moral Hubris?' (2004) 72 Medico-Legal Journal 3.

[99] Similarly, Del Mar observes that there is 'no such thing as an identifiable normative conflict that operates in isolation from the manner in which some sets of facts are constructed … Put another way, the positing of a normative conflict arises only when we establish the same factual platform'. See Maksymilian Del Mar, 'System Values and Understanding Legal Language' (2008) 21 Leiden Journal of International Law 29, 50–1.

Part I

The Definition of a Legal Dilemma

This part aims to answer the book's first question: 'What is a Legal Dilemma?' It frames the book's analysis by defining the term legal dilemma and by distinguishing the term from numerous related concepts (Section A). The first part also considers the circumstances that increase the potential frequency with which dilemmas may arise (Section B). Finally, this part introduces a distinction between dilemmas responding to epistemic undecidability and to metaphysical undecidability (Section C).

A. The Definition of a Legal Dilemma

This section defines the term legal dilemma and its constitutive components as a term of art. The first sub-section considers the merits of the term dilemma compared to the more technical concept of norm conflicts. It also acknowledges that the definition of a legal dilemma proffered here is a stipulative definition and explains how the adequacy of stipulative definitions should be assessed. The second sub-section then posits and elaborates upon the definition itself while the third sub-section distinguishes legal dilemmas from related concepts.

1. Terminology

The decision to name the concept under discussion 'legal dilemma' is a conscious choice,[1] based on a particular understanding of the problems posed by what is otherwise referred to as an irreconcilable,[2] unresolvable[3] or unavoidable[4] norm

[1] Agamben observes that 'terminology is the properly poetic moment of thought' and that 'terminological choices can never be neutral'. See Giorgio Agamben, *State of Exception* (University of Chicago Press 2008) 4.

[2] Joost Pauwelyn, *Conflict of Norms in Public International Law* (CUP 2003) 422; Anna Wyrozumska, 'Poland' in Dinah Shelton (ed), *International Law and Domestic Legal Systems* (OUP 2011) 490.

[3] Marko Milanovic, 'Norm Conflicts, International Humanitarian Law and Human Rights Law' in Orna Ben-Naftali (ed), *International Humanitarian Law and International Human Rights Law* (OUP 2011) 98, 107; Pauwelyn (n 2) 152.

[4] Milanovic (n 3) 108; Antonios Tzanakopoulos, 'Collective Security and Human Rights' in Erika de Wet and Jure Vidmar (eds), *Hierarchy in International Law: The Place of Human Rights* (OUP 2012) 58.

conflict, an inconvenience,[5] incompatibility,[6] or repugnancy.[7] The term 'legal dilemma' is chosen because it is associated with three particular aspects that are of specific importance to this book's argument.

First, the term legal dilemma approaches an underlying norm conflict from a holistic perspective. Compared to the notion of norm conflict (however defined), which implies a focus on the individual atomistic elements (norms) that trigger a particular norm conflict, legal dilemmas conceptualize underlying norm conflicts holistically, as a situational phenomenon on its own terms rather than as a fragmented, disparate constellation defined by and exclusively composed of its constitutive norms.[8] Used and understood in this more holistic sense, the term dilemma recognizes an underlying unity of the two or more conflicting prongs of an irresolvable norm conflict. This matters, because it avoids a binary characterization of norm conflicts and facilitates the identification and adoption of novel responses to legal norm conflicts. While conventional studies of norm conflicts assume an 'either-or' approach, the study of norm conflicts in dilemmatic terms is marked by an 'as-well-as' attitude. To illustrate, consider the *Distress at Sea* scenario where the ship master encounters multiple persons (A, B) in distress and is unable to render assistance to all imperilled persons. Describing such a situation as a conflict between the ship master's duty to rescue A and the ship master's duty to rescue B identifies the respective norms and stakeholders primarily by reference to the fact that they are in conflict, that they oppose each other. Describing such a situation as a dilemma subtly shifts the emphasis to a more holistic level that identifies the respective norms and stakeholders by reference to the fact that they form part of the same dilemmatic situation, that they collectively constitute a particular dilemma. The term dilemma thus expresses a relationship between two conflicting norms that is not only defined by competition and conflict but also by a shared fate of forming part of a particular dilemma.[9] In this sense, the term recognizes and reflects the paradoxical communion of those norms that mutually exclude each other.[10]

Second, compared to the more technical terms mentioned above, the term dilemma entails a notion of distress or crisis. Indeed, distress and dilemma share a prefix that indicates a tension between two or more poles: *dis-* (apart); *di-* (two).[11]

[5] Lon L Fuller, *The Morality of Law* (rev edn, Yale UP 1969) 69. [6] Fuller (n 5) 69.

[7] Jeremy Bentham, *The Limits of Jurisprudence Defined, Being Part Two of an Introduction to the Principles of Morals and Legislation* (Columbia UP 1945) 195–8. See also Fuller (n 5) 69.

[8] With reference to the related concept of the paradox, Hagenbüchle similarly observes that '[w]hile we can tolerate the thesis within the antithesis in the dialectical process, the contradiction in the paradox requires more radical endurance, because that which is mutually exclusive is—janiform—simultaneously connected in a remarkable manner.' See Roland Hagenbüchle, 'Was heißt "paradox"? Eine Standortbestimmung' in Roland Hagenbüchle and Paul Geyer (eds), *Das Paradox: eine Herausforderung des abendländischen Denkens* (2nd edn, Königshausen & Neumann 2002) 39 (tr by author).

[9] This is particularly beneficial in dilemmatic disputes involving several parties, when a declaration to the effect that each party's claim is equally strong can trigger renewed efforts to find mutually beneficial solutions to a particular conflict. See text to notes 203–206 in Part III.A.3.a.

[10] See also Hagenbüchle (n 8) 39.

[11] The etymological link is even stronger in German, where the term '*Verzweiflung*' (despair) contains the number two ('*zwei*'). Rhodes makes a similar observation regarding the Danish term for

This association is intended not just because it might capture the state of mind of a decision-maker responsible for deciding a particular dilemma, for example in the *Nuclear Weapons* scenario, but also because it expresses a systemic double consciousness that confronts international law and its actors with their own limitations in dilemmatic circumstances.

Finally, the term dilemma is chosen due to its connotations as a threshold concept, which crystallizes in the borderlands between the contradictions of different disciplines, normative spheres, norms, legal actors. This transcendental[12] dimension of a legal dilemma in its own right is lost to the more technical or descriptive terms above, which do not as obviously acknowledge the inter- and intra-systemic significance of the concept of a dilemma. For these reasons, the book favours the term 'legal dilemma' over the term 'irresolvable norm conflict'.[13]

The term legal dilemma has not previously been defined. Rather, it has been used loosely to refer to difficult legal questions or hard cases.[14] Departing from the conventional use of the term, this book prescribes a more precise, stipulative[15]—as opposed to descriptive[16]—definition[17] of a legal dilemma.

Descriptive definitions determine the meaning of a given term in a particular context based on common usage of the term in that same context.[18] They '[identify] what certain persons meant by a certain word at a certain less or more specified time and place'.[19] Stipulative definitions, in contrast, prescribe that a given term should have a specific meaning. While this meaning may be related to the actual use of a term, it could also represent an artificial construct.[20]

Consequently, descriptive definitions can be true or false to the extent that they accurately reflect the actual use of a term. Stipulative definitions, however, do not possess a truth-value.[21] Thus, authors of stipulative definitions

despair '*Fortvilelse*' where '*tvi*' refers to the number two. See Richard Rhodes, *The Making of the Atomic Bomb* (Simon & Schuster 1986) 61.

[12] Luhmann makes a similar observation concerning legal paradoxes. He notes that paradoxes 'take the place of the transcendental subject, to which Kant and his successors had attributed direct access to unconditioned, a priori valid knowledge'. See Niklas Luhmann, *Die Religion der Gesellschaft* (André Kieserling ed, Suhrkamp 2000) 132 (tr by Gunther Teubner, 'Dealing with Paradoxes of Law: Derrida, Luhmann, Wiethölter' in Oren Perez and Gunther Teubner (eds), Ian L Fraser (tr), *Paradoxes and Inconsistencies in the Law* (Hart 2006) 47).

[13] However, in more technical contexts, especially when considering international law's different norm conflict resolution devices in Part II, alternative labels may at times be used in order to relate to conventional discussions of norm conflicts.

[14] See Part I.A.3 on legal dilemmas and related concepts.

[15] Richard Robinson, *Definition* (Clarendon Press 1950) 59. Others use the terms 'prescriptive' (Ota Weinberger, *Rechtslogik* (Duncker & Humblot 1989) 360) or 'synthetic' (Ulrich Klug, *Juristische Logik* (Springer-Verlag 1982) 107; Erich Vranes, 'The Definition of "Norm Conflict" in International Law and Legal Theory' (2006) 17 EJIL 395, 396) to refer to stipulative definitions.

[16] Weinberger (n 15) 360. Others use the terms 'analytical' (Klug (n 15) 107; Vranes (n 15) 396) and 'lexical' (Robinson (n 15) 35) to refer to descriptive definitions.

[17] On the nature of definitions generally, see Weinberger (n 15) 358–9; Vranes (n 15) 396; Walter Dubislav, *Die Definition* (3rd edn, Felix Meiner 1931).

[18] Weinberger (n 15) 360. [19] Robinson (n 15) 35.

[20] Robinson (n 15) 59; Klug (n 15) 103; Vranes (n 15) 397; Weinberger (n 15) 360.

[21] Robinson (n 15) 39, 63; Weinberger (n 15) 360; Klug (n 15) 107; Jürgen Rödig, *Die Denkform der Alternative in der Jurisprudenz* (Springer-Verlag 1969) 3; Vranes (n 15) 397.

enjoy significantly more flexibility with respect to the definitions they craft.[22] Nonetheless, stipulative definitions do not entirely escape critical assessment. Apart from the general requirements that definitions need to satisfy,[23] stipulative definitions are judged by reference to teleological considerations.[24] This means that the adequacy of a stipulative definition should be assessed based on the stipulated definition's ability to capture or express what it was designed to capture or express.[25]

Given that this book introduces legal dilemmas as a novel term of art, there is no existing usage with which the definition could or should be directly associated. The following definition is thus a stipulative definition, which cannot be assessed on a truth-value scale but must, rather, be evaluated by reference to its utility in adequately capturing, communicating, and bringing into focus the phenomenon of international law that this book conceptualizes as a legal dilemma. The following stipulative definition is, then, the necessary first step in articulating the problem under review and identifying the best methodology for dealing with legal dilemmas.

2. The definition of a legal dilemma

A legal dilemma exists when an actor confronts an irresolvable and unavoidable conflict between at least two legal norms so that obeying or applying one norm necessarily entails the undue impairment of the other.[26]

Each element of the definition will be considered in turn.

a) An actor

For the purposes of this book, which investigates the concept of legal dilemmas in public international law, the relevant legal actors comprise only sovereign States, as represented by officials of a State acting in that capacity.[27] The element of the actor

[22] Dubislav (n 17) 21.

[23] Definitions should be precise and clear, free from contradictions and ambiguity; they should contain all essential elements of the defined object and they should be positively worded. See Weinberger (n 15) 368–71; Vranes (n 15) 397; Rödig (n 21) 3; Egon Schneider, *Logik für Juristen: die Grundlagen der Denklehre und der Rechtsanwendung* (Vahlen 2006) 51–4; Robinson (n 15) 80–92.

[24] Karl Engisch, 'Logische Überlegungen zur Verbrechensdefinition' in Paul Bockelmann, Arthur Kaufmann, and Ulrich Klug (eds), *Beiträge zur Rechtstheorie* (Vittorio Klostermann 1984) 161; Weinberger (n 15) 360; Vranes (n 15) 397; Ulrich Klug, 'Der Handlungsbegriff des Finalismus als methodologisches Problem' in Ulrich Klug (ed), *Philosophie und Recht—Festschrift zum 70. Geburtstag von Carl August Emge* (Franz Steiner 1960) 41; Albert Einstein, 'Physik Und Realität' (1936) 221 Journal of the Franklin Institute 313, 313, 315, 318.

[25] See also Vranes (n 15) 397.

[26] This is a modified version of the definition of a norm conflict by Vranes: 'There is a conflict between norms, one of which may be permissive, if in obeying or applying one norm, the other norm is necessarily or potentially violated.' See Vranes (n 15) 418.

[27] In principle, however, an actor could be any natural or legal person legally competent to make decisions and there is no reason to suppose that legal dilemmas may not also exist in other legal contexts, such as private international or domestic law.

is important since it reduces an abstract norm conflict to a concrete legal problem.[28] The actor's identity and location determine the factual and legal parameters[29] that influence the availability and utility of norm conflict avoidance techniques and resolution devices.[30]

The decision to limit the class of actors to States is based on States' still more or less exclusive privilege to create international legal norms.[31] Nonetheless, while, strictly speaking, only sovereigns can ultimately decide dilemmas, this book examines legal dilemmas through the lenses of judicial actors, such as international judges or arbitrators,[32] who are, in accordance with this book's argument, not charged with the responsibility for deciding, but rather with identifying, legal dilemmas in judicial settings. The analysis of legal dilemmas from a judicial point of view is most instructive for a consideration of the legal significance of legal dilemmas. However, the question of how sovereigns should eventually decide legal dilemmas is ultimately not a question that law or judicial actors can answer unequivocally.

Finally, the definition's focus on one actor facing a dilemma is not meant to exclude the possibility that a dilemma may arise, for instance, with respect to obligations that one actor owes to a second or third actor rather than the legal order itself. Indeed, many, if not all, one-person dilemmas can be construed as affecting other legal actors to the extent that almost every act engages other actors, directly or indirectly.[33] For example, while the conflicting norms in the *Nuclear Weapons* scenario do not derive from bilateral obligations, the consequences of a State's decision to utilize its right to self-defence are undoubtedly felt by other States. Likewise, the decisions of States facing conflicting treaty obligations of the kind involved in the *Canal Treaties* or *Military Alliances* scenarios engage at least the interests of those States party to the conflicting treaties. However, for the purposes of a jurisprudential analysis of the character of a legal dilemma, it is often sufficient to focus on the relationship of law and legal actors rather than the relationship of legal actors *inter se*. Nonetheless, inter-actor concerns are considered throughout this book and they play a particularly important role when new solutions to a given norm conflict need to be found once a given dilemma has arisen.[34]

[28] Alfred Verdross, 'Eine Antinomie der Rechtstheorie' in Hans R Klecatsky (ed), *Die Wiener Rechtstheoretische Schule* (Franz Steiner 2010) 1124. See also Hans Kelsen, 'Was ist ein Rechtsakt?' in Hans R Klecatsky (ed), *Die Wiener Rechtstheoretische Schule* (Franz Steiner 2010) 1129–32.

[29] Ronald P Loui, 'Alchurrón and von Wright on Conflict among Norms' in Donald Nute (ed), *Defeasible Deontic Logic* (Kluwer 1997) 350.

[30] See also Rödig on the importance of determining the time-space coordinates in the context of identifying alternatives, Rödig (n 21) 19. See further, Thomas Cornides, *Ordinale Deontik: Zusammenhänge zwischen Präferenztheorie, Normlogik und Rechtstheorie* (Springer-Verlag 1974) 143.

[31] For reasons that will become apparent later (see Part III.C.3), legal dilemmas confronting sovereign actors are slightly easier to justify than legal dilemmas confronting non-sovereign actors.

[32] Matthew Windsor has pointed out that legal advisors of governments can also face legal dilemmas. While their role is not considered in this work, it is hoped that the analysis offered here with respect to judges might, at least to some extent, be applicable to legal advisors as well. Comment from Matthew Windsor to author (23 June 2014).

[33] Ruth Barcan Marcus, 'Moral Dilemmas and Consistency' (1980) 77 The Journal of Philosophy 121, 122.

[34] See Part III.A.3.a. See also Part III.A.1.

b) Two legal norms

Conventionally, given the term's etymology,[35] discussions of dilemmas focus on the tension between two conflicting norms.[36] However, from an actor's point of view, the nature of the undecidability[37] that dilemmas entail, does not differ from the undecidability of polylemmas (trilemmas, for example)—except to the extent that an analysis of polylemmas requires the consideration of more pieces of information. With respect to the *Canal Treaties* case, for example, the nature of the issues involved would not have changed even if, in addition to Costa Rica, El Salvador, and Honduras, who also protested against the 1914 Nicaragua–US Treaty,[38] had intervened to assert their interests. In that case, Nicaragua could have faced conflicting obligations to four parties. However, attempts to ascertain the existence of irresolvable norm conflicts in that case would be undertaken in accordance with the same principles that govern conflicts between two norms. Thus, while the book focuses on dilemmas emerging from a conflict between two norms only, the same considerations could also apply *ceteris paribus* to polylemmas.

c) Legal norms

'Legal norms' refers to irreducible, concretized international legal norms of conduct. Norms of conduct are conventional or customary norms,[39] as defined by Article 38(1) of the ICJ Statute, that make a given course of conduct obligatory, permissible, or impermissible.[40] The reference to conduct norms is construed broadly, so as to include competence norms[41] and legal rules or principles[42] (including the general principles of law referred to by the ICJ Statute)[43] to the extent that they

[35] The word dilemma originates from the Greek dilēmma, 'from di- "twice" + lēmma "premise."'. See 'dilemma, n.' (*OED Online*, OUP December 2016) <http://www.oed.com/view/Entry/52772> accessed 27 January 2017.

[36] MV Dougherty, *Moral Dilemmas in Medieval Thought: From Gratian to Aquinas* (CUP 2011) 24; Daniel Statman, *Moral Dilemmas* (Rodopi 1995) 5–6.

[37] See also Part I.C.

[38] See Philip Marshall Brown, 'Costa Rica v. Nicaragua' (1917) 11 AJIL 156, 158.

[39] It is important to note that norm conflicts arise both among norms of the same source (eg two customary norms) and across different sources (eg conflicts between customary and conventional norms). See also Robert Kolb, 'Conflits Entre Normes de Jus Cogens' in Nicolas Angelet and others (eds), *Droit du pouvoir, pouvoir du droit: mélanges offerts à Jean Salmon* (Bruylant 2007) 483.

[40] The modes of conduct norms coincide with the three deontic modalities of deontic logic: Georg Henrik von Wright, 'Deontic Logic' (1951) 60 Mind 1, 1; Vranes (n 15) 398; Eugenio Bulygin, 'On Norms of Competence' (1992) 11 Law and Philosophy 201, 210, 211.

[41] Vranes (n 15) 415–18; Gerard Conway, 'Conflicts of Competence Norms in EU Law and the Legal Reasoning of the ECJ' (2010) 11 German Law Journal 966, 973; Bulygin (n 40) 202–3; Hans Kelsen, *Reine Rechtslehre* (Deuticke 1960) 150. It is not always easy to identify whether one deals with a competence norm or a conduct norm. See Bulygin (n 40) 215. See also John Gardner, 'Hart and Feinberg on Responsibility' in Matthew Kramer and others (eds), *The Legacy of H.L.A. Hart: Legal, Political and Moral Philosophy* (OUP 2008) 126.

[42] James W Harris, 'Kelsen and Normative Consistency' in Richard Tur and William L Twining (eds), *Essays on Kelsen* (Clarendon Press 1986) 224–6.

[43] Statute of the International Court of Justice (adopted 26 June 1945, entered into force 24 October 1945) 1946 UKTS 67 ('ICJ Statute') Art 38(1)(c).

entail irreducible conduct norms.[44] Conduct norms are irreducible once they, their scope, and their status have been identified[45] and once they are reduced to concrete provisions and applied to specific facts by means of interpretation.[46]

Interpretation is particularly crucial in the international legal context, where uncertainty frequently surrounds the existence, content, and applicability of legal norms.[47] As norm conflicts arise only between irreducible norms, norm interpretation precedes the identification of a norm conflict.[48] The operation and limits of international legal interpretation are considered here briefly and only in relevant part.[49]

Interpretation of norms in international law identifies the meaning of a given text with reference to one or all of the following: the words used in a text, the text's purpose, the author's intentions, or the text's conformity with previous practice.[50] In the international legal context, Articles 31–32 of the 1969 Vienna Convention on the Law of Treaties ('VCLT'),[51] which reflect customary international law,[52] encapsulate these different approaches.[53] Articles 31 and 32 provide:

[44] Norms not concretely applied could, of course, also conflict irreconcilably with each other. However, such conflicts raise issues of a more abstract kind (see, eg, Part 1.A.3.e.), compared to the concrete problems to which legal dilemmas relate. Note, further, that the focus on conflicting norms does not ignore that norm conflicts are often merely the legal manifestation of underlying policy conflicts. Pulkowski observes in this regard that norm conflicts might also be conceptualized as 'goal' or 'power struggles'. See Dirk Pulkowski, *The Law and Politics of International Regime Conflict* (OUP 2014) 19.

[45] In this regard, legal dilemmas are not concerned with any uncertainties pertaining to '[d]isputes about the existence and scope of rules', which are described by Weil in '"The Court Cannot Conclude Definitively ..." *Non Liquet* Revisited' (1998) 36 Columbia Journal of Transnational Law 109, 119. See also Part I.A.3.f.

[46] Karl Engisch, *Die Idee der Konkretisierung in Recht und Rechtswissenschaft unserer Zeit* (Winter 1953). See also Gadamer who observed that it is '[t]he work of interpretation ... to concretize the law in each specific case', Hans-Georg Gadamer, *Wahrheit und Methode: Grundzüge einer philosophischen Hermeneutik* (Mohr 1960) 335 (tr by Pulkowski (n 44) 279).

[47] Prosper Weil, 'Towards Relative Normativity in International Law?' (1983) 77 AJIL 413, 415; Pauwelyn (n 2) 89–94.

[48] ILC, Report of the Study Group of the International Law Commission finalized by Martti Koskenniemi, *Fragmentation of International Law: Difficulties Arising from the Diversification and Expansion of International Law* (13 April 2006) UN Doc A/CN.4/L.682 ('*Fragmentation Report*') paras 411–12; Harris (n 42) 222.

[49] For a comprehensive introduction to international legal interpretation, see Andrea Bianchi, Daniel Peat, and Matthew Windsor, *Interpretation in International Law* (OUP 2015).

[50] Robert Yewdall Jennings and Arthur Watts, *Oppenheim's International Law*, vol 1 (9th edn, Longman 1992) para 632; Jan Klabbers, *International Law* (CUP 2013) 52; ILC, *Fragmentation Report* (n 48) paras 411–12; Ralf Günter Wetzel and Dietrich Rauschning, *The Vienna Convention on the Law of Treaties: Travaux Préparatoires* (Metzner 1978) 251; Matthias Herdegen, 'Interpretation in International Law' in Rüdiger Wolfrum (ed), *Max Planck Encyclopedia of Public International Law* (Max Planck Institute for Comparative Public Law and International Law 2013) paras 11–26; Albert Bleckmann, 'Zur Feststellung und Auslegung von Völkergewohnheitsrecht' (1977) 37 Zeitschrift für ausländisches öffentliches Recht und Völkerrecht 504, 526–8.

[51] Vienna Convention on the Law of Treaties (opened for signature 23 May 1969, entered into force 27 January 1980) 1155 UNTS 331 ('VCLT') Art 31.

[52] *Territorial Dispute (Libyan Arab Jamahiriya/Chad)* (Judgment) [1994] ICJ Rep 6 [41]; *Oil Platforms (Islamic Republic of Iran v United States of America)* (Preliminary Objection) [1996] ICJ Rep 803 [23]; *Sovereignty over Pulau Ligitan and Pulau Sipadan (Indonesia/Malaysia)* (Judgment) [2002] ICJ Rep 625 [37]; ILC, *Fragmentation Report* (n 48) para 427.

[53] Strictly speaking, the provisions of the VCLT apply only to the interpretation of treaties. The rationale that informs the VCLT's approach to interpretation can be extended, however,

Article 31 **(General rule of interpretation)**

1. A treaty shall be interpreted in good faith in accordance with the ordinary meaning to be given to the terms of the treaty in their context and in the light of its object and purpose.
2. The context for the purpose of the interpretation of a treaty shall comprise, in addition to the text, including its preamble and annexes:
   a. Any agreement relating to the treaty which was made between all the parties in connexion with the conclusion of the treaty;
   b. Any instrument which was made by one or more parties in connexion with the conclusion of the treaty and accepted by the other parties as an instrument related to the treaty.
3. There shall be taken into account, together with the context:
   a. Any subsequent agreement between the parties regarding the interpretation of the treaty or the application of its provisions;
   b. Any subsequent practice in the application of the treaty which establishes the agreement of the parties regarding its interpretation;
   c. Any relevant rules of international law applicable in the relations between the parties.
4. A special meaning shall be given to a term if it is established that the parties so intended.

Article 32 **(Supplementary means of interpretation)**

Recourse may be had to supplementary means of interpretation, including the preparatory work of the treaty and the circumstances of its conclusion, in order to confirm the meaning resulting from the application of article 31, or to determine the meaning when the interpretation according to article 31:

a. Leaves the meaning ambiguous or obscure; or
b. Leads to a result which is manifestly absurd or unreasonable.

These provisions give judicial actors a lot of flexibility when interpreting contentious terms. Indeed, some have questioned the VCLT's utility to facilitate an adequate interpretative process[54] and it has been claimed that although 'it goes too far to suggest that "anything goes" under these provisions [articles 31 and 32, VCLT], still, "quite a bit goes" would be a fairly accurate synopsis'.[55] This is problematic

to the interpretation of norms beyond the treaty context. d'Aspremont observes, eg, that '[i]t does not seem unreasonable to submit that the principles governing the interpretation of customary international law and unilateral acts mirro[r] the interpretative principle devised for international treaties'. See Jean d'Aspremont, 'Articulating International Human Rights and International Humanitarian Law: Conciliatory Interpretation under the Guise of Conflict of Norms-Resolution' in Malgosia Fitzmaurice and Panos Merkouris (eds), *The Interpretation and Application of the European Convention of Human Rights* (Martinus Nijhoff 2013) 15. Similarly, Orakhelashvili states that '[t]he rationale underlying the interpretation of a treaty and of custom is the same'. See Alexander Orakhelashvili, *The Interpretation of Acts and Rules in Public International Law* (OUP 2008) 497. See also Bleckmann (n 50) 526–8. For a more critical view, see Herdegen (n 50) 61.

[54] See, eg, Christopher J Borgen, 'Resolving Treaty Conflicts' (2005) 37 George Washington International Law Review 573, 578.

[55] Jan Klabbers, 'Virtuous Interpretation' in Malgosia Fitzmaurice, Olufemi Elias, and Panos Merkouris (eds), *Treaty Interpretation and the Vienna Convention on the Law of Treaties 30 Years On*

since the abstract nature of these provisions increases the difficulty of maintaining a separation between the judicial task of norm-interpretation and the lawmaker's task of norm-modification and norm-creation.[56] This is particularly problematic in international law, where interpreters belonging to 'one or several interpretive communities',[57] each with its own distinct policy objectives,[58] are often asked to consider norms crafted by different interpretive communities and belonging to different legal regimes. While '"[o]bjective" interpretation is impossible',[59] judicial interpreters need to take great care not to exceed their 'judicial function' since over-ambitious interpretations can prevent the recognition of a legal dilemma.[60]

This risk exists, in particular, with respect to Article 31(3)(c) of the VCLT, commonly considered to embody the principle of 'systemic integration'.[61] According to the systemic integration principle, when interpreting 'a particular instrument, [a court] must always *interpret* and *apply* that instrument in its relationship to its normative environment',[62] consisting of 'any relevant rules of international law applicable ... between the parties'.[63] In the past, the systemic integration principle has been used to enlist general principles of law[64] to assist with the harmonious interpretation of conflicting terms. For example, several judges in the *Nuclear Weapons Advisory Opinion* sought to overcome the tension between the general prohibition of nuclear weapons and the inherent right to self-defence by interpreting the relevant provisions with reference to various general principles of law. Referring to Article 38(1)(c), ICJ Statute, one judge submitted, for example, that the conflict between norms of humanitarian law and the right to use nuclear weapons in extreme circumstances of self-defence should be resolved in favour of the latter

(Martinus Nijhoff 2010) 34; Philip Allott, 'Interpretation—an Exact Art' in Andrea Bianchi, Daniel Peat, and Matthew Windsor (eds), *Interpretation in International Law* (OUP 2015) 377.

56 *Interpretation of Peace Treaties with Bulgaria, Hungary and Romania (Advisory Opinion)* (Second Phase) [1950] ICJ Rep 221, 229; *South West Africa (Ethiopia v South Africa; Liberia v South Africa)* (Second Phase) ('*South West Africa*') [1966] ICJ Rep 6 [91].

57 Michael Waibel, 'Interpretive Communities in International Law' in Andrea Bianchi, Daniel Peat, and Matthew Windsor (eds), *Interpretation in International Law* (OUP 2015) 147.

58 Pulkowski (n 44) 16.

59 Waibel (n 57) 147. Going further, Waibel observes that '[i]n law, the choice of an interpretive method is the continuation of the politics of international law by other means.' See Waibel (n 57) 147. See also Ingo Venzke, *How Interpretation Makes International Law: On Semantic Change and Normative Twists* (OUP 2012) 60; Martti Koskenniemi, *From Apology to Utopia: The Structure of International Legal Argument* (CUP 2005) 18, 531.

60 See Part II.A.1 and Part III.A.2.b–c. which consider several problems posed by the existence of different interpretive and legislative communities in international law in the context of legal dilemmas.

61 ILC, *Fragmentation Report* (n 48) para 423.

62 ILC, *Fragmentation Report* (n 48) para 423 (emphasis in original).

63 VCLT (n 51) Art 31(3)(c).

64 ICJ Statute (n 43) Art 38(1)(c). General principles of law are often also invoked by those who argue in favour of the completeness of international law. For an overview of this argument, see Daniel Bodansky, 'Non Liquet and the Incompleteness of International Law' in Laurence Boisson de Chazournes and Philippe Sands (eds), *International Law, the International Court of Justice and Nuclear Weapons* (CUP 1999) 165–6. See also *Legality of the Threat or Use of Nuclear Weapons (Advisory Opinion)* [1996] ICJ Rep 226 ('*Nuclear Weapons Advisory Opinion*'), Declaration of Judge Herczegh, 275.

based on the general principle of law 'that no legal system is entitled to demand the self-abandonment, the suicide, of one of its subjects'.[65] Similarly, in the eyes of some, in the *Frontier Dispute Advisory Opinion (Interpretation of Article 3 of the Treaty of Lausanne)*,[66] the Permanent Court of International Justice ('PCIJ') was able to avoid a conflict between two norms by reference to the general principle that nobody may be a judge in his own cause.[67]

General principles and Article 31(3)(c) of the VCLT are without doubt important to maintaining the systemic nature of international law by 'looking beyond the individual case'.[68] However, given that it has been suggested that general principles can be used even to the extent of interpreting inconvenient legal norms 'out of existence',[69] it is important to acknowledge that, when interpreting legal norms, judicial actors must remain within 'the bounds of normal judicial action'.[70]

Accordingly, the ICJ has made it explicitly clear that it cannot 'go beyond what can reasonably be regarded as being a process of interpretation'[71] and that judicial interpretation must not lead to the 'rectification or revision'[72] of the interpreted terms. For example, when Bulgaria, Hungary, and Romania refused to appoint their own representatives to arbitration commissions established in accordance with the terms of the three countries' respective peace treaties[73] with the Allied Powers of the Second World War, the ICJ 'declined to find that an intended three-member commission could properly be constituted with two members only'.[74] According to the ICJ, to hold otherwise would have been contrary to the 'letter and spirit'[75] of the concerned treaties. Rejecting the claims of Ethiopia and Liberia, the ICJ subsequently confirmed this approach in the *South West Africa Advisory Opinion*.[76]

[65] See *Nuclear Weapons Advisory Opinion* (n 64), Separate Opinion of Judge Fleischhauer [5]. Judge Shahabuddeen also argued that the ICJ could have resolved the norm conflict by reference to particular general principles of international law. See *Nuclear Weapons Advisory Opinion* (n 64), Dissenting Opinion of Judge Shahabuddeen 377, 391–7.

[66] *Interpretation of Article 3, Paragraph 2 of the Treaty of Lausanne (Advisory Opinion)* [1925] PCIJ Series B No 12 ('*Interpretation of Article 3*').

[67] Hersch Lauterpacht, *The Development of International Law by the International Court* (CUP 1982) 159–60. See also *Interpretation of Article 3* (n 66) 32.

[68] ILC, *Fragmentation Report* (n 48) para 480.

[69] Lauterpacht (n 67) 165–6. For a strong critique of Lauterpacht's view, see Manfred Zuleeg, 'Vertragskonkurrenz im Völkerrecht. Teil I: Verträge zwischen souveränen Staaten' (1977) 20 German Yearbook of International Law 246, 271–4; Jan Klabbers, *Treaty Conflict and the European Union* (CUP 2009) 89.

[70] *South West Africa* (n 56) [91].

[71] *South West Africa* (n 56) [91].

[72] *South West Africa* (n 56) [91].

[73] Treaty of Peace with Bulgaria (signed 10 February 1947, entered into force 15 September 1947) 41 UNTS 21; Treaty of Peace with Hungary (signed 10 February 1947, entered into force 15 September) 41 UNTS 135; Treaty of Peace with Romania (signed 10 February 1947, entered into force 15 September 1947) 42 UNTS 3.

[74] *South West Africa* (n 56) [91].

[75] *Interpretation of Peace Treaties with Bulgaria, Hungary and Romania (Advisory Opinion)* (n 56), 229.

[76] *South West Africa* (n 56) [91].

Judicial interpreters should, guided by a presumption against the existence of a norm conflict[77] and by the corresponding principle of effective or harmonious interpretation, unquestionably 'eliminate … sham contradictions'[78] to the best possible extent. However, the presumption against conflict and in favour of harmony is rebutted when judicial actors encounter not 'sham' but 'genuine conflicts'[79] between the 'core of settled meaning[s]'[80] or the 'clear meaning'[81] of two norms.[82] Just as it has been observed that '[r]ights cannot be presumed to exist merely because it might seem desirable that they should',[83] the book argues that conflicts cannot be presumed not to exist merely because it might seem desirable that they should not. In other words, the principle of harmonious interpretation cannot justify the reconfiguration of norms,[84] or an attribution of a meaning to them that 'would be contrary to their letter and spirit'.[85]

Thus, when all interpretative efforts have been exhausted in the course of concretizing conduct norms and when it has proved impossible to identify a 'smallest common denominator'[86] within the bounds of the judicial function, interpretative efforts must be suspended even if, as a result, the purpose of particular clauses is 'thereby frustrated',[87] or if it emerges that a given pair of interpreted, concretized, norms may trigger a legal dilemma.

d) A conflict

International legal norm conflicts can be classified in at least four different ways (see Figure I.3). The first classification concerns the binary[88] division between contrary and contradictory norm conflicts. Contrary norm conflicts exist where two

[77] C Wilfred Jenks, 'The Conflict of Law-Making Treaties' (1953) 30 BYIL 401, 428; Michael Akehurst, 'The Hierarchy of the Sources of International Law' (1974) 47 BYIL 273, 275–6; Pauwelyn (n 2) 240–4.

[78] Hans Kelsen, *General Theory of Law and State* (Harvard UP 1945) 375. Kelsen believed, of course, that all contradictions between norms were ultimately 'sham' contradictions.

[79] ILC, *Fragmentation Report* (n 48) para 42; Borgen (n 54) 639; Joseph Raz, *Between Authority and Interpretation: On the Theory of Law and Practical Reason* (OUP 2009) 262.

[80] HLA Hart, *The Concept of Law* (2nd edn, Clarendon Press 1994) 123, 134, 144.

[81] Pauwelyn (n 2) 245–6. See also Borgen (n 54) 639.

[82] Julius Stone, 'Non Liquet and the Function of Law in the International Community' (1959) 35 BYIL 124, 133. At least originally, even Dworkin conceded that interpretation cannot harmonize conflicting legal provisions where 'two different political theories … each provide [different, but] exactly as good a justification of the settled law as the other'. See Ronald Dworkin, 'No Right Answer?' in PMS Hacker and Joseph Raz (eds), *Law, Morality and Society—Essays in Honour of H.L.A. Hart* (Clarendon Press 1977) 83.

[83] *South West Africa* (n 56) [91].

[84] Pauwelyn (n 2) 251, 273.

[85] *Interpretation of Peace Treaties with Bulgaria, Hungary and Romania (Advisory Opinion)* (n 56) 229.

[86] *Nuclear Weapons Advisory Opinion* (n 64), Separate Opinion of Judge Fleischhauer [5]. For Judge Fleischhauer, the smallest common denominator between the prohibition of nuclear weapons and the right to self-defence in the *Nuclear Weapons Advisory Opinion* consisted in the permission to use nuclear weapons as a last resort in extreme situations.

[87] *South West Africa* (n 56) [91].

[88] While Pauwelyn identifies 'four situations' of norm conflict (Pauwelyn (n 2) 179), they are simply four different manifestations of the two conflict types discussed here.

prescriptive norms (obligations, prohibitions) conflict.[89] This is the case, for example, with respect to Egypt's competing obligations towards Israel and the members of the Arab League in the *Military Alliances* scenario. Contradictory conflicts exist between prescriptive and permissive conduct norms, where the negation of one conduct norm results in the second conduct norm.[90] For example, the *Nuclear Weapons* scenario could be construed as a contradictory conflict between the permissive norm to use a nuclear weapon in self-defence and a prescriptive norm that prohibits the use of such weapons.

The distinction and relationship between contrary and contradictory conflicts is often[91] illustrated[92] with reference to the Deontic Square (see Figure I.1)[93]—a variant of the Traditional Square of Opposition.[94]

For the purposes of this analysis, it is, however, sufficient to illustrate legal norm conflicts by means of a Deontic Triangle (see Figure I.2).[95]

It is uncontroversial that contrary conflicts generate legally recognizable norm conflicts. Until recently,[96] however, many[97] have disputed the possibility of

[89] Ewald Wiederin, 'Was ist und welche Konsequenzen hat ein Normenkonflikt?' (1990) 21 Rechtstheorie 311, 319–20.

[90] Wiederin (n 89) 319–20.

[91] Vranes (n 15) 409; Pauwelyn (n 2) 179; Charles Leonard Hamblin, 'Quandaries and the Logic of Rules' (1972) 1 Journal of Philosophical Logic 74, 78.

[92] The Deontic Square is referred to here merely for illustrative purposes since the utility of classical (deontic) logic to illuminate the legal process is very limited. See Part III.B.1. See also LFE Goldie, 'Legal Pluralism and "No-Law" Sectors' (1958) 32 Australian Law Journal 220, 225; Oren Perez, 'Law in the Air: A Prologue to the World of Legal Paradoxes' in Oren Perez and Gunther Teubner (eds), *Paradoxes and Inconsistencies in the Law* (Hart 2005) 16–17; Dieter Krimphove, 'Grenzen der Logik' (2013) 44 Rechtstheorie 315; ILC, *Fragmentation Report* (n 48) para 25.

[93] The utility of deontic logic to contribute to legal theory is frequently called into question (see also Part III.B.1). However, even strong critics agree that deontic logic can be useful and even 'essential' when it comes to the identification of norm conflicts. See, eg, Pavlos Eleftheriadis, *Legal Rights* (OUP 2008) 96–7.

[94] Hamblin (n 91) 75; Vranes (n 15) 409; Terence Parsons, 'The Traditional Square of Opposition' in Edward N Zalta (ed), *The Stanford Encyclopedia of Philosophy* (Spring edn, 2014) <http://plato.stanford.edu/archives/spr2014/entries/square/> accessed 24 May 2017.

[95] The deontological trend appears to favour more rather than fewer relations. See Joachim Hruschka, *Das deontologische Sechseck bei Gottfried Achenwall im Jahre 1767* (Vandenhoeck & Ruprecht 1997); Hans Lenk, 'Konträrbeziehungen und Operatorengleichungen im deontologischen Sechseck' in Hans Lenk (ed), *Normenlogik. Grundprobleme der deontischen Logik* (Verlag Dokumentation 1974); Joachim Hruschka and Jan C Joerden, 'Supererogation: Vom deontologischen Sechseck zum deontologischen Zehneck: Zugleich ein Beitrag zur strafrechtlichen Grundlagenforschung' (1987) 73 Archiv für Rechts- und Sozialphilosophie 93.

[96] Christopher J Borgen, 'Treaty Conflicts and Normative Fragmentation' in Duncan Hollis (ed), *The Oxford Guide to Treaties* (OUP 2012) 455–6; Pauwelyn (n 2) 175–6, 198–9; Friedrich Klein, 'Vertragskonkurrenz' in Karl Strupp and H-J Schlochauer (eds), *Wörterbuch des Völkerrechts* (De Gruyter 1962) 555; Rüdiger Wolfrum and Nele Matz, *Conflicts in International Environmental Law* (Springer 2003) 6; Vranes (n 15) 415; ILC, *Fragmentation Report* (n 48) para 25.

[97] Emer de Vattel, *The Law of Nations* (Luke White 1792) para 312; Jenks (n 77) 426; Władysław Czapliński and Gennady M Danilenko, 'Conflicts of Norms in International Law' (1990) 21 Netherlands Yearbook of International Law 3, 12; Gabrielle Marceau, 'Conflicts of Norms and Conflicts of Jurisdictions—The Relationship between the WTO Agreement and MEAs and Other Treaties' (2001) 35 Journal of World Trade 1081, 1084, 1086; Wolfram Karl, 'Conflicts between Treaties' in Rudolf Bernhardt (ed), *Encyclopedia of Public International Law*, vol 7 (North-Holland

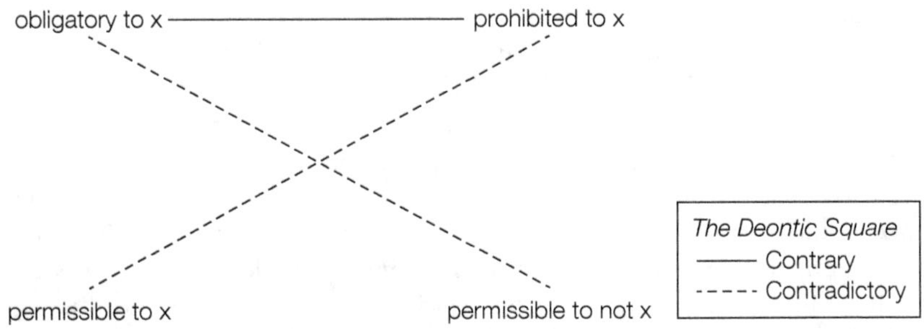

Figure I.1: The Deontic Square modifies the Traditional Square of Opposition to illustrate the different types of relationships between conduct norms.

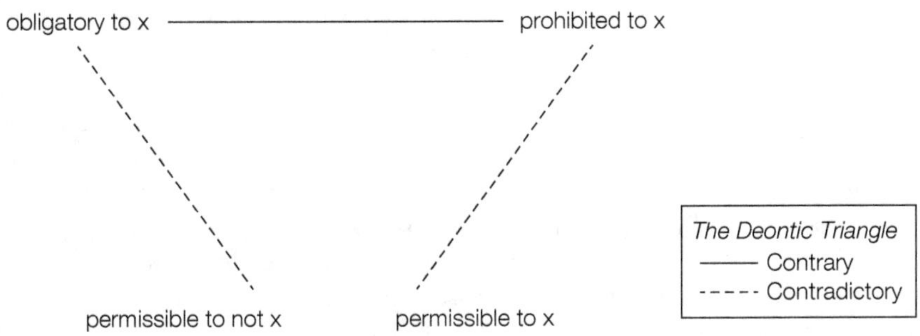

Figure I.2: For the purposes of this book, a Deontic Triangle suffices to illustrate the structure of dilemmatic norm conflicts, since there cannot be dilemmatic norm conflicts between permissive norms.

contradictory conflicts at least in international law,[98] since they involve permissive norms. Considering, however, that the definition proffered here is prescriptive, the definition of a legal dilemma should include contradictory norm conflicts—that is, conflicts between permissive and prescriptive norms.

This is so because the inclusion of permissive norms avoids stipulating that conflicts between permissions and prescriptive norms are always resolved in favour of the latter.[99] The subordination of permissions to prescriptions would

1984) 468; Guyora Binder, 'The Dialectic of Duplicity: Treaty Conflict and Political Contradiction' (1985) 34 Buffalo Law Review 329, 340. For additional references, see also Pauwelyn (n 2) 167.

[98] In legal theory, it is widely accepted that permissions can form part of conflicts of norms. See, eg, Wiederin (n 89) 322; Vranes (n 15) 409; Karl Engisch, *Die Einheit der Rechtsordnung* (Winter 1935) 46. For a more critical view, see Hamblin (n 91) 75.

[99] Boudreault applies this analysis to the ICJ's decision in *Jurisdictional Immunities of the State (Germany v Italy: Greece Intervening)* (Judgment) [2012] ICJ Rep 99. See François Boudreault, 'Identifying Conflicts of Norms: The ICJ Approach in the Case of the Jurisdictional Immunities of the State (Germany v. Italy: Greece Intervening)' (2012) 25 Leiden Journal of International Law 1003, 1009–12.

be difficult to justify if one considers that the inability to utilize a permission may 'reduce … [a given norm] to inutility'[100] and may, indeed, 'be as serious as a conflict'.[101] It would be particularly difficult to justify with respect to permissions that derive from rights.[102] For example, if an actor in the *Nuclear Weapons* scenario faced the choice between exercising the right to self-defence[103] and complying with the prohibition of the use of force, the existence of the right to self-defence would entail the permission to use force in self-defence.[104] The resulting *de facto* subordination of rights to prescriptions[105] would deprive rights of the force that they must by definition possess in situations of norm conflicts. If it were denied that permissions and, by extension, rights could irreconcilably conflict with prescriptive norms, rights would be entirely unsuitable to protect the interests they are designed to protect.[106] In fact, the existence *vel non* of a right would be completely irrelevant if a permission supported by a right conflicted with prescriptive norms. The outcome, the prescriptive norm prevailing, would let it appear as if no right ever existed.[107] Moreover, the view that rights would always have to give way to prescriptive norms comes at the expense of sacrificing a right-holder's fundamental freedom to choose independently whether or not to exercise a right. While it is correct to observe that permissions make 'behaviour in some sense optional',[108] it is not correct to argue that, because of the inherent optionality of permissions, permissions cannot form part of legal dilemmas. The very essence of the optionality of the permission's exercise is the freedom to choose whether or not to exercise a given permission. Therefore, the definition of a legal dilemma should recognize the possibility of conflicts between prescriptive and permissive norms.

In addition to the distinction between contrary and contradictory norms, one can, second, distinguish conflicts between different norms (A, B) and norm conflicts between twin norms (B, B). Twin norms are symmetrical norms that impose congruent obligations upon the norm-addressee with respect to two (or more)

[100] Vranes (n 15) 404. [101] Jenks (n 77) 426–7.

[102] While rights are not to be equated with permissions, rights can appear in the Deontic Triangle, to the extent that rights entail permissions. Rights could also be considered in order to identify prohibitions. For example, if actor A is entitled by virtue of the existence of a right to engage in a certain kind of conduct 1, this might lead to the prohibition of B to engage in a certain kind of conduct 2, which would impair A's exercise of A's right. See also Hamblin (n 91) 78.

[103] Incidentally, in the international legal context, a State's right to self-defence could also be construed as a State's obligation to protect the State's population. See, eg, Nico Schrijver, 'The Changing Nature of State Sovereignty' (1999) 70 BYIL 65, 97–8. See generally *Island of Palmas (United States of America v the Netherlands)* (1928) 2 RIAA 329, 839.

[104] The argument is not that permissions and rights are the same. There are permissions that are not rights (the permission to enter a friend's house for a dinner party, for example).

[105] Pauwelyn also makes an argument in favour of the equal status of rights and obligations in international law, Pauwelyn (n 2) 171–2.

[106] Thus, in *SAS v France* the European Court of Human Rights observed that the French law prohibiting the burka confronted the applicant 'with a dilemma …: either [the applicant] complies with the ban' and accepts the infringement of her right to practice her religion or 'she refuses to comply and faces criminal sanctions'. *SAS v France* (2015) 60 EHRR 11 [110].

[107] Pulkowski (n 44) 150. [108] Eleftheriadis (n 93) 86.

different objects. For example, a sovereign might be under an obligation to protect two particular citizens' inherent rights to life. The source of the two duties may be one and the same norm: Article 6 of the 1966 International Covenant on Civil and Political Rights ('ICCPR'),[109] for example. A situation of this kind could arise in relation to the *Hijacked Airplane* scenario. Similarly, the *Distress at Sea* scenario, concerning a ship master's obligation to rescue persons in distress at sea, could also be characterized as a legal dilemma resulting from a conflict between twin norms (Regulation 33, SOLAS) with which the master cannot simultaneously comply. This way, twin norms generate conflicts where the factual circumstances render it impossible (perhaps due to lack of time or resources) to honour both twin norms.

Third, one can distinguish conflicts that arise between norms authored by exactly the same (group of) legal persons, also called A/B conflicts, and conflicts between norms each authored by different (groups of) legal persons, also called AB/AC conflicts. For reasons that will become apparent shortly,[110] this distinction influences the availability of certain norm conflict resolution devices. The *lex posterior* principle,[111] for instance, might be applied regarding conflicting treaty provisions where the treaty membership of the earlier treaty mirrors that of the later treaty. However, the principle could not, for example, be applied regarding conflicting provisions of the 2007 Treaty on the Functioning of the European Union ('TFEU')[112] and the 1969 American Convention on Human Rights ('ACHR'),[113] since the membership of the TFEU differs from that of the ACHR. In contrast, norm conflict resolution devices based on conflict-of-laws approaches are applicable only to norms created by different legal persons.[114] This distinction is of relevance only for conflicts arising between different norms since twin norms are by definition symmetrical and must therefore have been created by the same legal person(s).[115]

Fourth, norm conflicts can be divided into contingent and intrinsic conflicts. Contingent conflicts arise between norms that are generally compatible but that conflict if specific circumstances arise. For example, in the *Nuclear Weapons* scenario a State's inherent right to self-defence and the prohibition to use nuclear weapons do not generally conflict unless a State can defend itself only by means of nuclear weapons. In contrast, intrinsic conflicts exist per se and irrespective of any factual circumstances. For example, in the *Submarine Warfare* scenario one clause of the 1922 Submarine Treaty sanctioned the attack of merchant vessels in times of war, while another clause of the same treaty prohibited such conduct. In the

[109] International Covenant on Civil and Political Rights (adopted 16 December 1966, entered into force 23 March 1976) 999 UNTS 171 Art 6.

[110] See Part II.A.1. [111] See Part II.A.1.

[112] Consolidated Version of the Treaty on the Functioning of the European Union [2012] OJ 326/1 ('TFEU').

[113] American Convention on Human Rights (concluded 21 November 1969, entered into force 18 July 1978) 1144 UNTS 123.

[114] See Part II.A.2. [115] See also Figure I.3.

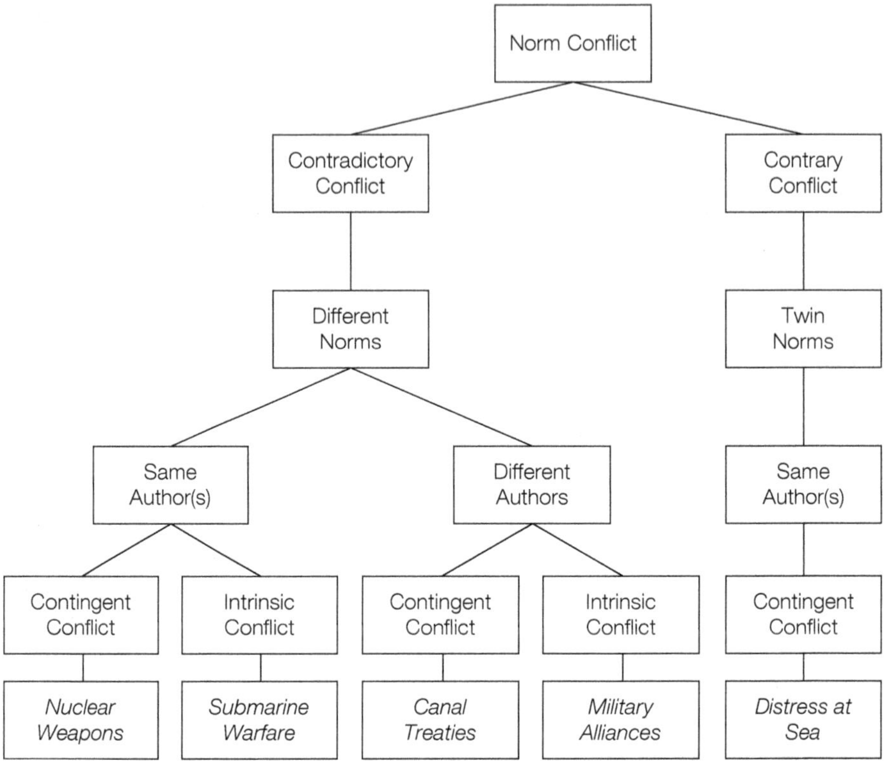

Figure I.3: The chart illustrates the four levels of distinction, the five types of potentially dilemmatic norm conflicts, and their corresponding examples.

first case, factual circumstances set two otherwise compatible norms on a collision course. In the second case, factual circumstances merely determine whether or not a conflict between two otherwise conflicting norms crystallizes. Again, this distinction is of particular relevance for norm conflicts arising between different rather than twin norms. Intrinsically conflicting twin norms would equate to a self-contradictory norm similar to a '*dispositio perplexa*'[116] ('a self-defeating expression of will'),[117] which would probably not qualify as a conduct norm, since it is incomprehensible.[118]

Each of these four distinctions is important. The first distinction highlights the necessity of considering permissions and, by extension, rights when studying

[116] Gottfried Wilhelm Leibniz, 'Inaugural Dissertation on Perplexing Cases in the Law' in Alberto Artosi, Bernardo Pieri, and Giovanni Sartor (eds), *Leibniz: Logico-Philosophical Puzzles in the Law* (Springer 2013) 137.

[117] Leibniz (n 116) 63, 83–6. See also Part III.B.2.

[118] In this regard, see also the discussion of the limited utility of the agglomeration principle in Part III.B.2.

legal dilemmas. The second, third, and fourth distinctions matter, in particular, as they condition the availability of norm conflict resolution devices and of norm conflict avoidance techniques.[119]

e) *Unavoidable*

Unavoidable conflicts are conflicts, that, before they have arisen, could not or simply have not been obviated by means of an actor's alternative response to one or both of the two norms at issue. Depending on the circumstances, such responses could include inaction, delegating the decision-making power to a third party, authorizing the modification of a given norm, reversing the steps that led to the dilemma, utilizing incompatibility clauses, or, if the issue is before a court, choosing—without exceeding the confines of the judicial function[120]—alternative interpretations of the norms in question.[121]

Conflicts that could not have been avoided are likely to arise in situations where two or more conflicting norms were created at different moments in time such that the emergence of a subsequent norm conflict was difficult to predict. For example, EU member States, who concluded energy related intergovernmental agreements with non-EU member States several years ago, could not have predicted that certain provisions of those intergovernmental energy agreements could subsequently violate provisions of EU law enacted decades later.[122] A good example of a conflict that could have been, but was not, avoided is the *Canal Treaties* scenario: Nicaragua could have, but did not, consult Costa Rica before concluding the 1914 Treaty with the US.

Apart from the questions raised by judicial interpretation considered previously, whether or not a conflict can be avoided is primarily a factual question. Although it is by no means always easy to identify the limits of a conflict's avoidability, these questions will not be considered here in any detail, for two reasons. First, irrespective of the avoidability of norm conflicts in principle, norm conflicts are *de facto* often not avoided. Were it otherwise, courts would never invoke norm conflict resolution devices. The very fact that norm conflict resolution devices are resorted to shows that, even if it were possible to avoid every conflict, at least in practice, conflicts are frequently not avoided. It follows, second, that the more difficult argument to prove for the purposes of this book, which argues in favour of the recognition of

[119] See Part II for a detailed analysis of international law's different norm conflict resolution devices.

[120] See also Part III.A.2.a.

[121] Czapliński and Danilenko (n 97) 13.

[122] For a discussion of the details concerning this norm conflict, see Valentin Jeutner, 'A Critique of the EU Commission's Proposal Concerning Intergovernmental Energy Agreements' (2016) 9 International Energy Law Review 181, 185–7. For the EU Commission's assessment of the situation, see Commission, 'Impact Assessment Accompanying the Proposal for a Decision of the European Parliament and of the Council on Establishing an Information Exchange Mechanism with Regard to Intergovernmental Agreements and Non-Binding Instruments between Member States and Third Countries in the Field of Energy and Repealing Decision No 994/2012/EU' (Commission Staff Working Document) SWD(2016) 27 final, 16.

legal dilemmas, is not that certain norm conflicts are unavoidable, but rather, that certain norm conflicts are irresolvable due to the inherent limitations of norm conflict resolution devices. These will be addressed in Part II.

f) Irresolvable

Irresolvable norm conflicts are conflicts, that, once they have arisen, cannot and/or should not be resolved by means of international law's norm conflict resolution devices.[123] Although factual considerations can be very important (in particular regarding contingent conflicts such as those relating to the *Nuclear Weapons* or *Military Alliances* scenarios), the resolvability of a given norm conflict is primarily a question of law. While it is commonly accepted that norm conflict avoidance mechanisms are either inherently limited or not utilized, the fundamental[124] problems related to the limitations of norm conflict resolution devices are not conventionally expounded. Thus, compared to proving the limitations of avoidability, it is more challenging and more important for the purposes of this book to establish the limitations of norm conflict resolution devices. This is why the entire second part of the book is dedicated to a detailed analysis of international law's norm conflict resolution devices and accommodation mechanisms in order to identify which conflicts are irresolvable.

g) Undue impairment

Neither avoidance mechanisms nor resolution devices must lead to an undue impairment of the norms concerned.[125] A norm is impaired[126] if an actor has violated or

[123] The reference to both the impossibility ('cannot') and the undesirability ('should not') is important here, as some norm conflict resolution devices cannot resolve conflicts (*lex superior*, eg, cannot resolve a conflict between two norms of the same rank) while others could in principle, but should not resolve a conflict. Residual rules, eg, could solve certain conflicts, but should not be used when their application would lead to undesirable consequences. Part II addresses this issue in detail.

[124] The limitations of specific norm conflict resolution devices, such as the traditional *leges specialis, posterior*, and *superior* principles, are, however, more frequently considered. See, eg, Pulkowski (n 44) 343; Henning Grosse Ruse-Khan, 'A Conflict-of-Laws Approach to Competing Rationalities in International Law: The Case of Plain Packaging between Intellectual Property, Trade, Investment and Health' (2013) 9 Journal of Private International Law 309, 312; Adolf Merkl, 'Die Rechtseinheit des österreichischen Staates. Eine staatsrechtliche Untersuchung auf Grund der Lehre von der lex posterior' (1918) 37 Archiv des öffentlichen Rechts 56, 76.

[125] This norm-impairment test as the definitive indicator that a norm conflict exists has also been favoured by Hans Kelsen, *General Theory of Norms* (Clarendon Press 1991) 123; Vranes (n 15) 418; Wiederin (n 89) 318; Pauwelyn (n 2) 175–6; Pulkowski (n 44) 149–50.

[126] Some argue that, *strictu sensu*, norms cannot impair other norms as much as ideals cannot impair ideals and that it would be more adequate to refer to one norm's proposition impairing another norm's proposition. See, eg, Jörg Kammerhofer, 'Unearthing Structural Uncertainty through Neo-Kelsenian Consistency: Conflicts of Norms in International Law' 3 <http://www.esil-sedi.eu/sites/default/files/Kammerhofer.pdf> accessed 23 January 2017. For the purposes of this book, however, the controversial distinction between norm propositions and norms is of little consequence, as long as it is clear that any reference to norm conflicts, or to the impairment of norms, accepts that impairing a legal norm, or norm proposition, does not necessarily affect the validity or the metaphysical integrity of the impaired norm. On the distinction between norms and norm propositions in general, see Pablo E Navarro and Jorge L Rodríguez, *Deontic Logic and Legal Systems* (CUP 2014) ch 3.

has been authorized to violate a norm such that a norm is deprived of its 'intended effect'.[127] A norm is unduly impaired if the impairment occurs as a result of violating the different parameters of the norm conflict resolution devices which will be considered in great detail in Part II.[128] Sometimes, it will be comparatively easy to determine whether attempts to resolve a norm conflict impair a norm unduly. For example, it might be obvious that a norm requiring three commission members cannot be read to mean that two members suffice.[129] Also, when the norms in question are legally absolute (for example, the legally unqualified prohibition of genocide)[130] or protect factually indivisible interests (for example, the right to life),[131] it will not be difficult to identify when one norm is unduly impaired, since legally absolute or factually indivisible norms cannot be impaired in degrees.[132]

However, difficult cases will inevitably arise. For example, whether, and to which extent, the prohibition of the use of nuclear weapons in the *Nuclear Weapons* scenario could equate to an undue impairment of States' right to self-defence[133] is a question that cannot be answered in the abstract. In difficult cases of this kind, judicial actors must be particularly cautious not to exceed their judicial competence by reconfiguring conflicting norms. In this regard, the caveats mentioned previously concerning the limitations of interpretative techniques apply here in particular.

Alongside the 'norm-impairment test' proposed here, at least three different tests have been suggested to identify a norm conflict: the logical contradiction test, the joint compliance test, and the default test. They will be briefly considered and rejected in turn. First, the 'logical contradiction test' 'translate[s] two norms into declarative statements to determine whether their conjunction results in a *logical* contradiction'.[134] This test is problematic, because beyond its ability to identify certain abstract norm conflicts, (deontic) logic is unable to account for the diversity of considerations that determine whether or not a concrete conflict exists. For example, a test purely based on logic would not be able to identify contingent conflicts, such as those involved in the *Distress at Sea* or *Military Alliances* scenarios, that are *prima facie* compatible.[135] Further, a considered analysis of whether or not,

[127] Pauwelyn (n 2) 251, 273. As argued previously, permissive norms are impaired if the freedom to choose whether or not to exercise a given permission—the essence of the optionality of permissions—is infringed by competing prescriptive norms.

[128] See Table II.1 in the final section of Part II for a comprehensive overview of the limitations of norm conflict resolution devices which, if disrespected, lead to the undue impairment of a norm.

[129] *South West Africa* (n 56) [91].

[130] See, eg, the Convention on the Prevention and Punishment of the Crime of Genocide (adopted 9 December 1948, entered into force 12 January 1951) 78 UNTS 277.

[131] It is factually impossible to infringe the right to life in degrees. See the discussion of the proportionality principle in Part II.A.3.

[132] See Part II.A.3 for a more detailed discussion of legally absolute and factually indivisible interests.

[133] *Nuclear Weapons Advisory Opinion* (n 64), Separate Opinion of Judge Guillaume [8]; *Nuclear Weapons Advisory Opinion* (n 64), Separate Opinion of Judge Fleischhauer [3], [5]; *Nuclear Weapons Advisory Opinion* (n 64), Dissenting Opinion of Judge Shahabuddeen, 416.

[134] Vranes (n 15) 413. According to Tammelo, the Australian High Court once adopted the logical contradiction test in *Australian Boot Trade Employees' Federation v Whybrow* (1910) 11 CLR 311 (Australian High Court). See Ilmar Tammelo, 'The Test of Inconsistency Between Commonwealth and State Laws' (1957) 30 Australian Law Journal 496, 498.

[135] Vranes (n 15) 413.

and to what extent, a given norm could justifiably be impaired, which takes into account the factual indivisibility and relative importance of competing norms, is beyond the capabilities of formal logic.[136] In any event, norm conflicts are not limited to contradictory relationships, but also include contrary conflicts.[137] Against this background, the impairment test is preferable.

Second, the 'joint compliance test' asks whether 'it is impossible for one norm subject to comply with both of a pair of norms'.[138] This test is problematic, because, depending on the definition of 'possible', it could result in the non-recognition of contradictory conflicts between permissions and prescriptions such as the one involved in the *Nuclear Weapons* scenario. In a situation where an actor chooses to comply with a prescription rather than a permission or right, no conflict would exist as the obligation is complied with, and as it would not be adequate to speak of an actor's 'non-compliance' with a permission that has not been exercised. Indeed, strictly speaking, joint compliance would be possible if the actor simply waived the competing permission. In contrast, the focus on the impairment of a norm detects such conflicts by identifying that a non-exercised right has been or will be impaired. Thus, the impairment test is preferable.[139]

Third, according to the 'default test', a conflict exists when compliance with either norm would lead to a judicial sanction.[140] Again, this test is insufficient, as the non-application of an actor's permission or right in the case of a contradictory conflict would not be covered. An actor who did not utilize a permission due to compliance with an obligation, such as States who forgo the utilization of their right to self-defence in favour of complying with the general prohibition of nuclear weapons in the *Nuclear Weapons* scenario, would normally not be held accountable by a court. Thus, the default test would be unable adequately to protect permissive norms in contradictory conflict situations. Similarly, a ship master in the *Distress at Sea* scenario, who rescues person A rather than person B, where either person but not both could have been rescued, may not necessarily face a judicial sanction. However, the potential lack of a sanction does not result in the extinction of the master's duty to rescue person A and person B. In other words, if the master rescues person A it would still be accurate to observe that the master also ought to have rescued person B so that the master's failure to do so violates the master's obligation to rescue person B.[141] In this sense, the norm-impairment test is preferable, too, since it distinguishes the question whether norms are impaired for the purposes of establishing the existence of a dilemma from the subsequent question, addressed in Part III, that concerns the most appropriate judicial characterization of an actor's decision of a particular dilemma.

[136] Krimphove (n 92) 323–30; Pulkowski (n 44) 146–7. See also Part III.B.1.

[137] See Part I.A.2.d.

[138] H Hamner Hill, 'A Functional Taxonomy of Normative Conflict' (1987) 6 Law and Philosophy 227, 227; Vranes (n 15) 413–14. This test is favoured, *inter alia*, by Vattel and Crawford. See Vattel (n 97) para 311; James Crawford, Second Report on State Responsibility, ILC Ybk 1999/II(1), 3 [313].

[139] Vranes (n 15) 413–14.

[140] Graham Priest, *In Contradiction* (OUP 2006) 182.

[141] See in this regard also the discussion concerning the 'ought implies can' maxim in Part III.B.2.

Overall, therefore, the impairment test is preferable, as it is able to capture the complexity of norm conflicts beyond the modalities of formal logic, provides adequate protection for permissive norms in contradictory conflict situations, and because it separates the questions concerning the existence of a conflict from subsequent questions concerning an actor's legal responsibility related to particular conflicts.

h) Obeying or applying one norm

The differentiation between obeying and applying a norm responds to the difference between prescriptive and permissive norms.[142] While prescriptive conduct norms are obeyed, permissive norms are applied. It would be inaccurate to say that a State applied (rather than obeyed) a prohibition when refraining from a prohibited course of conduct. Equally, it would be misleading to say that a State obeyed (rather than applied or exercised) a permissive norm by exercising a right. Thus, instances of obeying and instances of applying norms should be included in the definition of a legal dilemma.

It is with these considerations in mind that this book stipulates that a legal dilemma exists when an actor confronts an irresolvable and unavoidable conflict between at least two legal norms so that obeying or applying one norm necessarily entails the undue impairment of the other.

3. Legal dilemmas distinguished from related concepts

In the interest of clarity, this section briefly distinguishes legal dilemmas as defined above from related concepts. The terminological boundaries between these related concepts and legal dilemmas are often blurry. Thus, in its effort to distinguish legal dilemmas from related concepts, this section will focus on the central meanings of the terms in question while being fully aware that different readers may perceive the difference between dilemmas and related concepts to be larger or smaller.

a) Moral dilemmas

Compared to moral dilemmas, legal dilemmas concern a conflict between legal norms *inter se*. They do not concern conflicts between moral norms *inter se* or between a legal norm on the one side and a norm grounded exclusively in morality[143]

[142] Kelsen observes that '[a] person who behaves as a norm commands ... *observes* the relevant norm' and that a 'person who makes use of a permission granted to him' applies a norm. See Kelsen (n 125) 104–5.

[143] Conflicts between legal and moral norms raise questions about the links between morality and law famously discussed *inter alia* by Radbruch, Hart, and Fuller. See Gustav Radbruch, 'Gesetzliches Unrecht und übergesetzliches Recht' (1946) Süddeutsche Juristenzeitung 105; HLA Hart, 'Positivism and the Separation of Law and Morals' (1957) 71 Harvard Law Review 593; Lon L Fuller, 'Positivism and Fidelity to Law: A Reply to Professor Hart' (1958) 71 Harvard Law Review 630.

or utility,[144] for example, on the other. That does not mean, of course, that some legal dilemmas might not also exist as moral dilemmas and *vice versa*. The legal *Distress at Sea* scenario could, for example, also be discussed in moral terms,[145] and the philosophical *Trolley Problem*[146] could also be discussed in legal terms.[147] Similarly, in the *Nuclear Weapons Advisory Opinion* the Court's president explicitly noted that the advisory opinion reflects moral dilemmas in various ways.[148] This book focuses, however, exclusively on conflicts between legal norms. Conflicts between legal norms and moral norms will not be discussed, as they raise a separate set of questions.

b) *Conflicts of norms*

Legal dilemmas differ from general conflicts of norms in at least two respects. First, legal dilemmas concern only irresolvable and unavoidable conflicts. In this sense, the study of legal dilemmas begins where studies trying to identify norm conflict solutions and avoidance strategies end.[149] The book's focus on irresolvable conflicts thus assumes the opposite perspective by concentrating only on the limitations of norm conflict resolution devices. Second, the study of legal dilemmas goes beyond an abstract discussion of conflicting norms, by seeking to answer the concrete question of how the (international) legal order should respond to legal dilemmas when they arise.

c) *Indeterminacy*

Legal dilemmas are easily confused with cases of legal vagueness, relative indeterminacy, or uncertainty[150] regarding a norm's status or content. Further, legal dilemmas may appear to relate to cases of ambiguity concerning, for example, a norm's 'determining force',[151] equivocal 'linguistic expressions',[152] imprecise 'evaluative terminology',[153] or 'deontic indeterminacy'.[154] In contrast to these various forms

[144] Conflicts between legal norms and norms of utility raise the question of the state of exception discussed *inter alia* by Carl Schmitt, *Political Theology: Four Chapters on the Concept of Sovereignty* (George Schwab tr, University of Chicago Press 1985); Dietrich Bonhoeffer, *Ethik* (Eberhard Bethge ed, 2nd edn, Christian Kaiser Verlag 1953) 185; Agamben (n 1). See Part III.C.2.

[145] See, eg, Tracy Isaacs, *Moral Responsibility in Collective Contexts* (OUP 2011) 142.

[146] See, eg, Hans Welzel, 'Zum Notstandsproblem' (1951) 63 Zeitschrift für die gesamte Strafrechtswissenschaft 47; Philippa Foot, 'The Problem of Abortion and the Doctrine of the Double Effect' (1967) 5 Oxford Review 1.

[147] See, eg, the proceedings (*Case concerning the Aviation Security Act* (2005) Case No 1 BvR 357/05, BVerfGE 115, 118, [84ff]) before the German Constitutional Court concerning Article 14(3) of the 2005 German Aviation Security Act, which arguably sought to subordinate the right to life of civilians on board a hijacked aircraft to the right to life of civilians on the ground. See also Manuel Ladiges, *Die Bekämpfung nicht-staatlicher Angreifer im Luftraum: Unter besonderer Berücksichtigung des § 14 Abs. 3 LuftSiG und der strafrechtlichen Beurteilung der Tötung von Unbeteiligten* (Duncker & Humblot 2013).

[148] *Nuclear Weapons Advisory Opinion* (n 64), Declaration of Judge Bedjaoui [9].

[149] Pauwelyn's monograph is the most comprehensive contemporary study of the matter but Pauwelyn discusses irresolvable norm conflicts only in passing. See Pauwelyn (n 2) 419–22.

[150] See, eg, Jörg Kammerhofer, *Uncertainty in International Law: A Kelsenian Perspective* (Taylor & Francis 2010).

[151] Koskenniemi, *From Apology to Utopia* (n 59) 37–9.

[152] Koskenniemi, *From Apology to Utopia* (n 59) 38.

[153] Koskenniemi, *From Apology to Utopia* (n 59) 39.

[154] Tammelo (n 134) 500.

of indeterminacy, legal dilemmas arise only once a given norm's status and content have been ascertained, for example, by means of interpretation. In fact, given the irreducibility requirement,[155] vague or indeterminate norms are much less likely,[156] if not entirely unable, to generate norm conflicts.

Legal dilemmas could, however, be said to relate to 'legal indeterminacy' if such indeterminacy is defined as the absence of a 'single right answer'[157] to a legal question. This would not be an inaccurate description, since dilemmas could be described as situations in which there are two right (and two wrong) answers. However, to link legal dilemmas with legal indeterminacy in this manner can also be misleading to the extent that the absence of a 'single right answer' could suggest the existence of an undefined number of otherwise correct answers whereas, in the case of legal dilemmas, the number of right answers is distinctly determinate and finite.[158]

d) Gaps

Law's indecisiveness in dilemmatic circumstances could cause confusion between dilemmas and legal gaps. Legal gaps exist when no legal norm governs a particular factual state of affairs.[159] Just like actors facing dilemmas, actors facing legal gaps may have difficulties identifying what the law requires them to do. However, in the case of gaps, the difficulties arise due to a shortage of legal norms. In the case of dilemmas, they arise due to an abundance of legal norms.[160] While a gap is a legal state where 'the law support[s] neither side',[161] a legal dilemma reflects a state where the law supports both sides. The 1922 Treaty in the *Submarine Warfare* scenario,[162] for example, provided both for the permissibility and the

155 See Part I.A.2.c. 156 Perez (n 92) 5–6.

157 Timothy AO Endicott, *Vagueness in Law* (OUP 2000) 9.

158 The number of legal right answers to a dilemmatic norm conflict corresponds to the number of norms that constitute the dilemma.

159 There is a plethora of definitions of different kinds of legal gaps. For an overview, see Ulrich Fastenrath, *Lücken im Völkerrecht: zu Rechtscharakter, Quellen, Systemzusammenhang, Methodenlehre und Funktionen des Völkerrechts* (Duncker & Humblot 1991) 213–35; Stone (n 82) 140–3; Juliane Kokott, *The Burden of Proof in Comparative and International Human Rights Law: Civil and Common Law Approaches With Special Reference to the American and German Legal Systems* (Martinus Nijhoff 1998) 158–9; Claus-Wilhelm Canaris, *Die Feststellung von Lücken im Gesetz: eine methodologische Studie über Voraussetzungen und Grenzen der richterlichen Rechtsfortbildung praeter legem* (Duncker & Humblot 1964) 16; Alfred Verdross, *Völkerrecht* (5th edn, Springer 1964) 155; Karl Engisch, *Einführung in das juristische Denken* (9th edn, Kohlhammer 1997) 134.

160 With respect to norm conflicts, Loui observes, eg, that the 'problem is not … that there is no precedent that governs a case. The problem is that with no disingenuity, two or more precedents can be brought to bear on the case'. See Loui (n 29) 350. See also Neil MacCormick, 'Risking Constitutional Collision in Europe?' (1998) 18 Oxford Journal of Legal Studies 517, 530–1.

161 Bodansky (n 64) 161; Hugh Thirlway, 'The Nuclear Weapons Advisory Opinions: The Declarations and Separate and Dissenting Opinions' in Laurence Boisson de Chazournes and Philippe Sands (eds), *International Law, the International Court of Justice and Nuclear Weapons* (CUP 1999) 407–8.

162 Treaty relating to the Use of Submarines and Noxious Gases in Warfare (signed 6 February 1922) 25 LNTS 202 ('1922 Submarine Treaty').

prohibition of submarine warfare against merchant vessels. It would be inaccurate to characterize such a situation as a legal gap or as a state in which the law supports neither side. In this regard, legal dilemmas are diametrically opposed to legal gaps.[163]

Similarly, related concepts such as 'legal neutrality'[164] or 'silence'[165] do not capture the problem that legal dilemmas raise, as they refer equally to an absence rather than the superposition of legal norms. Likewise, the suggestion that international law might allow 'for the concept of toleration'[166] that transcends the 'binary understanding of permission/prohibition',[167] that provides 'for a range of non-prohibited options'[168] and that there might be a spectrum of 'degrees of non-prohibition'[169] or a 'middle ground'[170] between legality and illegality, does not adequately describe the problem posed by legal dilemmas. Conduct subject to dilemmatic regulation is not located on a spectrum between the legal conditions of legality and illegality. Dilemmatic conduct is both illegal and legal at the very same time—it occupies both ends of the legality spectrum (ranging from legality on the one side to illegality on the other) simultaneously. Nor is such conduct 'not-prohibited', as the concept of tolerance would suggest. There might well be other legal conditions, such as neutrality, toleration, vagueness, or indeterminacy but they raise issues quite distinct from legal dilemmas.

There is one concept of a legal gap that adequately captures certain aspects of a legal dilemma. Namely, the concept of a '*Kollisionslücke*',[171] which refers to the absence of a collision rule capable of resolving a given conflict of norms. Strictly speaking, however, it is misleading to describe such situations as '*Lücken*' as 'one does not actually have to deal with a gap but with a legal space which is occupied by two norms simultaneously.'[172] Further, the description of legal dilemmas as *Kollisionslücken* is undesirable, to the extent that the concept of a *Kollisionslücke* envisions that conflicting norms that are affected by a *Kollisionslücke* cancel each other out,[173] since the concept of a legal dilemma insists on the continued and simultaneous validity of both conflicting norms. Moreover, *Kollisionslücken* exist at a meta-level, removed from the primary rules applicable to a given situation.

163 Compare Quadrants II and IV of Figure IN.1 in the Introduction.

164 Stone (n 82) 136. For a distinction of dilemmas from indifference, see Marcus (n 33) 128.

165 *Accordance with International Law of the Unilateral Declaration of Independence in Respect of Kosovo (Advisory Opinion)* [2010] ICJ Rep 403 ('*Kosovo Advisory Opinion*'), Declaration of Judge Simma [9].

166 *Kosovo Advisory Opinion* (n 165), Declaration of Judge Simma [9].

167 *Kosovo Advisory Opinion* (n 165), Declaration of Judge Simma [9].

168 *Kosovo Advisory Opinion* (n 165), Declaration of Judge Simma [9].

169 *Kosovo Advisory Opinion* (n 165), Declaration of Judge Simma [8].

170 Goldie (n 92) 225.

171 Fastenrath (n 159) 227–9. Note that Raz's understanding of legal gaps also allows for the description of certain norm conflicts as gaps. Raz observes, eg, that 'unresolved conflict[s]' which exist 'when conflicting reasons fail to override each other … give rise to legal gaps'. See Joseph Raz, *The Authority of Law: Essays on Law and Morality* (2nd edn, OUP 2009) 75.

172 Fastenrath (n 159) 227 (tr by author).

173 See, eg, Christian Bumke, *Relative Rechtswidrigkeit: Systembildung und Binnendifferenzierungen im Öffentlichen Recht* (Mohr Siebeck 2004) 51.

In this regard, *Kollisionslücken* are similar to legal dilemmas but fundamentally different from legal gaps triggered by the absence of positive primary norms. For reasons that will be considered in detail below,[174] the distinction between legal gaps and legal dilemmas matters, in particular, because it means that *non liquet* declarations, which respond to legal gaps, are an inadequate response to legal dilemmas.

e) Paradoxes

Legal dilemmas, as defined here, do not refer—at least not directly—to systemic or structural contradictions of international law, which are sometimes described as dilemmatic[175] or paradoxical.[176] While legal dilemmas, like paradoxes, may concern contradictory and inconsistent elements of a legal system,[177] they focus specifically on concrete conduct norms,[178] rather than on abstract and general discussions of law's inherent systemic self-referential nature.

The paradoxical nature of certain legal questions can, of course, cause dilemmatic undecidability.[179] Indeed, some dilemmas may result from inherent, structural tensions within international law, such as the constant oscillation between the need to apologetically reflect State behaviour and to simultaneously prescribe normative conduct 'without being able to establish itself permanently in either position'.[180] Further, the acknowledgement of the concept of a legal dilemma certainly affects the way in which the international legal system is being conceptualized.[181] However, while legal dilemmas may often be linked to these systemic aspects, they could in principle exist even in perfectly coherent systemic

[174] See Part II.C.

[175] Koskenniemi, eg, named the first chapter of his seminal book on the structure of international legal argument, 'Objectivity in international law: conventional dilemmas'. See Koskenniemi, *From Apology to Utopia* (n 59) ch 1. See also the various meanings attributed to the term dilemma, most of which refer to intra-systemic paradoxes, by the various contributions in Gunther Teubner (ed), *Dilemmas of Law in the Welfare State* (Walter de Gruyter 1986). See, eg, Alberto Febbrajo, 'The Rules of the Game in the Welfare State' in Gunther Teubner (ed), *Dilemmas of Law in the Welfare State* (De Gruyter 1988) 144–146. Sylvest refers to international law's dilemma of the 'ecclesiastical dogma' stemming from the negative and positive effects of elastic and rigid interpretation, Casper Sylvest, 'International Law in Nineteenth-Century Britain' (2005) 75 BYIL 9, 9.

[176] Binder observes, eg, that '[t]he modern international legal system rests on a paradox—its legitimacy derives from the sovereignty of nations; yet, its function is the constraint of such sovereignty.' See Binder (n 97) 332–3. For a medieval engagement with law's supposedly contradictory nature, see Thomas Scott, *Foure Paradoxes of Art. Of Law. Of Warre. Of Service.* (Thomas Snodham 1611) ch 2.

[177] Perez (n 92) 14.

[178] Cf the definitions of the paradox offered by Hagenbüchle (n 8) and Paul Geyer, 'Historisch-systematische Grundlegung' in Roland Hagenbüchle and Paul Geyer (eds), *Das Paradox: eine Herausforderung des abendländischen Denkens* (2nd edn, Königshausen & Neumann 2002).

[179] On the different causes of dilemmatic undecidability, see Part I.C.

[180] Koskenniemi, *From Apology to Utopia* (n 59) 65. Other international legal de-stabilizing tensions exist between the territorial integrity of States and the peoples' right to self-determination or the consensual order of international law and the obligatory nature of international legal norms.

[181] See section B of the Conclusion.

contexts as a result of the occurrence of previously unconsidered events, for example, or due to a contradictory drafting of legal provisions (within a treaty, for instance).[182] Thus, some legal dilemmas may be related to structural contradictions or legal paradoxes. Nonetheless, legal dilemmas are in principle distinct from and should not be confused with paradoxes.

f) Disagreement

The most important difference between legal dilemmas and legal disagreement consists in the fact that legal dilemmas focus on the position of legal actors vis-à-vis the law, whereas disagreements[183] are '*intersubjective*'. They exist between legal actors *inter se* and 'oppose at least two people'.[184] Depending on the source of a dilemma, there can be links between intersubjective disagreements about law and legal dilemmas,[185] and legal dilemmas are certainly also intersubjective in the sense that they often affect the interests of more than one actor. However, once a legal dilemma has crystallized, the deliberative process of identifying (or disagreeing about) the precise content of norms has been completed. A legal actor facing a dilemma may negotiate with another actor about a mutually beneficial way of escaping a dilemma, but the actor does not dispute or disagree with another party about what the legal actor (legally) ought to do. Rather, the legal actor needs to make a choice between two or more equally justified courses of conduct, in the absence of a plurality of legal opinions concerning the relative weight which each option should be accorded. However, it is this plurality of equally justified, different, and conflicting legal opinions which disagreements are about. It would, of course, be possible to say that a legal actor facing a dilemma also disagrees (with itself) about what it should do in a dilemmatic situation. Yet this would be misleading, as a legal dilemma does not concern the subjective uncertainty about what a legal actor thinks it ought to do. Rather, legal dilemmas concern the question how two irresolvable norms, whose irreconcilability has been determined (by a court of law, if applicable) with reference to specific legal criteria and which are in that sense mind-independent, ought to be dealt with.[186]

[182] See Part I.B.1 and Part I.B.2.

[183] There are numerous definitions of legal disagreements; they 'come in all shapes and sizes'. See Jeremy Waldron, *Law and Disagreement* (OUP 1999) 149–51.

[184] Samantha Besson, *The Morality of Conflict: Reasonable Disagreement and the Law* (Hart 2005) 20. See also HE Mason, 'Responsibilities and Principles: Reflections on the Sources of Moral Dilemmas' in HE Mason (ed), *Moral Dilemmas and Moral Theory* (OUP 1996) 216.

[185] Specifically, disagreements can subsequently trigger legal dilemmas. See Part I.A.3.f. See also, Besson (n 184) 20.

[186] On the 'mind-independent' existence of incommensurability, see also Matthew H Kramer, 'When Is There Not One Right Answer?' (2008) 53 American Journal of Jurisprudence 49, 63. For an argument in favour of dilemmas being 'internal to individual conscience', see Besson (n 184) 20.

g) Hard cases

It might be tempting[187] to equate dilemmas with the 'hard cases'[188] that exist when legal provisions are vague, non-existent,[189] or located within a legal rule's 'penumbra of uncertainty'.[190] As established previously, however, legal dilemmas do not result from vague legal provisions or from the absence of norms. Instead, legal dilemmas arise from existing and determinate legal provisions. There is no doubt that certain potential legal dilemmas, such as the question concerning the legality of nuclear weapons, might concern factual scenarios that are 'hard' in the sense that they are 'ethically tragic'[191] but this is a corollary at best and not a constitutive element of legal dilemmas.

It should now be apparent that legal dilemmas may be similar to various other concepts, but that they are nonetheless distinct. Legal dilemmas do not concern non-existing, vague, indeterminate, moral, or paradox norms over which actors may disagree. Rather, legal dilemmas focus on an actor's relationship with unavoidable and irresolvable conflicts between existing, irreducible, and determinate legal conduct norms.

B. Factors Causing the Emergence of Dilemmas

This section considers four factors[192] that increase the probability that legal dilemmas occur within particular legal systems. The first two factors (prior fault, imperfect drafting) apply to legal systems in general. The latter two factors (the non-hierarchical nature of international law and fragmentation) apply to international law in particular.[193] The consideration of these factors at this stage is instructive, as the causes of a given dilemma to some extent inform the limitations of the norm conflict resolution devices discussed in the next part. Further, an actor's awareness of a dilemma's causes may influence how an actor responds to a given dilemma.

187 Pulkowski, eg, appears to conceptualize regime conflicts as 'hard cases'. See Pulkowski (n 44) 344. See also João Ernesto Christófolo, *Solving Antinomies between Peremptory Norms in Public International Law* (Schulthess 2016) 38–43. This might, perhaps, be defensible with respect to general regime conflicts and if one assumes that judicial actors decide regime conflicts in the same manner as they decide hard cases. However, it would certainly be misleading to describe dilemmas as hard cases and to compare the role of judicial actors observing dilemmas with that of judicial actors confronting hard cases. See Part III.A.2.a.

188 The concept of a 'hard case' and its implications has been hotly contested in recent decades by Hart and Dworkin amongst others. For an introduction to the debate, see Scott J Shapiro, 'The "Hart-Dworkin" Debate: A Short Guide for the Perplexed' (2007) Working Paper No. 77 Public Law and Legal Theory Working Paper Series. See also David Dyzenhaus, *Hard Cases in Wicked Legal Systems: Pathologies of Legality* (2nd edn, OUP 2010).

189 Ronald Dworkin, 'Hard Cases' (1975) 88 Harvard Law Review 1057, 1058.

190 Hart (n 80) 12, ch 7.

191 David Wolitz, 'Indeterminacy, Value Pluralism, and Tragic Cases' (2014) 62 Buffalo Law Review 529, 570.

192 The list of factors considered here is incomplete and merely aims to provide an overview of potential causes. Ultimately, the causes of dilemmas cannot be identified in the abstract and are likely to vary according to the particular circumstances. For additional lists of factors causing norm conflicts, see Conway (n 41) 980–1; Pauwelyn (n 2) 13–23; Anja Lindroos, 'Addressing Norm Conflicts in a Fragmented Legal System: The Doctrine of Lex Specialis' (2005) 74 Nordic Journal of International Law 27, 32.

193 These factors are nonetheless also good indicators of the likelihood of the occurrence of legal dilemmas in other legal contexts (such as domestic or regional systems).

1. An actor's prior fault

Even those who otherwise deny the possibility of dilemmas accept that an actor's prior fault can cause dilemmas to arise. Gratian's glossators[194] and Aquinas, for example, who categorically rejected the possibility of genuine dilemmas in principle, held the view that the only dilemmas that could possibly exist 'are those generated by an agent's prior misdeeds ... innocent agents never experience moral dilemmas'.[195] A cleric, for instance, who is obliged to baptize, but who has committed a sin, faces a self-induced dilemma, because owing to the 'serious sin he cannot baptize without committing an additional sin of irreverence'.[196]

Similarly, in international law, a State's previous unlawful conduct could contribute towards the occurrence of a subsequent dilemma. For example, if State X, in violation of a previous treaty$_1$ with State A, concludes a treaty$_2$ with State B, then international treaty law attributes[197] any resulting norm conflict triggered by State X's conclusion of treaty$_2$ to State X's prior defective behaviour (the conclusion of treaty$_2$).[198] The ILC's ARSIWA[199] and international law's debated[200] clean hands doctrine, according to which a State 'may not benefit from its own wrongful'[201] conduct, follow a similar rationale.

However, a State's prior fault does not necessarily have to be an unlawful activity in order to facilitate the emergence of a legal dilemma. Even a State's lawful conduct could make the occurrence of a dilemma more likely. For example, if State X, a member of the UN, joins the EU, State X exposes itself to the risk of encountering conflicts between norms deriving from the UN Charter,[202] on the one hand, and norms deriving from the EU Treaties,[203] on the other.[204] One might immediately

[194] Dougherty (n 36) 25–30.

[195] Dougherty (n 36) 139. Similarly, Hamblin considers the possibility of inconsistencies being caused by defective elements in a chain of causation of certain events, see Hamblin (n 91) 76–8. Aquinas's view presupposes, of course, that divine law is complete and coherent, a view—that some, like Gratian—disputed even at Aquinas's time. See Dougherty (n 36) 21.

[196] Dougherty (n 36) 123.

[197] As a result, international law normally does not recognize a norm conflict in such situations. However, there are significant exceptions. See Part II.

[198] See VCLT (n 51) Arts 61(2), 62(2)b.

[199] ILC, Articles on the Responsibility of States for Internationally Wrongful Acts annexed to UNGA Res 56/83 (12 December 2001) UN Doc A/Res/56/83 ('ARSIWA') Arts 25(2)b, 24(2)a, 23(2)a. See also Sandra Szurek, 'The Notion of Circumstances Precluding Wrongfulness' in James Crawford and others (eds), *The Law of International Responsibility* (OUP 2010) 436.

[200] James Crawford, *State Responsibility: The General Part* (CUP 2013) 278.

[201] ILC, Commentary to the ILC Articles on Responsibility of States for Internationally Wrongful Acts, ILC Ybk 2001/II(2) 31 ('*ARSIWA Commentary*') pt 1, ch 5 [9]. See also *Military and Paramilitary Activities in and against Nicaragua (Nicaragua v United States)* (Merits) [1986] ICJ Rep 14, Dissenting Opinion of Judge Schwebel [268–70]; Crawford (n 200) 278.

[202] Charter of the United Nations (adopted 26 June 1945, entered into force 25 October 1945) 1 UNTS XVI ('UN Charter').

[203] The EU Treaties are the Treaty on European Union (Consolidated Version of the Treaty on European Union [2012] OJ C326/01) and the TFEU (n 112).

[204] The *Kadi Cases* concerned this problem. See, Joined Cases C-402/05 P and C-415/05 P *Kadi and Al Barakaat International Foundation v Council of the European Union and Commission of the European Communities* [2008] ECR I-06351; Joined Cases C-584/10 P, C-593/10 P and C-595/10 P *Commission and Others v Kadi* (18 July 2013). See also Parts I.B.3 and II.A.2.

object that the link between State X's joining the EU and a subsequent, potential occurrence of a norm conflict is so tenuous that there is hardly any State activity that might not at some stage contribute to the occurrence of a dilemma. However, that is exactly the point. As soon as independent actors are introduced to a normative system and as soon as these actors start to act and start to make independent choices, they are inevitably increasing the risk of the occurrence of dilemmatic normative conflicts—whatever they do—even if they try to follow conscientiously every possible legal norm.[205] This is not necessarily a negative or positive thing. In fact, it is just part of the daily life of States that, at times, difficult decisions need to be taken. It is impossible to entirely avoid confronting dilemmatic predicaments.[206] The awareness that an actor's prior (faulty) conduct can facilitate the emergence of dilemmas is important, as it entails the acknowledgment that the creation of a dilemma-free world would require replacing States' independent will and autonomous conduct of their international relations with other States with a deterministic conception of law that leaves no room for any eventualities and unexpected developments.[207]

2. Imperfect drafting

This second factor, not unrelated to the previous one, concerns the risk that norm-creators may enact or adhere to potentially contradictory norms. While Aquinas and his contemporaries found it difficult to accept that the divine law creator could be guilty of incoherent lawmaking, positive international law is created by fallible humans.[208] It is inevitable, therefore, that drafting errors occur that can subsequently lead to dilemmatic situations. This can happen in two principal ways, corresponding to the previously established distinction between intrinsic and contingent norm conflicts: first, actors might (not necessarily unintentionally)[209] enact

[205] On the occurrence of norm conflicts despite an actor's unconditional norm-adherence, see Fabian Winter, Heiko Rauhut, and Dirk Helbig, 'How Norms Can Generate Conflict: An Experiment on the Failure of Cooperative Micro-Motives on the Macro-Level' (2012) 90 Social Forces 919, 924.

[206] This fact could in turn give rise to the question whether, if a State's engagement with international legal norms could lead to the confrontation with a legal dilemma and subsequent inevitable unlawful behaviour, States should (in the sense of Kant's categorical imperative) engage with international legal norms at all. While this question is not the focus of this book, Part III attempts to answer this question in the affirmative.

[207] Cf Ruth Barcan Marcus, 'More about Moral Dilemmas' in HE Mason (ed), *Moral Dilemmas and Moral Theory* (OUP 1996) 28–9.

[208] See, eg, Kedar who observed that '[t]he rule of law is always the rule of man. Law does not amend or justify itself; it is people who amend or justify their laws.' See Nir Kedar, 'The Political Origins of the Modern Legal Paradoxes' in Oren Perez and Gunther Teubner (eds), *Paradoxes and Inconsistencies in the Law* (Hart 2006) 102. Indeed, the rule of law is much more appropriately contrasted with the rule of power (physical or otherwise) than the rule of man, which, strictly speaking underpins both—the rule of law and the rule of power.

[209] Benvenisti and Downs observe, eg, that international law's intentional fragmentation, driven particularly by powerful States who conclude bilateral or multilateral treaties in conflict with existing agreements, is a powerful hegemonic tool. See Eyal Benvenisti and George W Downs, 'The Empire's New Clothes: Political Economy and the Fragmentation of International Law' (2007) 60 Stanford Law Review 595, 609. See also Borgen (n 96) 451; Surabhi Ranganathan, *Strategically Created Treaty Conflicts and the Politics of International Law* (CUP 2014). See also Part I.B.4.

inherently contradictory norms, triggering intrinsic conflicts, and, second, actors might draft norms that are incapable of dealing with certain factual events, leading to contingent conflicts.

The *Submarine Warfare* scenario provides a good example of an intrinsic norm conflict caused by imperfect drafting. Outlining first the conditions for a submarine's lawful attack of a merchant vessel in the 1922 Submarine Treaty's Article 1(1), Articles 1(2) and 4 of the 1922 Submarine Treaty subsequently prohibit the attack of merchant vessels outright.[210] This way, the 1922 Submarine Treaty simultaneously outlaws and legalizes—subject to certain conditions—submarine warfare against merchant vessels. Although the parties were acutely aware of that intrinsic contradiction at the drafting stage, the provisions of the 1922 Submarine Treaty were left unmodified.[211]

Further, it has been observed[212] that the Preamble of the Cartagena Protocol on Biosafety[213] contains an intrinsic contradiction. First, the Preamble states that the Protocol 'shall not be interpreted as implying a change in the rights and obligations of a Party under any existing international agreements'.[214] However, this passage is then followed by an '[u]nderstanding that the above recital is not intended to subordinate this Protocol to other international agreements'.[215] Either the parties' rights and obligations under existing international agreements remain unaffected (and the Protocol defers to such other agreements) or the Protocol has the same status as those agreements (as the second paragraph seems to suggest), in which case the parties' obligations would be affected (contrary to what the first paragraph suggests).

In domestic contexts, too, imperfect drafting can trigger norm conflicts. For example, where the federal legislature in a federal system issues laws in contradiction with State law, actors may confront conflicting norms deriving from federal and State law respectively.[216] However, inattentive drafting can even lead to contradictions within one and the same statute.[217] The recently disputed section 3

[210] 1922 Submarine Treaty (n 162) Art 4.

[211] Joel Ira Holwitt, *'Execute against Japan': The U.S. Decision to Conduct Unrestricted Submarine Warfare* (Texas A&M UP 2009) 34. See also Department of the Navy, 'An Attempt to Interpret the Treaty entered into to make more effective the Rules adopted by Civilized Nations for the Protection of the Lives of Neutrals and Noncombatants at Sea in time of war' (General Records of the Department of the Navy 1900–1947, General Board 438, Box: 168, Entry 281 A-1, 13 February 1922) 10.

[212] Pauwelyn (n 2) 334.

[213] Cartagena Protocol on Biosafety to the Convention on Biological Diversity (concluded 29 January 2000, entered into force 11 September 2003) 2226 UNTS 208 ('Cartagena Protocol').

[214] Cartagena Protocol (n 213), Preamble, para 10.

[215] Cartagena Protocol (n 213), Preamble, para 11.

[216] See, eg, *Case concerning the Constitutionality of Steering Taxes* (1998) Case No 2 BvR 1876/91, BVerfGe 98, 83, [139]–[141] (German Federal Constitutional Court) regarding a conflict between State and federal law in the context of the public management system of waste disposal.

[217] See also the decision of the German Federal Constitutional Court in a case concerning contradictory provisions of a statute that provided for a referendum regarding the re-structuring of three southern German federal States shortly after the Second World War, *Case concerning a Plebiscite on a German South-West State* (1951) Case No 2 BvG 1/51, BVerfGe 1, 14, 45, [82], [122] (German Constitutional Court). The case *Blake v National Bank* 90 US (23 Wall) 307 (1874) 311 (Supreme Court of the United States) refers to a contradictory provision in a US domestic statute (section 15 of the Internal Revenue Act 1870 (United States)).

of the 2002 Child Status Protection Act (US) provides a good example of such a 'Janus-Faced'[218] provision.[219] In that instance, it was not clear whether section 3, which concerned the freezing of visa application dates beyond a derivative beneficiary's twenty-first birthday, provided such an 'aged-out' applicant with an immediate remedy, or whether such an applicant could retain the original priority date of a visa application only if the applicant had an independent relationship with the initial petitioner. Feeling unable to resolve the conflict definitively, the US Supreme Court eventually deferred to the executive agency's restrictive interpretation.[220]

Similarly, imperfect drafting can cause contingent norm conflicts. In fact, just like innocent State conduct, almost every pair of provisions could be brought into conflict by an imaginative mind's construction of certain events. In addition to the *Nuclear Weapons, Military Alliances*, and *Distress at Sea* scenarios discussed above, a contingent conflict could, for example, also arise in the context of the 1997 International Watercourses Convention ('UNWC').[221] According to Articles 5 and 6 of the UNWC, States are entitled to utilize shared watercourses in an equitable and reasonable manner. While numerous factors assist with a determination of what might be equitable and reasonable,[222] 'requirements of vital human needs'[223] are of particular importance. At the same time, the UNWC imposes on States the obligation not to cause 'significant harm to other watercourse States'.[224] A contingent conflict arises in a situation where the 'vital human needs' of one State cannot be met without causing 'significant harm' in another watercourse State.[225]

With respect to each of the scenarios mentioned above, careful drafting could have reduced the risk that contingent conflicts will arise. Nonetheless, even careful drafting cannot entirely prevent at least the emergence of future contingent dilemmas. This is so, not just because human lawmaking is inevitably imperfect, but also because it is simply impossible to foresee the emergence of every factual scenario. This is particularly the case in international law, with its multiplicity of actors, decentralized legislation, and proliferation of adjudication instruments.

3. The non-hierarchical nature of international law

In addition to the two factors considered above, international law's non-hierarchical nature makes it particularly susceptible to the occurrence of norm conflicts.[226]

[218] *Scialabba v Cuellar de Osorio* 134 S. Ct. 2191 (2014) 14 (Supreme Court of the United States).

[219] *Scialabba v Cuellar de Osorio* (n 218) 14. See also 'Scialabba v Cuellar de Osorio' (2014) 128 Harvard Law Review 341.

[220] *Scialabba v Cuellar de Osorio* (n 218) 14.

[221] Convention on the Law of the Non-Navigational Uses of International Watercourses (adopted 21 May 1997, entered into force 17 August 2014) 36 ILM 700 ('UNWC').

[222] UNWC (n 221) Art 6. [223] UNWC (n 221) Art 10(2).

[224] UNWC (n 221) Art 7.

[225] Such a situation could arise when the upstream riparians of the Nile River Basin need to utilize more Nile water than they currently do, leading to water shortages with severe consequences in Egypt.

[226] Hafner identifies additional factors that contribute towards the likelihood of the occurrence of conflicts of norms in international law, including the lack of centralized organs, the specialization of regulations, the existence of different regimes of secondary rules, and the different structures

Most domestic legal systems possess a sophisticated hierarchy of norms, which helps resolving conflicts to the largest possible extent, for example, by means of the *lex superior* principle.[227] Most norms of international law, however, do not exist in hierarchical relationships.[228] Instead, they are, at least by default, of equal or innominate rank.[229] Conflicts between such international legal norms cannot be resolved within a hierarchical framework. Instead, they need to be resolved on a casuistic basis[230] or with reference to international law's 'informal hierarchy',[231] which accords priority first, to *ius cogens* obligations and, second, to obligations arising pursuant to the UN Charter. These will each be briefly considered in turn.

Ius cogens or 'peremptory norms' are norms[232] that are:

> accepted and recognized by the international community of states as a whole as a norm from which no derogation is permitted and which can be modified only by a subsequent norm of general international law having the same character.[233]

The Vienna Conventions on the Laws of Treaties[234] and the ARSIWA[235] refer explicitly to the concept of *ius cogens*, and the ILC states that:

> the concept of peremptory norms of general international law is recognized in international practice, in the jurisprudence of international and national courts and tribunals and in legal doctrine.[236]

Nonetheless, the precise effect[237] and definition[238] of *ius cogens* norms remain disputed. Further, although *inter alia* the prohibition of slavery, torture, genocide, and aggression are commonly cited[239] as examples of *ius cogens* norms, there is no

of international legal norms. See Gerhard Hafner, 'Pros and Cons Ensuing from Fragmentation of International Law' (2003) 25 Michigan Journal of International Law 849, 854–5.

227 See Part II.A.1.

228 ILC, *Fragmentation Report* (n 48) paras 323–4; Rüdiger Wolfrum, 'Sources of International Law' in Rüdiger Wolfrum (ed), *Max Planck Encyclopedia of Public International Law* (Online ed, Max Planck Institute for Comparative Public Law and International Law 2011) para 11; Czapliński and Danilenko (n 97) 7–8; Lindroos (n 192) 28–9.

229 ILC, *Fragmentation Report* (n 48) paras 323–4; Pauwelyn (n 2) ch 3.

230 Wolfrum (n 228) 11; Jorge E Viñuales, *Foreign Investment and the Environment in International Law* (CUP 2012) 141. For such cases, a plethora of norm conflict resolution devices exists.

231 ILC, *Fragmentation Report* (n 48) para 327; Lindroos (n 192) 28–9.

232 On *ius cogens* in general, see ILC, *Fragmentation Report* (n 48) para 361; Alexander Orakhelashvili, *Peremptory Norms in International Law* (OUP 2006).

233 ILC, *ARSIWA* (n 199) Art 26; VCLT (n 51) Arts 53, 64.

234 VCLT (n 51) Art 53; Vienna Convention on the Law of Treaties between States and International Organizations or between International Organizations (adopted 21 March 1986) (1986) 25 ILM 543 Art 53.

235 ILC, *ARSIWA* (n 199) Art 26; VCLT (n 51) Arts 53, 64.

236 ILC, *ARSIWA Commentary* (n 201) Art 40 [2].

237 Dinah Shelton, 'Normative Hierarchy in International Law' (2006) 100 AJIL 291, 304.

238 Ulf Linderfalk, 'The Effect of Jus Cogens Norms: Whoever Opened Pandora's Box, Did You Ever Think About the Consequences?' (2007) 18 EJIL 853; Czapliński and Danilenko (n 97) 8.

239 ILC, *ARSIWA Commentary* (n 201) Art 40 [4]–[6]; ILC, *Fragmentation Report* (n 48) paras 377–9. Additionally, the following norms are generally accepted as *ius cogens* norms: the right to self-determination, the prohibition of systematic racial discrimination, the prohibition of crimes against humanity. See Crawford (n 200) 316.

exhaustive agreement as to which norms enjoy the status of *ius cogens*.[240] Thus, while the concept of *ius cogens* norms does alleviate the risk of the occurrence of irresolvable norm conflicts between *ius cogens* norms and other norms, '[t]here are only a few *jus cogens* norms [and] their content is often unclear'.[241] Most problematically, it is unclear how conflicts between *ius cogens* norms *inter se* could be resolved.[242] Indeed, it will be shown below that conflicts between *ius cogens* norms are prone to trigger the most severe of norm conflicts.

Alongside *ius cogens* norms, Article 103 of the UN Charter[243] provides that 'obligations of the Members of the United Nations under [the UN Charter]' prevail over UN members' 'obligations under any other international agreement'.[244] The priority of UN members' obligations arising under the UN Charter includes the 'binding decisions by United Nations bodies'[245] and applies to UN members' future agreements and to agreements with non-UN members.[246] As result, a UN member State's obligations conflicting with UN obligations are suspended.[247] In a similar manner to *ius cogens* norms, Article 103 of the UN Charter can thus lower the risk of norm conflicts occurring in international law, despite the absence of a formal hierarchy.

However, even leaving aside questions as to the meaning the provision attributes to the term 'conflict',[248] the utility of Article 103, UN Charter, is undermined by numerous problems. First, the article does not assist with conflicts between two obligations, both of which arise under the UN Charter. Second, it is disputed whether Article 103, UN Charter, applies only to conflicting 'agreements' or whether it also establishes a priority of obligations arising under the UN Charter over those arising under general international law such as customary law.[249] It is comparatively more settled that obligations under the UN Charter cannot prevail over, and are subordinate to, *ius cogens* obligations.[250] Third, it is disputed whether

240 Shelton (n 237) 302; ILC, *Fragmentation Report* (n 48) para 375.

241 Lindroos (n 192) 28–9.

242 See Part II.A.1 and see generally Kolb (n 39); Christófolo (n 187).

243 For a historic contextualization of the provision, see Jenks (n 77) 436–7.

244 UN Charter (n 202) Art 103. See also VCLT (n 51) Art 30(1).

245 ILC, *Fragmentation Report* (n 48) para 331. See also *Questions of Interpretation and Application of the 1971 Montreal Convention arising from the Aerial Incident at Lockerbie (Libyan Arab Jamahiriya v United Kingdom)* (Request for the Indication of Provisional Measures: Order) [1992] ICJ Rep 3 [39].

246 ILC, *Fragmentation Report* (n 48) para 330. It is not clear whether Article 103, UN Charter, can also supersede the conventional obligations of a UN member to a non-UN-member (rather than to the UN or its members itself).

247 ILC, *Fragmentation Report* (n 48) para 333; Jure Vidmar, 'Norm Conflicts and Hierarchy in International Law' in Erika de Wet and Jure Vidmar (eds), *Hierarchy in International Law: The Place of Human Rights* (OUP 2012) 19.

248 Johann Ruben Leiss and Andreas Paulus, 'Article 103' in Bruno Simma and others (eds), *The Charter of the United Nations: A Commentary*, vol 2 (3rd edn, OUP 2012) 2122–3.

249 ILC, *Fragmentation Report* (n 48) paras 344–5; Rudolf Bernhardt, 'Article 103' in Bruno Simma and others (eds), *The Charter of the United Nations: A Commentary*, vol 2 (2nd edn, OUP 2002) 1298–9; Vidmar (n 247) 18; Leiss and Paulus (n 248) 2132–3. In practice, however, Article 103, UN Charter, would probably prevail in most cases to the extent that the UN Charter is applied as *lex specialis* vis-à-vis a less specific, conflicting customary norm.

250 ILC, *Fragmentation Report* (n 48) para 360; Vidmar (n 247) 22; Leiss and Paulus (n 248) 2119–20.

Article 103, UN Charter, can trump the obligations of a UN member to a non-UN member based on an agreement concluded between the UN member and the non-UN member[251] and whether Article 103 of the UN Charter could apply to agreements concluded between States who are not UN members.[252] Finally, the article cannot preclude the possibility that a State encounters a conflict between two norms, one of which is imposed by an organization, such as the EU, which is not a party to the UN Charter and is thus not bound by the Charter's Article 103. This question crystallized most famously in the *Kadi Cases*,[253] which concerned the imposition of sanctions on an individual by an EC Commission Regulation,[254] in accordance with two UN Security Council Resolutions.[255] Undeterred by the general priority of Article 103 obligations, the Court of Justice of the European Union ('CJEU') held,[256] and confirmed on appeal,[257] that the circumstances surrounding the listing of the applicant 'patently' violated the applicant's 'rights of the defence, in particular the right to be heard, and the right to effective judicial review of those rights'.[258] Apart from calling into question the supremacy of Article 103 obligations (although the CJEU avoided a direct discussion of Article 103, UN Charter and sought to limit itself to an indirect review of the UN Security Council resolution by focussing on the legality of the EC Commission Regulation),[259] *Kadi* put States that are UN and EU members in 'an impossible position as regards meeting their international obligations'.[260] The CJEU's refusal to subordinate EU obligations to Article 103, UN Charter, means that situations can arise where EU members must comply, for example, with UN Security Council Resolutions, while being simultaneously bound to comply with conflicting EU norms.

It follows that, although *ius cogens* norms and Article 103, UN Charter, can rein in the dilemma-inducing effects of the non-hierarchical nature of the international legal order in some respects, the extent of that ability is limited by numerous uncertainties and, most importantly, by the residual problem that concerns the possibility of conflicts arising between norms of the same or innominate rank. Another issue, which the two superior categories of norms leave unaddressed, concerns international law's lack of an institutional hierarchy.[261] This issue is especially exacerbated by international law's increasing fragmentation.

[251] Bernhardt (n 249) 1298; ILC, *Fragmentation Report* (n 48) para 343; Leiss and Paulus (n 248) 2129–30.

[252] In this case Article 103, UN Charter, could at best apply as a norm of customary law.

[253] *Kadi and Al Barakaat* (n 204); *Commission and Others v Kadi* (n 204).

[254] Commission Regulation (EC) 2062/2001 of 19 October 2001 amending for the third time Regulation 467/2001, Annex I [2001] OJ L277/25.

[255] UNSC Res 1267 (15 October 1999) UN Doc S/RES/1267; UNSC Res 1333 (19 December 2000) UN Doc S/RES/1333.

[256] *Kadi and Al Barakaat* (n 204) [334].

[257] *Commission and Others v Kadi* (n 204) [163].

[258] *Kadi and Al Barakaat* (n 204) [334].

[259] *Kadi and Al Barakaat* (n 204) [87], [314].

[260] *Commission and Others v Kadi* (n 204) [61].

[261] With the exception of UN Security Council action pursuant to Chapter VII, UN Charter (n 202).

4. Fragmentation

International law is to an extent 'fragmented', in the sense that there are various more or less disparate substantive sovereigns and regimes that are continuously created and modified by a multiplicity of different legal actors. Although this fragmentation is by no means a 'modern phenomenon',[262] recent decades have witnessed a notable extension of the material scope of international law. Likewise, the number of actors who are subject to, and shape, international law has increased significantly. This enlargement of international law's material and personal scope makes the occurrence of conflicts between norms originating from different[263] international legal regimes and enacted by different legal actors much more likely.

Materially, international law has diversified, both in terms of substantive subject matters now regulated by international law, such as international environmental law, international criminal law, or international economic law, and in terms of an increased number of regional legal regimes, including *inter alia* the EU, the Inter-American Human Rights Regime (comprised of the Inter-American Commission on Human Rights and the Inter-American Court of Human Rights ('IACtHR')) and the African Union.

International law's material diversification has been accompanied by a proliferation of the number and kind of legal actors who are subject to, and shape, international law. Many of international law's specialized subject areas now possess, for example, their own specialized institutions such as the World Trade Organization ('WTO'), the World Intellectual Property Organization, or the World Health Organization. Likewise, many of the regional and subject-matter specific regimes[264] have their own judicial bodies such as the European Court of Human Rights ('ECtHR'), the CJEU, the IACtHR, the International Criminal Court ('ICC'), and the International Tribunal for the Law of the Sea. Compared to 1945, when no more than ten[265] international judicial bodies existed,[266] there are now more than 100 international judicial bodies that make legal determinations based on international law.[267] In line with the observation that 'there

[262] Joost Pauwelyn, 'Fragmentation' in Rüdiger Wolfrum (ed), *Max Planck Encyclopedia of Public International Law* (Online ed, Max Planck Institute for Comparative Public Law and International Law 2006) para 7; ILC, *Fragmentation Report* (n 48) para 486.

[263] The likelihood of conflicts arising between norms of the same fragment or regime is of course unaffected by the phenomenon of fragmentation.

[264] Borgen (n 96) 451–3.

[265] This figure excludes ad hoc tribunals.

[266] The Permanent Court of International Justice, the Permanent Court of Arbitration, the Central American Tribunal, three bodies of the International Labour Organization (the Commission of Inquiry, the Committee of Experts on the Application of Conventions and Recommendations, the Conference Committee on the Application of Conventions), the International Joint Commission, the Bank for International Settlements Tribunal, the International Civil Aviation Organization Council, the League of Nations Administrative Tribunal. See Cesare PR Romano, 'The Project on International Courts and Tribunals: The International Judiciary in Context (A Synoptic Chart)' <http://www.pict-pcti.org/publications/synoptic_chart/synop_c4.pdf> accessed 27 January 2017.

[267] Romano (n 266); Andreas Fischer-Lescano and Gunther Teubner, 'Fragmentierung des Weltrechts: Vernetzung Globaler Regimes statt etatistischer Rechtseinheit' in Mathias Albert

are as many law-makers as there are subjects of international law',[268] the sheer number and the diverse and often divergent interests of different legal actors and judicial bodies who are involved in shaping international law contribute significantly to the risk that conflicts between legal norms of different specialized regimes will arise: for example, conflicts between human rights norms and economic norms; or conflicts between EU norms and norms of the European Convention on Human Rights ('ECHR')[269].[270] The relatively recent controversy concerning the environmental impact of the UK's MOX Plant, which triggered parallel proceedings in three regimes,[271] illustrates the effects of fragmentation very well.

Although the link between the ongoing fragmentation of international law and the occurrence of norm conflicts should not be overstated, and while numerous proposals[272] have been advanced to smooth the potential frictions between the different fragments of international law, it is beyond doubt that the fragmented nature of international law contributes significantly towards the likelihood of the occurrence of norm conflicts and legal dilemmas in international law.

C. Distinguishing Epistemic and Metaphysical Undecidability

Having considered various factors that make the occurrence of dilemmas more likely, this section briefly distinguishes two kinds of dilemmatic undecidability: epistemic undecidability and metaphysical undecidability.[273] Consideration of the nature of dilemmatic undecidability is instructive at this stage both because it influences an actor's response to a particular dilemma, and also because it allows for a better appreciation of the various limitations of the norm conflict resolution devices discussed in the next part.

Epistemic undecidability exists with respect to dilemmas that are caused by normative super-complexity and/or by an actor's 'limited ability to discern rightly

and Rudolf Stichweh (eds), *Weltstaat und Weltstaatlichkeit: Beobachtungen globaler politischer Strukturbildung* (Verlag für Sozialwissenschaft 2007) 37.

268 Pauwelyn (n 262) para 7.

269 Convention for the Protection of Human Rights and Fundamental Freedoms (signed 4 November 1950, entered into force 3 September 1953) 213 UNTS 221.

270 ILC, *Fragmentation Report* (n 48) para 489.

271 See also ILC, *Fragmentation Report* (n 48) paras 10–12 and Part II.A.2.

272 ILC, *Fragmentation Report* (n 48) paras 491–3; Joost Pauwelyn, 'Bridging Fragmentation and Unity: International Law as a Universe of Inter-Connected Islands' (2003) 25 Michigan Journal of International Law 903, 915–16; Grosse Ruse-Khan (n 124) 321. See generally Part II.

273 This distinction is not dissimilar to Gray's division of Berlin's value-conflicts into empirical and conceptual conflicts (John Gray, *Isaiah Berlin* (Princeton UP 1996) 55) or to da Silva's distinction between 'ontic' and 'epistemic' roughness. See Virgílio Afonso da Silva, 'Comparing the Incommensurable: Constitutional Principles, Balancing and Rational Decision' (2011) 31 Oxford Journal of Legal Studies 273, 295.

among information'.[274] In other words, it might be clear in principle what the law should and could regulate but the challenge is to ensure that positive law actually reflects such an underlying normative consensus. For example, if all States were to agree that nuclear weapons should be prohibited without exception, the currently existing dilemma concerning the threat or use of such weapons could be overcome by crafting a new treaty bringing positive law and States' views into line. Similarly, if States were to agree that the 1922 Submarine Treaty[275] should actually have prohibited submarine warfare against merchant vessels, States could amend that treaty accordingly. So epistemic undecidability can be cured (at least retrospectively) by modifying particular legal norms, by identifying already existing 'principles, not yet codified, which would [be able] to resolve such dilemmas',[276] or by researching altogether novel ways to regulate a given legal question.

Metaphysical undecidability, on the other hand, does not result from inadequate drafting processes or epistemic (mis-)understandings.[277] Rather, metaphysical undecidability responds to the deontological impossibility of establishing a preference between conflicting norms and/or to States' fundamental disagreements concerning the course of the world materializing within and among the international legal order(s), running alongside and across the contours of regional regimes, national legal systems, and specific subject-matter jurisdictions. Metaphysically undecidable dilemmas reflect entrenched conflicts of values,[278] rationalities,[279] political theories,[280] objectives,[281] principles,[282] or ideals[283] among relevant international legal actors. To the extent that international law contains conflicts of this kind, such underlying inconsistencies will be projected onto the firmament of positive law that arches over social reality. Such normative tensions call for direct engagement with the underlying controversies, explicitly going beyond the conventional parameters of legal reasoning.[284] In the *Nuclear Weapons* scenario, for example, such a controversy could relate to the question as to whether the survival

[274] Besson (n 184) 53. See also Roy Sorensen, 'Epistemic Paradoxes' in Edward N Zalta (ed), *The Stanford Encyclopedia of Philosophy* (Spring edn, 2014) <http://plato.stanford.edu/archives/spr2014/entries/epistemic-paradoxes/> accessed 24 May 2017.

[275] See Part I.B.2.

[276] Thomas Nagel, 'War and Massacre' (1972) 1 Philosophy & Public Affairs 123, 143.

[277] Alasdair MacIntyre, *Whose Justice? Which Rationality?* (Duckworth Gerald 1988) 142.

[278] Besson (n 184) 54; Wolitz (n 191) 554–5.

[279] Andreas Fischer-Lescano and Gunther Teubner, 'Regime-Collisions: The Vain Search for Legal Unity in the Fragmentation of Global Law' (2004) 25 Michigan Journal of International Law 999, 1003–4.

[280] Even Dworkin accepts that there are cases where there is no one right answer, eg, when 'two different political theories, which suggest different answers to that question, for some reason each provide exactly as good a justification of the settled law as the other.' See Dworkin (n 82) 83–4. However, Dworkin limits this concession to 'immature legal systems'.

[281] Wolitz (n 191) 554–5.

[282] Marcus (n 207) 25; Nagel (n 276) 143.

[283] Kammerhofer (n 126) 4.

[284] Correspondingly, the medieval Franciscan Raymond Lull argued that only the *deus ex machina*, only divine intervention, could save agents facing dilemmas resulting from a disordered moral universe (rather than the agent's limited perception of reality). See Dougherty (n 36) 108, 111.

of sovereign States should be more important than the protection of humans from unbearable suffering.[285] Indeed, in the *Nuclear Weapons Advisory Opinion* the ICJ attributed the difficulty of reaching an unequivocal decision to the 'continuing difference of views' between nuclear weapon States and the non-nuclear weapon States 'with regard to the legal status of weapons as deadly as nuclear weapons'.[286] Similarly, in the case of a contingent water law dilemma, one question could be whether it is desirable to prioritize the satisfaction of all riparians' vital human needs even if such prioritization would significantly harm the existing uses of certain riparians. The issue is more protracted still if there are insufficient water resources to satisfy the vital human needs of all riparians. In dilemmatic situations of this kind, judicial actors will not be able to find the answers to such questions in international legal texts or custom. Instead, dilemmas that concern metaphysical undecidability call for an 'explicitly political' debate[287] with all affected stakeholders (inside and outside of judicial fora) in order to identify whether and how a given conflict could be solved. For as long as these underlying metaphysical questions remain unresolved, and they may well turn out to be irresolvable when the interests concerned are incommensurable, absolute, or indivisible,[288] dilemmas which are rooted in such divergent views will remain uncured.

The distinction between epistemic and metaphysical undecidability matters, as it determines the kind of efforts that might be taken following the emergence of a dilemma.[289] States might sensibly hope to prevent the (re-)emergence of a dilemma caused by epistemic undecidability relating to a legally imperfect regulation of a particular legal issue by directing efforts towards bringing positive law in line with the actualities of a given situation. However, such hopes are less apposite when States deal with an undecided or undecidable metaphysical question.[290] In such cases, the focus must shift from norm modification efforts to concerted attempts to find ways to accommodate and to negotiate the existence of such metaphysical dilemmas within a polynormative[291] legal order in a productive and fruitful manner.

In an attempt to answer the book's first question 'What is a Legal Dilemma?', the first part stipulated a definition of a legal dilemma. The definition provides that a legal dilemma exists when an actor confronts an irresolvable and unavoidable conflict between at least two legal norms so that obeying or applying one norm necessarily entails the undue impairment of the other. In order to sharpen the concept of a legal dilemma further, the first part also distinguished jurisprudential concepts

[285] More poignantly, Judge Bedjaoui observed that the tension in the *Nuclear Weapons Advisory Opinion* concerned the conflict between a 'State's right to survival' on the one hand and the 'survival of all mankind' on the other. See *Nuclear Weapons Advisory Opinion* (n 64), Declaration of President Bedjaoui [22].

[286] *Nuclear Weapons Advisory Opinion* (n 64) [98].

[287] Fischer-Lescano and Teubner (n 279) 1003–4.

[288] See Part II.A.3.

[289] See also Part III.A.3.a.

[290] The nature of a given dilemma's undecidability might not always be apparent before attempts to rectify a given dilemma are undertaken.

[291] Weil (n 45) 118–19.

that are related to, and yet different from, legal dilemmas. The final two sections considered the causes of dilemmas and the nature of their undecidability. Against this background, the following part now seeks to answer the second question, 'Can legal dilemmas exist in contemporary international law?'. Thus, in order to test the adequacy of the definition of a legal dilemma proposed in the first part, the second part attempts to determine whether legal dilemmas can possibly feature in the international legal order, or whether the existence of contemporary international law's sophisticated norm conflict resolution devices and accommodation mechanisms precludes their possibility.

Part II

The Possibility of a Legal Dilemma

The aim of the second part is to validate the stipulative definition of Part I by identifying those norm conflicts which contemporary international law cannot satisfactorily resolve. In doing so, this part answers the second research question—whether legal dilemmas could exist in international law—in the affirmative and demarcates the doctrinal space that legal dilemmas occupy. The argument will be developed in three sections. The first section identifies the inherent limitations of norm conflict resolution devices. Norm conflict resolution devices deal with a norm conflict by establishing a hierarchy or a compromise between norms. They thereby identify a course of action that avoids impairing either norm unduly. The second section then considers the limitation of norm conflict accommodation devices. Norm conflict accommodation devices do not resolve conflicts. Instead, they provide actors facing a dilemma with a justification or an excuse to impair an otherwise protected norm. The third section then explains why measures of last resort do not preclude the possibility of the existence of legal dilemmas. Measures of last resort are default rules and *non liquet* declarations which courts could supposedly utilize in dilemmatic circumstances when no other device yields satisfactory results.

It should be noted at the outset that this section does not aim to establish the inherent unsuitability or defectiveness of the devices and mechanisms discussed. For the purposes of establishing the possibility of dilemmas, it suffices to show that there are certain types of norm conflict that contemporary international law's norm conflict resolution devices and accommodation mechanisms are unable or unsuitable to deal with. This is what this part aims to do.

A. The Limitations of Norm Conflict Resolution Devices

This section identifies the limits of three norm conflict resolution devices. First, the section considers the inherent limitations of international law's three traditional norm conflict resolution principles (*lex specialis, lex posterior*, and *lex superior*). Second, the inherent limitations of conflict-of-laws approaches will be evaluated. Finally, this section establishes the limited ability of solving norm conflicts by means of proportionality tests.

1. Traditional norm conflict resolution principles

International law's traditional norm conflict resolution principles are the *lex specialis* principle, the *lex posterior* principle, and the *lex superior* principle. The three principles resolve conflicts between two legal norms by establishing a hierarchy between conflicting norms in favour of the more specific norm (*lex specialis*),[1] the later[2] norm (*lex posterior*),[3] and the norm of higher rank (*lex superior*).[4] They thereby identify a course of action that avoids impairing either norm unduly. These three principles are the ones most commonly used and accepted.[5] However, their legal status,[6] rationale,[7] and their relationship *inter se*[8] are disputed in international law.[9]

[1] Justinian, *Digesta* (Theodor Mommsen and Paul Krüger eds, Weidmann 1954) 50.17.80, 48.19.41 (Papinianus); Emer de Vattel, *The Law of Nations* (Luke White 1792) para 316; Hugo Grotius, *The Rights of War and Peace* (Liberty Fund 2005) bk 2, ch XVI, s XXIX; Gerald Fitzmaurice, 'The Law and Procedure of the International Court of Justice 1951–4: Treaty Interpretation and Other Treaty Points' (1957) 33 BYIL 203; Dionisio Anzilotti, *Cours de Droit International*, vol 1 (Gilbert Gidel tr, Sirey 1929) 103; ILC, Report of the Study Group of the International Law Commission finalized by Martti Koskenniemi, *Fragmentation of International Law: Difficulties Arising from the Diversification and Expansion of International Law* (13 April 2006) UN Doc A/CN.4/L.682 ('*Fragmentation Report*') para 119; Joost Pauwelyn, *Conflict of Norms in Public International Law* (CUP 2003) 385; Gerard Conway, 'Conflicts of Competence Norms in EU Law and the Legal Reasoning of the ECJ' (2010) 11 German Law Journal 966, 985; C Wilfred Jenks, 'The Conflict of Law-Making Treaties' (1953) 30 BYIL 401, 446.

[2] Sometimes the reverse rationale, prioritizing not the newest but the older norm, is favoured instead. For contemporary examples, see Consolidated version of the Treaty on the Functioning of the European Union [2012] OJ 326/1 ('TFEU') Art 351; Convention on the Law of the Non-Navigational Uses of International Watercourses (adopted 21 May 1997, entered into force 17 August 2014) 36 ILM 700 Art 3.

[3] ILC, *Fragmentation Report* (n 1) para 225; Antonios Tzanakopoulos, 'Collective Security and Human Rights' in Erika de Wet and Jure Vidmar (eds), *Hierarchy in International Law: The Place of Human Rights* (OUP 2012) 46.

[4] See generally Ralf Michaels and Joost Pauwelyn, 'Conflict of Norms or Conflict of Laws?: Different Techniques in the Fragmentation of Public International Law' (2012) 22 Duke Journal of Comparative & International Law 349, 354; Conway (n 1) 984–5; MV Dougherty, *Moral Dilemmas in Medieval Thought: From Gratian to Aquinas* (CUP 2011) 19–20.

[5] Jörg Kammerhofer, 'Unearthing Structural Uncertainty through Neo-Kelsenian Consistency: Conflicts of Norms in International Law' 4 <http:/www.esil-sedi.eu/sites/default/files/Kammerhofer.pdf> accessed 23 January 2017. In addition to these principles, Zuleeg and Jenks list the autonomous operation principle, the 'pith and substance' principle, and the legislative intention principle. See Manfred Zuleeg, 'Vertragskonkurrenz im Völkerrecht. Teil I: Verträge zwischen souveränen Staaten' (1977) 20 German Yearbook of International Law 246, 265–6; Jenks (n 1) 436. For further variants see also Anja Lindroos, 'Addressing Norm Conflicts in a Fragmented Legal System: The Doctrine of Lex Specialis' (2005) 74 Nordic Journal of International Law 27, 38–9; Georg Schwarzenberger, *International Law as Applied by International Courts and Tribunals*, vol 1 (3rd edn, Stevens 1957) 472.

[6] Vranes identifies at least ten different statuses of these principles. See Erich Vranes, 'Lex Superior, Lex Specialis, Lex Posterior—Zur Rechtsnatur der "Konfliktlösungsregeln"' (2005) 65 Zeitschrift für ausländisches öffentliches Recht und Völkerrecht 391, 392–5. See also Jenks (n 1) 436; Schwarzenberger (n 5) 473.

[7] Marko Milanovic, 'The Lost Origins of *Lex Specialis*: Rethinking the Relationship between Human Rights and International Humanitarian Law' in Jens David Ohlin (ed), *Theoretical Boundaries of Armed Conflict and Human Rights* (CUP 2016) 30.

[8] Lindroos (n 5) 41; Jenks (n 1) 407, 436; Vranes (n 6) 391, 392, 394; Conway (n 1) 987; Karl Engisch, *Die Einheit der Rechtsordnung* (Winter 1935) 47; Christopher J Borgen, 'Treaty Conflicts and Normative Fragmentation' in Duncan Hollis (ed), *The Oxford Guide to Treaties* (OUP 2012) 467–8. Compare also Pauwelyn (n 1) 407, 408; Tzanakopoulos (n 3) 46.

[9] Kammerhofer (n 5) 1–2, 4; Vranes (n 6) 391.

Rather than outlining and analysing the general debate on the merits and shortcomings of these three particular principles, which has been amply done by others,[10] this section considers the principles' utility specifically and exclusively in the context of the debate about irresolvable norm conflicts.

There are two types of norm conflict that the principles are unable to resolve. First, the principles cannot be applied to situations where the conflicting norms were not created, or are not adhered to, by the same parties.[11] Second, even where the two norms were created, or are adhered to, by the same parties, the principles cannot resolve conflicts where the norms in question possess the same, unknown, or innominate respective indicators (specificity, age, rank). These limitations will be considered in turn.

First, the principles cannot resolve AB/AC conflicts. That is, the principles cannot be applied in situations where the conflicting norms were not created, or are not adhered to, by exactly the same party or parties.[12] The application of the principles presupposes that State A, to which State B owes an obligation or against which State B invokes a right, must have participated in the creation of, or consented to, the conflicting norm that impairs State B's obligation or supports State B's right vis-à-vis State A.[13] This limitation, also known as the concept of *res inter alios acta* or 'unity of parties' in treaty law,[14] of the principles' applicability to A/B conflicts derives from the principles' rationale.

[10] See, eg, ILC, *Fragmentation Report* (n 1); Vranes (n 6); Kammerhofer (n 5); Milanovic (n 7); Michaels and Pauwelyn (n 4).

[11] See also Part I.A.2.d.

[12] The focus on the unity of parties is preferable to a focus on the legal regime (where regimes are distinguished from each other by virtue of possessing different secondary rules) to which each norm belongs since the rationale of the traditional norm conflict resolution principles would still warrant the principles' utilization even across the boundaries of different legal regimes, as long as the norms belonging to different regimes were created by exactly the same parties. For example, France and Germany might first enter into a Bilateral Investment Treaty ('BIT') and subsequently into a bilateral Environmental Protection Treaty. Any subsequent conflict between France and Germany pertaining to the provisions of the BIT and the Environmental Treaty could still be resolved by means of the traditional conflict resolution principles (irrespective of the fact that the norms belong to different regimes) as the parties are identical for the purposes of the bilateral conflict.

[13] It could be argued that the same rationale informs the fundamental principle of international law that a State's non-compliance with international law cannot be excused by conflicting domestic provisions since international actors neither created nor adhere to the domestic provisions of a particular State. See, eg, *Treatment of Polish Nationals and Other Persons of Polish Origin or Speech in the Danzig Territory (Advisory Opinion)* [1932] PCIJ Series A/B No 44, 24; Vienna Convention on the Law of Treaties (opened for signature 23 May 1969, entered into force 27 January 1980) 1155 UNTS 331 ('VCLT') Art 27; ILC, 'Articles on the Responsibility of States for Internationally Wrongful Acts' annexed to UNGA Res 56/83 (12 December 2001) UN Doc A/Res/56/83 ('ARSIWA') Art 3; Statute of the International Court of Justice (adopted 26 June 1945, entered into force 24 October 1945) 1946 UKTS 67 ('ICJ Statute') Art 38(1)d.

[14] VCLT (n 13) Art 30(3); Borgen (n 8) 468; Surabhi Ranganathan, *Strategically Created Treaty Conflicts and the Politics of International Law* (CUP 2014) 12–13. The principle's counterpart, *pacta tertiis nec nocent nec prosunt*, is expressed in VCLT (n 13) Art 34. Discussing treaty conflicts, Borgen observes that, in the absence of a unity of parties, '[t]he VCLT would allow the obligations to each party to survive, thus there is no solution to the conflict in the VCLT, just a recognition that a conflict exists'. See Borgen (n 8) 468.

The rationale that informs the principles is that laws are made by lawmakers not only in appreciation of the principles' existence and operation, but also in appreciation of the totality of the lawmakers' otherwise existing obligations and rights.[15] In domestic systems, from where the principles originate,[16] this rationale works very well and facilitates the smooth operation of federal legal systems, for example, which possess multiple levels of legislation. In international law, however, norms are frequently created and amended by very different (groups of) legal actors and it cannot be presumed that the lawmakers of a treaty, for example, legislate 'with knowledge of [all] prior laws'[17] that may otherwise bind each and every other party to a given treaty.[18]

This means that if Egypt (A) in the *Military Alliances* scenario, for example, undertakes separate and conflicting treaty obligations, one obligation (X) vis-à-vis State B (a member of the Arab League) and one obligation (Y) vis-à-vis State C (Israel), Egypt cannot invoke the norm conflict resolution principles to prioritize either obligation over the other, since the identity of the creators of each obligation are not identical. The same analysis applies to Nicaragua's conflicting obligations towards Costa Rica and the US in the *Canal Treaties* scenario. Thus, when Costa Rica requested the Central American Court to declare the 1914 Treaty, which Nicaragua had concluded with the US, 'null and void', the Court observed that it could not do so since the US were not subject to the Court's jurisdiction.[19] In AB/AC conflicts of this kind, the legislative intent of the creators of obligation X cannot be transferred to the creators of obligation Y.[20] Article 30(5) of the VCLT[21] explicitly gives effect to this limitation with respect to the operation of *lex posterior* in treaty law, but, by virtue of the rationale that underpins all three principles, this limitation extends to the *lex specialis* and *lex superior* principles in and beyond the law of treaties.

For example, consider the case of a newly independent State that, upon independence, gained a customary entitlement to receive a certain volume of water from a shared watercourse. If the existing riparians have already distributed the entirety of the available waters by means of several bilateral and multilateral treaties, a contingent conflict arises between the newly independent State's customary

[15] Charles Rousseau, 'De la Compatibilité des Normes Juridiques Contradictoires dans l'Ordre International' (1932) 39 Revue Générale de Droit International Public 133, 177; ILC, *Fragmentation Report* (n 1) paras 61, 226; Michaels and Pauwelyn (n 4) 354; Pauwelyn (n 1) 96, 387–8; Lindroos (n 5) 36; Conway (n 1) 986, 987. All additional and more specific rationales, eg, that the more specific norm represents a more considered view of a given situation (*lex specialis*), that the highest authority has the best understanding of a given situation (*lex superior*), or that the latest norm embodies the most recent and most informed view of a legislator, are merely corollaries of the legislative intent rationale.

[16] Jenks (n 1) 436–7.

[17] Michaels and Pauwelyn (n 4) 356; Pauwelyn (n 1) 97.

[18] Tzanakopoulos (n 3) 46; ILC, *Fragmentation Report* (n 1) paras 115, 226, 243; Zuleeg (n 5) 266, 267; Michaels and Pauwelyn (n 4) 360–1.

[19] *Costa Rica v Nicaragua* (1917) 11 AJIL 181, 228.

[20] Zuleeg (n 5) 266; ILC, *Fragmentation Report* (n 1) para 115.

[21] VCLT (n 13). See also Zuleeg (n 5) 268. Zuleeg proposes the utilization of the 'political decision principle' ('das Prinzip der politischen Entscheidung') to resolve such conflicts. See text to note 34 in the Introduction.

entitlement and the treaty obligations or entitlements of the existing riparians. In a dispute between the existing riparians and the newly independent State, the traditional conflict resolution principles would be inapplicable, as the existing States' legislative intent informing the creation of the treaty provisions cannot be transferred to the newly independent State.[22] A similar example could be constructed with respect to conflicts concerning customary norms *inter se*, relating, for example, to the impossibility of utilizing the traditional principles in support of a customary norm (for example, regarding the scope of a State's territorial waters) that the State against which the norm is invoked has never accepted.[23]

Therefore, the principles' utility is limited to conflicts between norms that where created, or are adhered to, by the same parties. This makes sense. Were it not the case, States could be released from certain obligations simply by entering into conflicting obligations—be they more specific, later, or of seemingly higher rank—with other States. A related problem would arise for judicial actors of a particular treaty system, who could be asked to determine 'whether one field of law or norm should have prevalence over another',[24] based on the traditional conflict resolution principles. In accordance with the view that '[i]n international law, every tribunal is a self-contained system',[25] in such situations 'it becomes difficult to devise a neutral perspective from which conflict solutions could be formulated'[26] as the judicial actors of one regime would be asked to assess the legislative intention informing a norm of a foreign system vis-à-vis the legislative intention informing the norm belonging to the judicial actors' system. This problem is exacerbated by

[22] This problem could arise in the Jordan River Basin if Palestine advanced a claim to access an increased volume of the Jordan River based on international law. See Valentin Jeutner, 'Water Claims of an Independent Palestine in Practice: Reconciling Conflicting Water Claims in the Region' in Mutaz Qafisheh (ed), *Palestine Membership in the United Nations: Legal and Practical Implications* (Cambridge Scholars Publishing 2013). See also Mark Eugen Villiger, *Customary International Law and Treaties: A Study of Their Interactions and Interrelations, with Special Consideration of the 1969 Vienna Convention on the Law of Treaties* (Brill 1985) 161–2.

[23] See, eg, the Norwegian argument and its assessment by the ICJ in *Fisheries (United Kingdom v Norway)* (Merits) [1951] ICJ Rep 116, 131. The rationale could be extended further to cover conflicts between regional *ius cogens* norms that conflict with general *ius cogens* norms. See Giorgia Gaja, *Jus Cogens Beyond the Vienna Convention* (Brill 1981) 289; Kirsten Schmalenbach, 'Article 53' in Oliver Dörr and Kirsten Schmalenbach (eds), *Vienna Convention on the Law of Treaties: A Commentary* (Springer 2012) 940.

[24] Nancie Prud'homme, 'Lex Specialis: Oversimplifying a More Complex and Multifaceted Relationship' (2007) 40 Israel Law Review 356, 380–1. See also Lindroos (n 5) 28, 42, 43; ILC, *Fragmentation Report* (n 1) para 34; Bruno Simma and Dirk Pulkowski, 'Of Planets and the Universe: Self-Contained Regimes in International Law' (2006) 17 EJIL 483, 489.

[25] *Prosecutor v Tadic* (Jurisdiction) (1995) 105 ILR 419 [11]. See also the observation of Jennings concerning the 'tendency of particular tribunals to regard themselves as different, as separate little empires which must as far as possible be augmented', Robert Yewdall Jennings, 'The Proliferation of Adjudicatory Bodies: Dangers and Possible Answers' in *Implications of the Proliferation of International Adjudicatory Bodies for Dispute Resolution* (1995) 9 ASIL Bulletin 2. See also Michael Waibel, 'Interpretive Communities in International Law' in Andrea Bianchi, Daniel Peat, and Matthew Windsor (eds), *Interpretation in International Law* (OUP 2015) 162. See also Martti Koskenniemi, 'Hegemonic Regimes' in Margaret A Young (ed), *Regime Interaction in International Law* (CUP 2012) 317.

[26] Michaels and Pauwelyn (n 4) 367–8.

the fact that different international judicial fora possess adjudication mechanisms with varying levels of sophistication. This means that the views of particularly well developed and prolific fora could ' "coloniz[e]" ... the fabric of international law'[27] in the future. So the principles' inapplicability to conflicts between norms created or adhered to by different actors is not a mere technicality, but it protects norms from illegitimate interference by judicial actors or States who are prevented from subordinating conflicting norms in cases where not all affected parties created, or adhere to, the conflicting norms. As a result, the conclusion that the traditional norm conflict resolution principles are inapplicable to conflicts between norms created by different parties is important and ensures that norms are modified by legitimate means.[28]

There is no question that there are also many cases where the principles' rationale justifies the principles' utilization. For example, specific bilateral agreements may displace conflicting general norms in accordance with the *lex specialis* principle;[29] the later of two treaties concluded by the same actors may prevail in accordance with the *lex posterior* principle as codified by Article 30(3) of the VCLT; and UN Security Council resolutions generally enjoy a higher status than other norms in accordance with the *lex superior* principle.[30]

However, and this is second limitation of the principles' utility, even where conflicting norms were created by the same party or parties, the principles are unable to resolve conflicts between norms possessing the same, unknown, or an innominate specificity (*lex specialis*), age (*lex posterior*), or rank (*lex superior*).

The utility of the *lex specialis* principle depends on the possibility of distinguishing general from specific norms.[31] However, the degree of specificity of the subject matter regulated[32] by two or more norms can be very difficult to ascertain[33] given the absence of any criteria that could assist with the measurement of specificity.[34] For example:

> there may be little point in trying to define the *lex specialis* in the interaction between trade agreements and environmental agreements. From the perspective of the trade agreement,

[27] Michaels and Pauwelyn (n 4) 367–8.

[28] See also Part III.A.2.

[29] In the *Gabčíkovo-Nagymaros Project Case*, eg, the ICJ held that the Treaty Concerning the Construction and Operation of the Gabčikovo-Nagymaros System of Locks (Hungary–Czechoslovakia) (signed 16 September 1977, entered into force 30 June 1978) 1109 UNTS 211 governed the legal relations between Hungary and Slovakia as *lex specialis*. See *Gabčíkovo-Nagymaros Project (Hungary/Slovakia)* (Judgment) [1997] ICJ Rep 7 [132].

[30] Charter of the United Nations (adopted 26 June 1945, entered into force 25 October 1945) 1 UNTS XVI ('UN Charter') Art 25.

[31] Martti Koskenniemi, *The Function and Scope of the Lex Specialis Rule and the Question of 'Self-Contained Regimes': An Outline* (2004) UN Doc ILC(LVI)SG/FIL/CRD.1 and Add. 1, 5.

[32] There is also the related difficulty of determining whether two or more norms actually apply to the same subject matter. See Koskenniemi (n 31) 6; Simma and Pulkowski (n 24) 488; Borgen (n 8) 468.

[33] Koskenniemi (n 31) 5; Prud'homme (n 24) 374; Lindroos (n 5) 44; ILC, *Fragmentation Report* (n 1) para 58; Robert Yewdall Jennings and Arthur Watts, *Oppenheim's International Law*, vol 1 (9th edn, Longman 1992) para 633 (p 1280); Simma and Pulkowski (n 24) 489.

[34] Prud'homme (n 24) 384.

the trade rule will be more specific ... [F]rom the viewpoint of the environmental treaty, the environmental rule will be more specific.[35]

Even if degrees of specificity could be determined with certainty, the *lex specialis* principle could not resolve a conflict between two equally specific or two equally general norms.[36] This would, for example, be the case in any conflict that arises between twin norms. The conflicting norms in the *Distress at Sea* scenario, for instance, are a mirror image of each other. Both obligations, O_1 to save person A and O_2 to save person B, derive from Regulation 33 of the SOLAS Convention. Thus, it is impossible to distinguish these obligations on the basis of their specificity.

Similarly, the *lex posterior* principle cannot operate between two norms that were created at the same time. Again, this is the case where the conflicting norms are twin norms, as is the case in the *Distress at Sea* scenario, for example, or where the conflicting norms were enacted simultaneously as provisions of the same legal instrument. This was the case in the *Submarine Warfare* scenario.[37]

Moreover, the *lex posterior* principle cannot be applied when the age of at least one of the conflicting norms is uncertain, or when at least one norm is of 'continuing' or 'eternal'[38] validity, so that, even if a creation date can be ascertained, such a norm cannot be displaced by a later norm.[39] Uncertain time stamps could be a problem in disputes concerning historic titles to territory. In the *Minquiers and Ecrehos* case, for example, the parties had asked the ICJ to determine the rights and obligations of the parties *inter alia* based on various thirteenth century treaties.[40]

A conflict between 'continuing' norms existed between prescriptions of environmental law and prescriptions of the law governing the use of force in the context of the *Nuclear Weapons Advisory Opinion*.[41] Although the environmental conventions in question were of a much more recent character than the law governing the use of force and self-defence, the ICJ observed that 'the [environmental] treaties in question could [not] have intended to deprive a State of the exercise of its right of self-defence under international law because of its obligations to

[35] Michaels and Pauwelyn (n 4) 367–8. For the purposes of this book, the example must be taken to presuppose that both the norms of the environmental regime and the norms of the trade regime have been created by all parties to the dispute. Otherwise, the traditional principles would not apply in any case in accordance with this section's first argument.

[36] Lindroos (n 5) 42.

[37] A fictional domestic example, concerning a land registry that issues two contradictory deeds simultaneously, is provided by Wiethölter: Rudolf Wiethölter, 'Begriffs-oder Interessenjurisprudenz—Falsche Fronten im IPR und Wirtschaftsverfassungsrecht: Bemerkungen zur Selbstgerechten Kollisionsnorm' in Alexander Lüderitz and Jochen Schröder (eds), *Festschrift für Gerhard Kegel* (1977) 215.

[38] For domestic examples of eternity clauses, see, eg, Basic Law for the Federal Republic of Germany 1949 Art 79(3) (Germany); Constitution of the Federative Republic of Brazil 1988 Art 60(4) (Brazil); Constitution of the Islamic Republic of Iran 1979 Art 177(5) (Iran).

[39] Pauwelyn (n 1) 97; Jenks (n 1) 444. 'Continuing' or 'eternal' norms prevail in any case where they are also the applicable *lex superior*.

[40] See *Minquiers and Ecrehos (France/United Kingdom)* (Judgment) [1953] ICJ Rep 47, 53–7.

[41] Pauwelyn (n 1) 408.

protect the environment'.[42] Nonetheless, States still had to 'take environmental considerations into account'[43] when engaging in military activities.

As for the *lex superior* principle, limitations arise in circumstances where two norms of the same or of innominate rank conflict with each other. In a largely non-hierarchical order like international law[44] this limitation applies to conflicts between almost all norms that are not ranked and are thus of the innominate rank.[45] To that extent, there are only very few situations in which the *lex superior* principle can play a meaningful role in international law.[46] However, as established previously,[47] there are certain circumstances in which legal norms are compared with reference to their respective rank.[48] In particular, customary and conventional norms tend to prevail[49] over general principles;[50] and *ius cogens* norms[51] and obligations arising pursuant to Article 103 of the UN Charter[52] prevail over all other norms. While it is generally accepted that *ius cogens* norms prevail over obligations arising pursuant to Article 103, UN Charter, conflicts between two *ius cogens* norms are completely irresolvable.[53]

[42] *Legality of the Threat or Use of Nuclear Weapons (Advisory Opinion)* [1996] ICJ Rep 226 ('*Nuclear Weapons Advisory Opinion*') [30].

[43] *Nuclear Weapons Advisory Opinion* (n 42) [30].

[44] James Crawford, *Brownlie's Principles of Public International Law* (8th edn, OUP 2012) 22–3; Malcolm N Shaw, *International Law* (7th edn, CUP 2014) 87–8; Władysław Czapliński and Gennady M Danilenko, 'Conflicts of Norms in International Law' (1990) 21 Netherlands Yearbook of International Law 3, 7–8; Mónica García-Salmones Rovira, *The Project of Positivism in International Law* (OUP 2013) ch 8.

[45] See Part I.B.3. [46] Czapliński and Danilenko (n 44) 7–8. [47] See Part I.B.3.

[48] Note, eg, the ICJ's reference to obligations based on 'elementary considerations of humanity' in *Corfu Channel (United Kingdom v Albania)* (Merits) [1949] ICJ Rep 4, 22. See also *Nuclear Weapons Advisory Opinion* (n 42) [79]; Case T-306/01 *Ahmed Ali Yusuf and Al Barakaat International Foundation v Council of the European Union and Commission of the European Communities* [2005] ECR II-3544 [281]–[282]; ILC, *Fragmentation Report* (n 1) paras 326–7.

[49] In many cases, conventional and customary norms would of course also prevail in virtue of their comparative specificity.

[50] ICJ Statute (n 13) Art 38(1)(c). Pellet observes that, although general principles 'are a direct source of rights and obligations ... they are subsidiary in the sense that the Court will usually only resort to them in order to fill a gap in the treaty or customary rules available'. See Alain Pellet, 'Article 38' in Andreas Zimmermann and others (eds), *The Statute of the International Court of Justice: A Commentary* (OUP 2012) 850.

[51] Lindroos (n 5) 28–9; Jorge E Viñuales, *Foreign Investment and the Environment in International Law* (CUP 2012) 142.

[52] Jure Vidmar, 'Norm Conflicts and Hierarchy in International Law' in Erika de Wet and Jure Vidmar (eds), *Hierarchy in International Law: The Place of Human Rights* (OUP 2012) 18, 19; ILC, *Fragmentation Report* (n 1) paras 330–1. Sometimes *erga omnes* obligations are also said to represent an example of the 'informal hierarchy of international law'. The *erga omnes* status of a norm does not, however, reflect a norm's comparative qualitative status within international law, but speaks instead to the norm's ability to be invoked by all States.

[53] ILC, *Fragmentation Report* (n 1) para 367; Anthony E Cassimatis, 'International Humanitarian Law, International Human Rights Law, and Fragmentation of International Law' (2007) 56 ICLQ 623, 630. Note, however, that the VCLT provides, in (implicit) accordance with the *lex posterior* principle, that existing *ius cogens* norms can be modified by subsequently emerging *ius cogens* norms (VCLT (n 13) Arts 53, 64). Nonetheless, the details of the *ius cogens* norm modification process itself are also uncertain. See Schmalenbach (n 23) 917; Villiger (n 22) 672–3. In any event, the VCLT cannot accommodate *ius cogens* conflicts when the *lex posterior* principle is inapplicable. This will be the case, in particular, when a contingent conflict emerges between two existing *ius cogens* norms (as opposed to one existing and one emerging *ius cogens* norm) or when the age of two conflicting

Even so, conflicts between two *ius cogens* norms are rarely discussed.[54] It has been argued, for example, that the ILC, when preparing the ARSIWA,[55] 'did not envisage the possible conflict between peremptory norms'.[56] However, this is not entirely accurate. While the ILC's latest reports on the Responsibility of States for Internationally Wrongful Acts did ignore this possibility, draft Article 4, ARSIWA, as proposed in the Third Report on State Responsibility,[57] expressly contemplated conflicts between *ius cogens* norms:

> An internationally wrongful act of a State does not entail an obligation for that State or a right for another State to the extent that the performance of that obligation or the exercise of that right would be incompatible with a peremptory norm of general international law unless the same or another peremptory norm of general international law permits such performance or exercise in that case.[58]

The ILC's Special Rapporteur explains:

> The present article [4] ... states that no derogation from a peremptory norm is permitted even as a legal consequence of an internationally wrongful act. Obviously, one cannot exclude that the same peremptory norm or a later one permits such derogation, particularly as a legal consequence of conduct of a State which is itself incompatible with a peremptory norm.[59]

The report suggested that conflicts between *ius cogens* norms should be resolved by construing one norm as the exception to the other.[60] However, this proposal is limited to specific cases in which the *ius cogens* norms in question lend themselves to such a reconfiguration. Further, commenting on this draft article, some UN members doubted the possibility that situations of this kind could in fact arise.[61] Others accepted the possibility of the existence of *ius cogens* conflicts in principle, but

norms is unknown or identical, or when it is—in the case of continuing obligations—irrelevant. See ILC, Draft Articles on the Law of Treaties with Commentaries, ILC Ybk 1966/II 187, comment on draft Art 50.

[54] For important exceptions, see Robert Kolb, 'Conflits Entre Normes de Jus Cogens' in Nicolas Angelet and others (eds), *Droit du Pouvoir, Pouvoir du Droit: Mélanges offerts à Jean Salmon* (Bruylant 2007); Cezary Mik, 'Jus Cogens in Contemporary International Law' (2013) 33 Polish Yearbook of International Law 27, 82–3; João Ernesto Christófolo, *Solving Antinomies between Peremptory Norms in Public International Law* (Schulthess 2016).

[55] ILC, *ARSIWA* (n 13).

[56] Paul Tavernier, 'Relevance of the Intertemporal Law' in James Crawford and others (eds), *The Law of International Responsibility* (OUP 2010) 402–3.

[57] Willem Riphagen, Third Report on the Content, Forms and Degrees of International Responsibility (Part Two of the Draft Articles), ILC Ybk 1982/II(1), 22 ('*Third Report*') 47.

[58] Riphagen, *Third Report* (n 57) 47.

[59] Riphagen, *Third Report* (n 57) 47.

[60] Riphagen, *Third Report* (n 57) 47.

[61] The delegate of Madagascar stated, eg, that 'his delegation found it difficult to believe that the international legal order could admit at the same time of a peremptory norm of general international law prohibiting the fulfilment of an obligation or the exercise of a right, and another peremptory norm authorizing the same fulfilment or exercise'. See UNGA, 'Sixth Committee, Summary Records of Meetings' (16 November 1982) UN Doc A/C.6/37/SR.46 para 119, p 27 (Mr Razanakoto); UNGA, 'Sixth Committee, Summary Records of Meetings' (17 November 1982) UN Doc A/C.6/37/SR.47 para 49, p 14 (Mr Gonzales Galvez, Mexico).

expressed concern about their irreconcilability[62] or asked the Special Rapporteur to provide specific examples.[63]

Eventually, having skipped over draft Article 4 in the report on its 35th session,[64] the ILC withdrew draft Article 4. The Special Rapporteur observed:

> that the matter dealt with in draft article 4 as submitted in this report (*jus cogens*) ... could very well be dealt with within the framework of the articles on reciprocity and reprisals (see articles 8 and 9 as submitted below).[65]

However, the draft articles that the Special Rapporteur refers to (Articles 8 and 9—respectively, the suspension of performance in response to internationally wrongful acts and reprisals), contain no reference to *ius cogens* conflicts.[66] Article 9 subjects reprisals *inter alia* to limitations contained in Article 12.[67] Article 12 in turn provides that injured States are not entitled to suspend obligations that exist 'by virtue of a peremptory norm of general international law' (Article 12(b)).[68] So, while *ius cogens* norms still limit the exercise of reprisals (which is also reflected in the ILC's final report),[69] the reference to the possibility of a conflict between *ius cogens* norms *inter se* has disappeared.

Against that background, some have argued that conflicts between *ius cogens* norms are merely a 'theoretical possibility'[70] and that it would be difficult to find a 'realistic illustration' of such a conflict.[71] Indeed, the suggestion that a contingent conflict could arise between a *ius cogens* norm prohibiting the use of force and an alleged 'right to humanitarian intervention' of *ius cogens* nature, for example, in the context of NATO's activities in Kosovo,[72] is not very persuasive, given the probable absence of a 'right to humanitarian intervention'.[73] More convincingly, however, it could be argued that a contingent conflict could arise between the 'intransgressible principles of international customary law',[74] embodied in the

[62] UNGA, 'Sixth Committee, Summary Records of Meetings' (17 November 1982) UN Doc A/C.6/37/SR.47 para 67 p 19 (Mr Mahbouli, Tunisia).

[63] UNGA, 'Sixth Committee, Summary Records of Meetings' (9 November 1982) UN Doc A/C.6/37/SR.40 para 47, pp 11–12 (Mr Economides, Greece); UNGA, 'Sixth Committee, Summary Records of Meetings' (5 November 1982) UN Doc A/C.6/37/SR.38 para 15, p 6 (Mr Museux, France); UNGA, 'Sixth Committee, Summary Records of Meetings' (18 November 1982) UN Doc A/C.6/37/SR.49 para 9, p 5 (Mr Mazilu, Romania).

[64] ILC, 'Report of the International Law Commission on the Work of Its 35th Session' (3 May–22 July 1983) UN Doc A/38/10, 90–3.

[65] Willem Riphagen, Fifth Report on the Content, Forms and Degress of International Responsibility (Part Two of the Draft Articles), ILC Ybk 1984/II(1), 1 ('*Fifth Report*') para 5, p 1.

[66] Riphagen, *Fifth Report* 3.

[67] Riphagen, *Fifth Report* 3.

[68] Riphagen, *Fifth Report* 4.

[69] ILC, *ARSIWA* (n 13) Art 26.

[70] Cassimatis (n 53) 630.

[71] Cassimatis (n 53) 630.

[72] Tavernier (n 56) 402–3. See also Christófolo (n 54) 253–304; Christian Tomuschat, *International Law: Ensuring the Survival of Mankind on the Eve of a New Century* (Brill 1999) 218–26; Kolb (n 54) 495–7.

[73] For a recent suggestion that a 'hypothetical peace agreement between Israel and Palestine' could trigger an irresolvable conflict between the (alleged) *ius cogens* norms concerning a) the obligatory non-recognition of forceful territorial acquisitions and b) the Palestinian recognition of such a state of affairs in a future peace treaty with Israel, see Christófolo (n 54) 322–34.

[74] *Nuclear Weapons Advisory Opinion* (n 42) [79].

Hague and Geneva Conventions[75] concerning *inter alia* the obligation to avoid unnecessary suffering,[76] as well as the prohibition of weapons unable to distinguish between civilians and combatants[77] on the one hand, and a 'State's inherent right to self-defence'[78] in a situation where a State can defend itself only by means which are incapable of complying with the distinction principle or which cause unnecessary suffering, on the other hand.[79] One might question the frequency with which such conflicts could arise,[80] but this does not undermine the validity of the argument that the *lex superior* principle's utility is limited to situations where conflicting norms possess different ranks.[81]

The overall utility of the three traditional principles to resolve norm conflicts in international law is therefore limited in two ways. First, the principles cannot resolve conflicts between norms that have not been created, or are not adhered to, by all parties that the legal dilemma affects. Second, the principles cannot resolve conflicts where the norms in question possess the same, unknown, or no respective indicators (specificity, age, rank).

2. Conflict-of-laws approaches

In contrast to international law's traditional norm conflict resolution mechanisms discussed in Part II.A.1 above, private international law's conflict-of-laws approaches were designed specifically to resolve conflicts between different legal regimes. They aim to resolve conflicts between 'questions [of the] jurisdiction of courts, recognition and enforcement of foreign judgments, and of applicable law for legal relations which have a link to more than one national law.'[82] Examples of conventional conflict-of-laws devices include the 'traditional method',[83] the 'governmental interest'[84] test, and the 'functional approach'.[85]

In brief, the 'traditional method' identifies a preference between competing laws by assessing which of two norms has the 'closest and most real connection to the particular claim'[86] or which norm had the 'closest connection to the particular issue to be adjudicated'.[87] The 'governmental interest' test establishes a preference

[75] *Nuclear Weapons Advisory Opinion* (n 42) [78].

[76] See, eg, Declaration Renouncing the Use, in Time of War, of certain Explosive Projectiles under 400 Grammes Weight (1868) 18 Martens 474 para 1.

[77] See, eg, Protocol Additional to the Geneva Conventions of 12 August 1949, and relating to the Protection of Victims of International Armed Conflicts (adopted 8 June 1977, entered into force 7 December 1978) 1125 UNTS 3 Arts 48, 51(1), 52(2).

[78] UN Charter (n 30) Art 51.

[79] See the discussion of the *Nuclear Weapons* scenario in Section B.1 of the Introduction.

[80] James Crawford, *State Responsibility: The General Part* (CUP 2013) 316.

[81] See also Part I.B.3.

[82] Henning Grosse Ruse-Khan, 'A Conflict-of-Laws Approach to Competing Rationalities in International Law: The Case of Plain Packaging between Intellectual Property, Trade, Investment and Health' (2013) 9 Journal of Private International Law 309, 321.

[83] Michaels and Pauwelyn (n 4) 358.

[84] Grosse Ruse-Khan (n 82) 325–6; Michaels and Pauwelyn (n 4) 359.

[85] Michaels and Pauwelyn (n 4) 360.

[86] Adrian Briggs, *The Conflict of Laws* (3rd edn, OUP 2013) 40. Grosse Ruse-Khan (n 82) 322.

[87] Briggs (n 86) 40; Grosse Ruse-Khan (n 82) 322. See also Michaels and Pauwelyn (n 4) 358.

between competing laws by assessing to which extent a particular law would further a particular government's interest.[88] Finally, the 'functional approach', of which there are multiple variants,[89] establishes a preference between competing laws *inter alia* by identifying 'the proper law, the law most appropriate to govern the issue in question'.[90]

There is little disagreement that these conventional conflict-of-laws approaches are not easily transplanted into the public international law sphere.[91] An assessment of the degree of 'close connection',[92] 'asking whose interest would be more significantly affected',[93] or a 'comparative evaluation of ... asserted policies'[94] all involve 'value judgment[s] ... prone to be driven by the bias of the rule-system to which the tribunal belongs'.[95] As such, the legitimacy deficit that would exist if the *lex specialis* principle, for example, were applied across legal regimes, is left unremedied. In addition, some of the factors on the basis of which conflict-of-laws approaches seek to assign a priority between different systems may not exist in international law to the same extent, or else the factors may, again, be of equal value.

However, some[96] have recently proposed that slightly modified conflict-of-laws approaches could overcome certain limitations of the traditional norm conflict resolution devices identified above.[97] Suggestions include the 'conflict rule of integration'[98] and the 'appropriate application'[99] test. Again, very briefly, the 'conflict rule of integration' provides that, where two norms conflict, the 'underlying rule-system'[100] should apply 'which is more able to integrate the other system's rules'.[101] The 'appropriate application' test, in turn, maintains that one should not consider 'whether an issue "really" belongs to trade or environmental law', but rather that the question should be 'which regime is more appropriate to be applied to the particular fact pattern'.[102]

These approaches may well be of considerable utility in the sphere of private international law and even in non-dilemmatic public international legal contexts.

[88] Michaels and Pauwelyn (n 4) 359. See also Brainerd Currie, 'Notes on Methods and Objectives in the Conflict of Laws' (1959) Duke Law Journal 171, 178.

[89] Michaels and Pauwelyn distinguish an English, a US-American, and a European approach: Michaels and Pauwelyn (n 4) 360.

[90] Michaels and Pauwelyn (n 4) 360. See also FA Mann, 'The Proper Law in the Conflict of Laws' (1987) 36 ICLQ 437; JHC Morris, 'The Proper Law of Tort' (1951) 64 Harvard Law Review 881.

[91] Andreas Fischer-Lescano and Gunther Teubner, 'Regime-Collisions: The Vain Search for Legal Unity in the Fragmentation of Global Law' (2004) 25 Michigan Journal of International Law 999, 1023.

[92] Grosse Ruse-Khan (n 82) 322.

[93] Grosse Ruse-Khan (n 82) 326; ILC, *Fragmentation Report* (n 1) paras 488, 14–15.

[94] Michaels and Pauwelyn (n 4) 360.

[95] Grosse Ruse-Khan (n 82) 329; ILC, *Fragmentation Report* (n 1) paras 488, 14–15.

[96] Fischer-Lescano and Teubner (n 91); Michaels and Pauwelyn (n 4); Grosse Ruse-Khan (n 82).

[97] Michaels and Pauwelyn (n 4) 357, 367–8.

[98] Grosse Ruse-Khan (n 82) 330–1. Pulkowski appears to favour a slightly similar approach: Dirk Pulkowski, *The Law and Politics of International Regime Conflict* (OUP 2014) 341.

[99] Michaels and Pauwelyn (n 4) 369.

[100] Grosse Ruse-Khan (n 82) 330–1.

[101] Grosse Ruse-Khan (n 82) 330–1.

[102] Grosse Ruse-Khan (n 82) 330–1.

With respect to irresolvable norm conflicts, however, they are limited in at least three ways.

First, conflict-of-laws approaches cannot be applied to conflicts between norms belonging to the same regime since the operation of conflict-of-laws approaches presupposes and relies on the existence of at least two legal regimes. This may be stating the obvious but this limitation is significant considering that it restricts the potential utility of conflict-of-laws approaches to the scenarios concerning the *Canal Treaties* and *Military Alliances*. Conversely, conflicts between twin norms in the *Distress at Sea* scenario, for example, or conflicts of the kind considered in the *Submarine Warfare* and *Nuclear Weapons* scenario could not be resolved by conflict-of-laws approaches.

Second, even when the conflicting norms belong to different regimes, the conflict-of-laws approaches cannot preclude the possibility of legal dilemmas where the decision in favour of one norm by one particular judicial actor or legal forum does not settle the conflict definitively in the sense that there is still the possibility of the same conflict forming the subject matter of proceedings in different judicial fora. Situations of this kind can arise in various situations. For example, in the *Canal Treaties* scenario, the Central American Court had, on the basis of the 1858 Cañas–Jerez Treaty,[103] no difficulty to determine that Nicaragua's subsequent conclusion of the 1914 Bryan-Chamorro Treaty[104] with the US violated Costa Rica's rights.[105] At the same time, however, there was no question that the Central American Court could not declare the offending 1914 Treaty 'null and void', as requested by Costa Rica, since the US was not subject to the court's jurisdiction and did not participate in the proceedings.[106] As a result, the Central American Court's decision leaves the norm conflict, which Nicaragua faces, unaffected. In Nicaragua's situation, the traditional norm conflict principles cannot be applied to establish a preference between the two conflicting norms because there is no unity of parties and because the competing norms derive from two different treaties. But even though conflict-of-laws approaches could in principle provide for a resolution of a norm conflict across two treaties, they cannot do so in cases of AB/AC conflicts where the involvement of a third party's interest prevents a given conflict to be settled definitively.

The *Kadi Cases*[107] are a second example of this limitation. Here the issue was not the involvement of a third party but rather that the CJEU's decision to insist on the UK's compliance with the UK's EU law obligations did not dispose of the question whether the UK, by honouring its EU law obligations, would violate its obligations under Article 103 of the UN Charter. Even if the CJEU had applied

[103] Treaty of Territorial Limits (Costa Rica–Nicaragua) (signed 15 April 1858) (1858) 118 CTS 439.

[104] Convention on Interoceanic Canal (US–Nicaragua) (signed 5 August 1914, entered into force 22 June 1916) (1914) 10 Bevans 379.

[105] *Costa Rica v Nicaragua* (n 19) 223.

[106] *Costa Rica v Nicaragua* (n 19) 228.

[107] Joined Cases C-402/05 P and C-415/05 P *Kadi and Al Barakaat International Foundation v Council of the European Union and Commission of the European Communities* [2008] ECR I-06351; Joined Cases C-584/10 P, C-593/10 P, and C-595/10 P *Commission and Others v Kadi* (18 July 2013).

one of the modified conflict-of-laws approaches to determine that EU law should be applied to the particular facts of the case, this determination would not preclude the possibility that a different court, asked to determine whether the UK violated its obligations under the UN Charter, could not reach the opposite conclusion thus making it 'impossible' for countries in the position of the UK to meet 'their international obligations'.[108]

A final example of this limitation relates to the recent controversy between Ireland and the UK concerning the environmental impact of the UK's MOX Plant, which triggered parallel proceedings in three regimes.[109] One the one hand, the matter was adjudicated[110] by an arbitration panel established pursuant to the United Nations Convention on the Law of the Sea.[111] On the other hand, proceedings were initiated[112] in accordance with the provisions of the dispute settlement procedure of the Convention for the Protection of the Marine Environment of the North-East Atlantic Convention.[113] Additionally, the matter was also brought before the CJEU,[114] based on the EC Treaty[115] and the Treaty establishing the European Atomic Energy Community.[116] In each of these three proceedings the application of the modified conflict-of-laws approaches may help to identify the most appropriate solution for each of the respective cases. However, the solution identified by each one of the three judicial fora cannot claim validity beyond the realm of the specific forum within which a particular decision was reached.

Third, even when the conflicting norms belong to different regimes, when all parties concerned created, or adhere to, the conflicting norms and when there is no risk of parallel proceedings, conflict-of-laws approaches cannot preclude the possibility of dilemmas when the comparative 'appropriateness' or the comparative ability to integrate a given set of norms cannot be measured on a scale. For example, even if the jurisdiction of the Central American Court of Justice in the *Canal Treaties* would have extended to the US or if the US had joined the proceedings, it is still difficult to imagine just on which judicial basis the court would have established a preference between the conflicting norms given that the obligations, at least in that case, were mutually exclusive. Even if the conflicting norms would not have been mutually exclusive, the Central American Court would have had to engage in a quintessential political assessment concerning the comparative merit

[108] *Commission and Others v Kadi* (n 107) [61].

[109] See also ILC, *Fragmentation Report* (n 1) paras 10–12.

[110] *The MOX Plant Case (Ireland v United Kingdom)* (Request for Provisional Measures: Order) [2001] ITLOS Rep 95; *The MOX Plant Case (Ireland v United Kingdom)* (Order) (2003) 126 ILR 310.

[111] United Nations Convention on the Law of the Sea (opened for signature 10 December 1982, entered into force 16 November 1994) 1833 UNTS 3.

[112] *Dispute concerning Access to Information under Article 9 of the OSPAR Convention (Ireland v United Kingdom)* (Final Award) (2003) 23 RIAA 59.

[113] Convention for the Protection of the Marine Environment of the North-East Atlantic (opened for signature 22 September 1992, entered into force 25 March 1998) 2354 UNTS 67.

[114] C-459/03 *Commission of the European Communities v Ireland* [2006] ECR I-04635.

[115] Now the TFEU (n 2).

[116] Treaty establishing the European Atomic Energy Community (signed 25 March 1957, entered into force 1 January 1958) 298 UNTS 167.

of Nicaragua's foreign policy interest in order to determine which legal instrument should prevail. The various problems associated with judicial assessments of this kind in dilemmatic circumstances will be the main subject of discussion in the following sub-sections.

For now, it suffices to note that reformed conflict-of-laws approaches may be of considerable utility with respect to non-dilemmatic norm conflicts in public international law. However, they are unable to preclude the possibility that legal dilemmas, as defined by Part I, may arise.

3. Proportionality tests

The previous two sections considered mechanisms which establish priorities between conflicting legal norms. This section focuses on the proportionality principle. The proportionality principle does not seek to create priorities, but compromises between conflicting norms.[117] International lawyers know proportionality primarily as a technique to determine the adequacy of military activities in the law of war and the law of armed conflict.[118] However, proportionality can also play a more general role in norm conflict scenarios. In norm conflict settings, proportionality facilitates a balancing process designed to identify the most adequate way to reconcile two or more conflicting norms. The appeal of the proportionality principle is that it allows for the balancing of competing norms where the more rigid conflict resolution mechanisms discussed above fail to provide a solution.[119] For example, in a situation where two norms are of the same degree of specificity, the proportionality principle could identify a solution by striking

[117] The German concept of '*praktische Konkordanz*', which 'aim[s] at a solution that gives both rights effective protection to the possible extent', exemplifies this approach. See Stephan W Schill and Benedict Kingsbury, 'Public Law Concepts to Balance Investors' Rights with State Regulatory Actions in the Public Interest—the Concept of Proportionality' in Stephan W Schill (ed), *International Investment Law and Comparative Public Law* (OUP 2010) 93.

[118] Beyond the law of war and armed conflict, proportionality also features, *inter alia*, in the fields of human rights law, maritime delimitation, trade and investment disputes and in the jurisprudence of the WTO, the European Court of Human Rights, or the European Court of Justice. See Rosalyn Higgins, *Problems and Process: International Law and How We Use It* (Clarendon Press 1995) 228–35; Judith Gail Gardam, *Necessity, Proportionality and the Use of Force by States* (CUP 2004) 2–3; Thomas M Franck, 'On Proportionality of Countermeasures in International Law' (2008) 102 AJIL 715, 719; Jan Klabbers, 'Setting the Scene' in Jan Klabbers, Anne Peters, and Geir Ulfstein (eds), *The Constitutionalization of International Law* (OUP 2009) 35; Emily Crawford, 'Proportionality' in Rüdiger Wolfrum (ed), *Max Planck Encyclopedia of Public International Law* (Online ed, Max Planck Institute for Comparative Public Law and International Law 2010); Anne Peters, 'Verhältnismäßigkeit als Globales Verfassungsprinzip (Proportionality as a Global Constitutional Principle)' in Björnstern Baade and others (eds), *Verhältnismäßigkeit im Völkerrecht* (Mohr Siebeck 2015); UNHRC, 'General Comment 29: States of Emergency (Article 4)' (2001) UN Doc CCPR/C/21/Rev.1/Add.11; Stephan W Schill, 'Cross-Regime Harmonization through Proportionality Analysis: The Case of International Investment Law, the Law of State Immunity and Human Rights' (2012) 27 ICSID Review 87.

[119] Klabbers remarks that proportionality does not 'ultimately [favour] one interest over another ... [but] ... prevent[s] this from happening by achieving a balancing of (typically) rights'. See Klabbers (n 118) 35; Schill and Kingsbury (n 117) 78.

an adequate balance between the extent to which one norm is impaired in favour of a second norm. However, it is exactly proportionality's inherent flexibility that renders it difficult to apply and unsuitable to solve certain types of norm conflicts.

The core of both the domestic as well as the international proportionality principle—the idea of balancing—is an established legal method with a very long history.[120] Despite, or perhaps because of, the principle's popularity, however, no universally accepted definition of the principle exists.[121] Even within the comparatively small field of modern international law, and even within the still smaller and highly specialized area of the law of war and armed conflict, there is little consensus about the exact definition of proportionality and the principle's legal status.[122] However, it is undisputed that proportionality tests are frequently employed in legal practice[123] and, for the purposes of assessing proportionality's utility as a norm conflict resolution mechanism, it is not necessary to attempt to provide a precise definition of the concept. Rather, the observations below regarding proportionality's limited ability to assist with the resolution of specific norm conflicts focuses

[120] The idea of balancing was already employed by the philosophers of Ancient Greece. Later proponents of the concept include Cicero, Augustine, Aquinas, Grotius. Cf Aharon Barak, *Proportionality: Constitutional Rights and Their Limitations* (CUP 2012) 176; Crawford (n 118) paras 4–5; Stavros Tsakyrakis, 'Proportionality: An Assault on Human Rights?' (2009) 7 International Journal of Constitutional Law 468, 469. Proportionality also plays an important role in numerous domestic jurisdictions. In the domestic context, consider especially Germany's doctrine of '*praktische Konkordanz*' referred to in note 117 above. See also, eg, Andreas Kulick, *Global Public Interest in International Investment Law* (CUP 2012) 191–2; Schill and Kingsbury (n 117) 93; Konrad Hesse, *Grundzüge des Verfassungsrechts der Bundesrepublik Deutschland* (20th edn, CF Müller Verlag 1999) 28. Regional and institutional legal orders also employ proportionality tests. See, eg, Julian Rivers, 'Proportionality and Discretion in International and European Law' in Nicholas Tsagourias (ed), *Transnational Constitutionalism* (CUP 2007); Higgins (n 118) 236.

[121] Franck (n 118) 716; Michael Newton and Larry May, *Proportionality in International Law* (OUP 2014) 3; Gardam (n 118) 2–3. For attempts to define the concept in different contexts, see, eg, Robert Alexy, 'Constitutional Rights, Balancing, and Rationality' (2003) 16 Ratio Juris 131, 135; Barak (n 120) 369; Madhav Khosla, 'Proportionality: An Assault on Human Rights?: A Reply' (2010) 8 International Journal of Constitutional Law 298, 299; Crawford (n 118) para 2; Talal Asad, 'Thinking about Terrorism and Just War' (2010) 23 Cambridge Review of International Affairs 3, 10; Chris Jochnick and Roger Normand, 'The Legitimation of Violence: A Critical History of the Laws of War' (1994) 35 Harvard International Law Journal 49, 56.

[122] Franck (n 118) 734. While Franck (ibid 716) ponders whether proportionality could be a general principle, Higgins questions that conclusion. See Higgins (n 118) 236. Barak maintains that proportionality is a 'general concept' of international law. See Barak (n 120) 202. In the context of the ECHR, Tsakyrakis argues that the principle of proportionality 'has acquired the status of general principle': See Tsakyrakis (n 120) 475. In the context of the law of war and of armed conflict, Gardam argues that proportionality is both a 'conventional and a customary law principle': Judith Gail Gardam, 'Proportionality and Force in International Law' (1993) 87 AJIL 391, 391. Green echoes her assessment. See James Green, *The International Court of Justice and Self-Defence in International Law* (Hart 2009) 88.

[123] Franck (n 118) 734. In the *Nuclear Weapons Advisory Opinion*, the ICJ identified proportionality, at least in the context of the law of armed conflict, as an 'intransgressible [principle] of international customary law'. See *Nuclear Weapons Advisory Opinion* (n 42) [78]–[79]. In Nolte's view, whether or not proportionality is a general principle or a rule depends 'on the context in which it is applied'. See Georg Nolte, 'Thin or Thick? The Principle of Proportionality and International Humanitarian Law' (2010) 4 Law & Ethics of Human Rights 245, 247.

on the core component of proportionality: the balancing of conflicting values and norms.[124]

The argument with respect to proportionality and its various sub-tests is not that they are by definition flawed.[125] Rather, the argument is that there are certain types of norm conflicts that proportionality cannot satisfactorily resolve.[126] Most problematic are conflicts involving legally absolute[127] and/or factually indivisible[128] norms. Against that background, proportionality's ability to resolve norm conflicts is limited in four ways. First, proportionality cannot resolve conflicts between norms that are legally absolute and thus immune to balancing exercises. Second, proportionality cannot be employed where at least one of the two norms in question protects a factually indivisible interest. Third, proportionality cannot be employed with respect to incommensurable norms. Finally, proportionality cannot resolve conflicts between norms, which—though not incommensurable—are of exactly the same importance.

As regards the first reason, the proportionality principle cannot be applied to norms that a given legal system renders categorically immune from balancing[129] by protecting it with a legal 'firewall'.[130] Some might generally question the utility of such categorical prohibitions.[131] However, it is a fact that international law contains a limited class of norms,[132] most importantly *ius cogens* norms,[133] from which 'no derogation is permitted'.[134] The preclusion of balancing is not limited to *ius*

[124] Matthias Klatt and Moritz Meister, *The Constitutional Structure of Proportionality* (OUP 2012) 1; Nolte (n 123) 247.

[125] For an outright rejection of the proportionality test, see Tsakyrakis (n 120).

[126] Reinhard Merkel, '§14 Abs. 3 Luftsicherheitsgesetz: Wann und warum darf der Staat töten?' (2007) 62 JuristenZeitung 373, 374; Mattias Kumm, 'What Do You Have in Virtue of Having a Constitutional Right? On the Place and Limits of the Proportionality Requirement' (2006) Paper 46 New York University Public Law and Legal Theory Working Papers 30; Barak (n 120).

[127] 'Legally absolute' here refers both to norms that are non-derogable (norms that cannot be disapplied) and to norms that can in principle be disapplied but that, if they apply, cannot be qualified.

[128] 'Factual indivisibility' exists where the interest a norm protects cannot be meaningfully partitioned into sub-interests.

[129] Grégoire CN Webber, 'Proportionality, Balancing, and the Cult of Constitutional Rights Scholarship' (2010) 23 Canadian Journal of Law and Jurisprudence 179, 199; Klabbers (n 118) 36. In the domestic context Calabresi's and Melamed's 'inalienable entitlements' would also fall within this category. See Guido Calabresi and A Douglas Melamed, 'Property Rules, Liability Rules, and Inalienability: One View of the Cathedral' (1972) 85 Harvard Law Review 1089, 1092. The avoidance of consequentialist reasoning is one of the main reasons for positing that certain norms are immune from balancing. See, eg, Klabbers (n 118) 36; Kumm (n 126) 28, 39.

[130] Jürgen Habermas, *Between Facts and Norms: Contributions to a Discourse Theory of Law and Democracy* (William Rehg tr, Polity 1996) 256, 258.

[131] Klatt and Meister (n 124) 31–8. Similarly, Schill accepts that the application of proportionality tests to balance State immunity and investment interests presupposes the abandonment of 'absolute forms of immunity'. See Schill (n 118) 119.

[132] The special status the German Basic Law accords the protection of human dignity is a domestic example of a norm that is by stipulation (at least *prima facie*) exempt from balancing exercises. See Barak (n 120) 27; Khosla (n 121) 300, 306; Kai Möller, 'Balancing and the Structure of Constitutional Rights' (2007) 5 International Journal of Constitutional Law 453, 466.

[133] See Part I.B.3 and Part II.A.1.

[134] VCLT (n 13) Art 53. See also *Jurisdictional Immunities of the State (Germany v Italy: Greece Intervening)* (Judgment) [2012] ICJ Rep 99 [95]. By distinguishing between substantive and procedural

cogens norms. The absolute prohibition of chemical weapons,[135] for example, which is not necessarily of *ius cogens* character, also precludes the possibility that the use of chemical weapons may ever feature in a balancing exercise.[136] Hence, once at least one norm has been identified as a norm that the law precludes from being balanced (and this identification might indeed happen at the first stages of a proportionality test), it cannot be 'relativized'[137] and cannot feature in a proportionality test. In certain cases, this limitation of proportionality might not result in a dilemma. Sometimes the *lex superior* principle can, for example, resolve such conflicts, to the extent that a *ius cogens* norm in question takes precedence.[138] However, dilemmas can exist in constellations where both norms are immune from balancing.[139] These can be situations where two *ius cogens* norms conflict[140] or where two non-derogable norms conflict. In these cases, it will not be possible to resolve the conflict by means of a proportionality test.

Second, norms that protect a factually indivisible interest are not susceptible to balancing. The most obvious example in this regard is the right to life which protects the factually indivisible interest of life. A person's life cannot be infringed in degrees. A person is either dead or alive. The interest in this case does not admit of a spectrum of different stages of infringement. Consequently, it is impossible to establish a compromise between a particular person's life and a competing necessity to violate a person's life.[141] In a similar manner, some judges in the *Nuclear Weapons Advisory Opinion* argued that the outright prohibition of nuclear weapons would not constitute a mere limitation of a State's right to self-defence but rather a complete denial of such a right in situations when recourse to a nuclear weapon 'was the last available means by way of which the victimized State could exercise its right under Article 51 of the Charter'.[142] If one accepts, for the sake of argument, that the rights to self-defence (in certain circumstances) and life can protect indivisible interests, the violation of such interests may still be justified or excused[143] but

law, the ICJ was able to avoid commenting on Italy's argument that *ius cogens* norms would always prevail 'over any inconsistent rule of international law'. See ibid, [92]–[93].

[135] Convention on the Prohibition of the Development, Production, Stockpiling and Use of Chemical Weapons and on their Destruction (adopted 3 September 1992, entered into force 29 April 1997) 1974 UNTS 45 Art 1(1)(b).

[136] Similarly, the ICCPR stipulates that certain rights are non-derogable, International Covenant on Civil and Political Rights (adopted 16 December 1966, entered into force 23 March 1976) 999 UNTS 171 ('ICCPR') Art 4(2).

[137] Kulick (n 120) 192. See also Habermas (n 130) 160.

[138] Note the limitations of the *lex superior* principle identified previously. See Part II.A.1.

[139] Möller (n 132) 467.

[140] See Part II.A.1.

[141] See section B.5 of the Introduction for examples of conflicts involving competing rights to life.

[142] *Nuclear Weapons Advisory Opinion* (n 42), Separate Opinion of Judge Fleischhauer [3]. The extent to which the right to self-defence is indivisible eventually depends, of course, on the specific facts of a given situation and on the extent to which an attack would lead to the partial or complete destruction of a State.

[143] An excuse or a justification (depending on the domestic system) may exist, eg, where an attacker is killed in self-defence, , or duress etc. and where the eventual death of the attacker is attributed to the attacker who, by attacking the victim, assumed the risk that she/he might die as a result of the attack. See, eg, Merkel (n 126) 377.

such a violation will certainly not be susceptible to measurement on a proportionality scale that aims to identify a compromise between two conflicting norms.[144] A compromise presupposes that at least one unit of each of the negotiated interests survives the balancing exercise. Otherwise, there would be no difference between a compromise and the victory of one norm over another. However, that condition is not fulfilled when indivisible interests feature in a proportionality test. Persons proportionately deprived of their right to life are dead. States proportionately deprived of the only means by which they might exercise their right to self-defence are deprived of that right.

The fact that no unit of a proportionately infringed indivisible interest survives, also leads to a legitimacy problem if it is accepted that the legitimacy of a legal system relies on the conferment of benefits (however marginal) on the legal system's subjects.[145] If the legal subject is dead (in the case of human persons) or ceases to exist (in the case of legal persons) as the result of the proportionate infringement of that subject's indivisible interest, then 'the legitimacy-constituting relationship between the legal order and a legal subject'[146] collapses. It is not possible to speak of the relative or proportionate infringement of a dead person's or a right-holder's indivisible interest,[147] since only one norm emerges victorious. However, it is exactly on that part of an otherwise impaired norm, which survives a proportionality test, that the legitimacy of a proportionality test relies. If no unit of an infringed interest survives—and especially if the legal subject itself is extinguished[148]—then the measure whose proportionality a proportionality test seeks to establish is illegitimate.

Third, even where a norm's indivisible character (legal or empirical) does not preclude balancing, proportionality cannot resolve conflicts between incommensurable norms. Norms are incommensurable when there is no '*rationally* identified

[144] With respect to the right to life, in particular, there is also the much more fundamental problem regarding the justifiability of a proportionate killing to the person killed, who derives absolutely no benefit from the measure. The argument is essentially that the legitimacy of a measure that results in the extinction of a legal subject cannot be established vis-à-vis that legal subject. See Merkel (n 126) 375.

[145] This is certainly the case if proportionality 'defin[es] the relationship between the state and its citizens' (Schill and Kingsbury (n 117) 80) or if proportionality 'sets material limits on the interference of public authorities into the private sphere of the citizen'. See Mads Andenas and Stefan Zleptnig, 'Proportionality and Balancing in WTO Law: A Comparative Perspective' (2007) 42 Texas International Law Journal 371, 383.

[146] Merkel (n 126) 375 (tr by author).

[147] This does not, of course, preclude the argument that the deprivation of a person's right to life might be proportionate (eg, within the meaning of Art 2(2), ECHR) vis-à-vis the interests of third persons or the general public. However, such arguments cannot establish the legitimacy of the 'proportionate' measure vis-à-vis the deprived right-holder. Thus, in *McCann*, eg, the ECtHR tested whether the UK's killing of the suspects was 'strictly proportionate to the aim of protecting persons [the inhabitants of Gibraltar] against unlawful violence' and not whether the UK's conduct was strictly proportionate vis-à-vis the suspects' rights to life. See *Case of McCann and Others v the United Kingdom* [1996] 21 EHRR 97 [194].

[148] In the *Nuclear Weapons Advisory Opinion*, this view was concisely expressed by Judge Fleischhauer, who observed that 'no legal system is entitled to demand the self-abandonment, the suicide, of one of its subjects'. See *Nuclear Weapons Advisory Opinion* (n 42), Separate Opinion of Judge Fleischhauer [5]. See also *Nuclear Weapons Advisory Opinion* (n 42), Separate Opinion of Judge Guillaume [8].

metric for measuring, or scale for "weighing", the goods and bads in issue'.[149] If there is no 'identified metric' that could aid the balancing process, it is impossible to identify objectively a way to reconcile conflicting norms. Thus, in the context of proportionality's role in the law of armed conflict, it has been observed that '[d]issimilar entities cannot be compared absent a common currency of evaluation'.[150] The problem is that dilemmatic norm conflicts are very likely to involve a choice between two different options that cannot be measured on one scale—particularly in conflicts involving norms belonging to different legal regimes, created by different legal persons[151] or relating to conflicts between twin norms. In the *Military Alliances* scenario, for example, it is impossible for a judicial actor to determine which of Egypt's two conflicting obligations Egypt should prefer. Similarly, in the *Canal Treaties* scenario it is difficult to imagine just on which legal basis Nicaragua's conflicting treaty obligations could be balanced. In such cases, when there is no '*rationally* identified metric'[152] for balancing a particular set of conflicting norms, judicial actors asked to undertake a proportionality assessment, would necessarily have to make a decision based on a subjective[153] metric in the sense that the eventual determination is based on personal, not legal, judgment. Although subjective decisions are, as will be argued later,[154] the only means to resolve dilemmatic situations, a judicial actor's subjective decision cannot form the grounds for an international legal judgment.[155] This is especially so, given that international legal dilemmas often affect[156] several different parties with several different sets of interests.

This observation is also the response to the argument that incommensurability does not equal incomparability.[157] Even if comparability could be achieved by means of a 'common metric'[158] created, for example, 'qua moral reasoning'[159] in

[149] John Finnis, 'Natural Law and Legal Reasoning' in Robert P George (ed), *Natural Law Theory: Contemporary Essays* (Clarendon Press 1992) 146 (emphasis in the original). Raz defines incommensurability as a state of affairs where 'it is neither true that one is better than the other nor true that they are of equal value'. See Joseph Raz, *The Morality of Freedom* (Clarendon Press 1986) 322. See also Virgílio Afonso da Silva, 'Comparing the Incommensurable: Constitutional Principles, Balancing and Rational Decision' (2011) 31 Oxford Journal of Legal Studies 273, 278; Paul-Erik N Veel, 'Incommensurability, Proportionality, and Rational Legal Decision-Making' (2010) 4 Law & Ethics of Human Rights 178, 184; Matthew H Kramer, 'When Is There Not One Right Answer?' (2008) 53 American Journal of Jurisprudence 49, 63.

[150] Michael N Schmitt, 'Fault Lines in the Law of Attack' in Susan C Breau and Agnieszka Jachec-Neale (eds), *Testing the Boundaries of International Humanitarian Law* (British Institute of International & Comparative Law 2006) 293. See also Franck (n 118) 729; Newton and May (n 121) 17; Klabbers (n 118) 35–6; Green (n 122) 86–96; ICTY Review Committee, 'Final Report to the Prosecutor by the Committee Established to Review the NATO Bombing Campaign Against the Federal Republic of Yugoslavia' (2000) para 48 <http://www.icty.org/x/file/Press/nato061300.pdf> accessed 1 June 2017.

[151] Michaels and Pauwelyn (n 4) 368.

[152] Finnis (n 149) 146 (emphasis in the original).

[153] Klatt and Meister (n 124) 62; Robert Alexy, *A Theory of Constitutional Rights* (OUP 2002) 404–5; Finnis (n 149) 145.

[154] See Part III.A.2.

[155] See particularly Part III.A.2.a.

[156] See the examples in section B of the Introduction.

[157] da Silva (n 149) 283; Klatt and Meister (n 124) 62.

[158] Klatt and Meister (n 124) 62.

[159] Klatt and Meister (n 124) 62.

domestic law, in fragmented international legal contexts, subjective 'moral reasoning' as a legal strategy is very problematic, due to the presence of extremely diverse conceptualizations of morality.[160] The concession that comparability can be achieved only by subjective means would also entail acceptance of the argument of numerous critics that proportionality is essentially a smoke screen for subjective decision-making processes;[161] that proportionality assessments take place in a 'black box'[162] and that, at least in nuclear weapons related scenarios, ' "softening" of the absolute rule by a flexible standard ("proportionality") leaves everything ultimately up to the person with the button'.[163] For this reason, proportionality can resolve conflicts between incommensurable norms only at the cost of accepting subjective decisions by judicial actors.[164]

Fourth, even if one rejected the notion of incommensurable norms, or if a decision-maker faced a choice between two commensurable norms, there can still be 'stalemate';[165] situations of complete equality that proportionality cannot decide, such that a decision-maker faces a 'dilemmatic or tragic [choice]'.[166] Stalemates may occur seldom, but they do occur.[167] With respect to domestic systems, it was pointed out that '[t]he imperative of peaceful coexistence cannot always tell us which of multiple compromises strikes a better "balance" between clashing values.'[168] Similarly, it has been observed that '[c]onstitutional rights are not a subject-matter, which is so finely distinguished that it excludes structural, that is, real balancing stalemates to such an extent as to make them practically insignificant'[169] and that courts should defer to the legislature[170] in such cases. If this is true for domestic law, where the judiciary is an integral part of the domestic legal systems, it is especially true for international law, where judicial institutions possess fewer competences compared to domestic courts, and where conflicts can arise not just within one system but across multiple legal regimes. Therefore, when a norm

[160] Rivers (n 120) 119. See also Part III.A.1.

[161] Klabbers (n 118) 35; T Alexander Aleinikoff, 'Constitutional Law in the Age of Balancing' (1986) 96 Yale Law Journal 943, 976–8; Tsakyrakis (n 120) 489, 493.

[162] Aleinikoff (n 161) 976.

[163] Martti Koskenniemi, 'Case Analysis: Faith, Identity, and the Killing of the Innocent: International Lawyers and Nuclear Weapons' (1997) 10 Leiden Journal of International Law 137, 152. This is a particularly fitting description of the operation of a proportionality test in a nuclear self-defence scenario. See section B.1 of the Introduction.

[164] For a more detailed consideration of why subjective judicial decisions are problematic in dilemmatic circumstances, see in particular Part III.A.2.

[165] da Silva (n 149) 292; Alexy (n 153) 408, 411; Klatt and Meister (n 124) 37.

[166] da Silva (n 149) 292. [167] Alexy (n 153) 412; Kramer (n 149) 56.

[168] David Wolitz, 'Indeterminacy, Value Pluralism, and Tragic Cases' (2014) 62 Buffalo Law Review 529, 592.

[169] Alexy (n 153) 411.

[170] da Silva (n 149) 292, 293, 300. The concept of the 'margin of appreciation' may be the international equivalent of the domestic notion of judicial deference. For an example, see *Oil Platforms (Islamic Republic of Iran v United States of America)* (Judgment) [2003] ICJ Rep 161, Separate Opinion of Judge Kooijmans [44]. See also Franck (n 118) 731; Schill (n 118) 166; Rivers (n 120). On the idea of judicial deference to domestic legislatures in response to contradictory norms, see also *Scialabba v Cuellar de Osorio* 134 S. Ct. 2191 (2014) (Supreme Court of the United States); 'Scialabba v Cuellar de Osorio' (2014) 128 Harvard Law Review 341.

conflict arises where both norms, though commensurable and divisible (legally or empirically) possess exactly the same importance within the parameters of a given legal regime, proportionality tests will be able to identify how to balance such conflicting norms only at the cost of subjective judicial lawmaking, thereby exceeding the parameters of a given legal regime.[171]

The ability of proportionality tests to overcome dilemmatic conflicts by identifying a compromise between irresolvable conflicting norms is therefore limited in at least four ways. That does not mean that proportionality tests are per se unsuitable norm conflict resolution devices. However, the section has shown that, although proportionality tests may assist with the resolution of conflicts both within and across regimes, proportionality tests are inapplicable when conflicts involve legally absolute, factually indivisible, or incommensurable norms, or when an actor faces a stalemate situation.

B. Limitations of Norm Conflict Accommodation Mechanisms

Against the backdrop of the shortcomings of norm conflict resolution devices identified in the previous section, accommodating rather than resolving norm conflicts might seem preferable. In contrast to norm conflict resolution devices, which aim to establish a priority or a compromise between conflicting norms, the mechanisms discussed in this section accommodate conflicts by providing actors facing a dilemma with a justification or an excuse[172] to impair an otherwise protected norm. In that regard, the methods discussed here correspond to some extent[173] to the concept of the 'lesser evil'[174] of medieval theologians and

[171] Schill and Kingsbury, eg, admit that proportionality may lead to a '*gouvernement des juges*' in excess of international judicial actors' competences. However, they submit that proportionality assessments are better than an analysis 'without rationalization' at all. See Schill and Kingsbury (n 117) 102–3. This book argues that a '*gouvernement des juges*' is problematic, at least in dilemmatic circumstances, and that the rejection of a '*gouvernement des juges*' does not entail accepting decisions 'without [any] rationalization'. See Part III.A.2.

[172] The important debate on the distinction between justifications and excuses does not need to be settled here, even if one might argue that it is misleading to refer to justifications—which, strictly speaking, prevent the emergence of a norm conflict in the first place—as an accommodation mechanism. What unites the approaches discussed in this section (and what unites excuses and justifications for the purposes of dilemmas) is that they identify avenues that allow for the impairment of otherwise protected norms, thereby preventing a dilemma from arising. The ILC assumed a similar approach when drafting the ARSIWA, making no 'categorical distinction between justifications and excuses'. See Crawford (n 80) 280.

[173] The similarity exists merely to an extent because 'lesser evil resolutions' furnish excuses only, whereas some of the mechanisms discussed here also provide justifications.

[174] Indeed, it could be argued that Article 24(2)(b) of the ARSIWA expressly reflects the 'lesser evil' approach by providing that measures taken in distress must not be 'likely to create a comparable or greater peril'. Similarly, in the context of the ICCPR, it has been observed that Art 4, ICCPR (n 136) 'may represent a necessary evil'. See Sarah Joseph and Melissa Castan, *The International Covenant on Civil and Political Rights: Cases, Materials, and Commentary* (3rd edn, OUP 2013) 910. See also Diane A Desierto, *Necessity and National Emergency Clauses: Sovereignty in Modern Treaty Interpretation* (Martinus Nijhoff 2012) 252; Rosalyn Higgins, 'Derogations under Human Rights Treaties' (1977) 48 BYIL 281, 281. Compare McGoldrick, who argues that derogations (at least in the context of the ICCPR) are not necessary evils, but rather involve the 'complete or partial

philosophers.[175] According to the 'lesser evil resolution',[176] otherwise applicable sanctions can be dispensed with when agents face unresolvable moral dilemmas. However, '[t]he dispensation is not a dispensation from committing evil, but is a dispensation from the prohibition [that] outside the dilemma' would normally apply to 'the action that is the lesser evil'.[177] In other words, dispensation does not allow the actor to escape the dilemma 'morally unscathed';[178] it simply removes the threat of the sanction from the lesser evil, while acknowledging the undesirable consequences of the lesser evil at the same time. Thus, normative systems, which provide that irresolvable norm conflicts may be dissolved in favour of a lesser evil, preclude true dilemmas, since the impairment of that norm which the actor does not apply or comply with is excused.

Similarly, some of the methods discussed here address norm conflicts not by effectively removing one norm from the equation,[179] but by precluding a State's responsibility under international law that would otherwise attach to the conduct in question. As a result, it could be argued that these mechanisms could preclude legal dilemmas if it can be shown that, all other things being equal, the mere fact of an actor facing an irresolvable norm conflict—the mere impossibility of complying with or applying two norms simultaneously—could lead to the preclusion of wrongfulness otherwise associated with the impairment of that norm.

However, this section shows that an actor's inability to comply with two norms simultaneously does not engage contemporary international law's norm conflict accommodation mechanisms. In other words, it is, in principle, not possible for an actor to justify or to excuse an actor's non-compliance with a norm merely by pointing towards a conflicting norm that compelled the actor to do so. The argument will be developed with reference to three customary norm conflict accommodation mechanisms,[180] as reflected in the ILC's 2001 ARSIWA,[181] the 1969 VCLT,[182] and the 1966 ICCPR.[183]

elimination' of the obligation in question: Dominic McGoldrick, 'The Interface between Public Emergency Powers and International Law' (2004) 2 International Journal of Constitutional Law 380, 383.

175 Dougherty (n 4) 21–5. 176 Dougherty (n 4) 171. 177 Dougherty (n 4) 24.

178 Dougherty (n 4) 24.

179 That is why it would be inadequate to say that an actor who chooses to comply with norm A rather than norm B, which has been disapplied in accordance with, eg, the *lex superior* principle, impairs norm B. Norms disapplied in accordance with the norm conflict resolution devices discussed above effectively drop out of the picture so that no conflicting norm remains that could be impaired by not complying with it.

180 In addition to the general accommodation mechanisms considered here, there are of course numerous specific mechanism such as the right to self-defence (eg, UN Charter (n 30) Art 51) or security interest clauses in investment treaties (see, eg, Treaty Concerning the Reciprocal Encouragement and Protection of Investment (Argentina–US) (signed 14 November 1991, entered into force 20 October 1994) (1992) 31 ILM 124 Art 11) that could accommodate certain conflicts in a similar manner. However, in order to make the argument in favour of the possibility of legal dilemmas, it suffices to show that there can be conflicts that particular norm conflict accommodation devices cannot accommodate.

181 ILC, *ARSIWA* (n 13). 182 VCLT (n 13). 183 ICCPR (n 136).

It is, no doubt, unusual to evaluate these three mechanisms in the context of norm conflicts, as they are principally designed to accommodate tensions between legal norms and facts,[184] rather than conflicts between legal norms *inter se*. Nonetheless, their consideration at this stage is instructive, to the extent that the three sub-sections rebut the argument that an actor's impairment of a given norm can always be justified or excused in dilemmatic circumstances.

1. The ARSIWA

The ARSIWA list six circumstances that preclude the wrongfulness of otherwise wrongful acts. These six circumstances are consent,[185] self-defence,[186] counter-measures,[187] force majeure,[188] distress,[189] and necessity.[190] If at least one of these six circumstances can be established, the wrongfulness of an otherwise wrongful act is precluded. As a result, States are not responsible for violating international law,[191] although the 'primary obligation'[192] remains unaffected and compensation may still be payable.[193] Evidently, however, the legal impossibility of complying with or applying two norms simultaneously is not among the circumstances precluding wrongfulness. Thus, the ability of the ARSIWA to preclude the emergence of legal dilemmas is limited to the six circumstances to which the ARSIWA apply. In all other cases, 'applicable rules of international law continue to govern questions concerning the responsibility of a State for an internationally wrongful act'.[194] Rules of this kind can be found in customary law,[195] or in treaties,[196] such as the

[184] The distinction between conflicts between norms and facts and norms *inter se* is not always easy to maintain. For example, if a provision of a BIT provides that a State's BIT obligations may be suspended in a public emergency, then it is true that a specific set of facts (the public emergency) leads to the suspension of the State's BIT obligations. In that regard, the BIT's public emergency provision negotiates the relationship between the treaty obligation (a norm) and a fact (the public emergency). However, legally it is not merely the occurrence of a specific set of events but the fact that the concerned State exercises a right to be released from its BIT obligations in the event of a public emergency that suspends the State's obligations. Thus, in that regard, the BIT's provision also negotiates the relationship between the treaty obligation (a norm) and the State's right to be released from that treaty obligation (another norm).

[185] ILC, *ARSIWA* (n 13) Art 20.

[186] ILC, *ARSIWA* (n 13) Art 21.

[187] ILC, *ARSIWA* (n 13) Art 22.

[188] ILC, *ARSIWA* (n 13) Art 23.

[189] ILC, *ARSIWA* (n 13) Art 24.

[190] ILC, *ARSIWA* (n 13) Art 25.

[191] Crawford (n 80) 282.

[192] James Crawford, Second Report on State Responsibility, ILC Ybk 1999/II(1), 3, [224]–[226]; *Case Concerning the Difference between New Zealand and France Concerning the Interpretation or Application of two Agreements, concluded on 9 July 1986 between the two States and which related to the Problems arising from the Rainbow Warrior Affair (New Zealand/France)* (1990) 20 RIAA 217 [76]. However, the distinction between primary and secondary obligations is not undisputed. See Crawford (n 80) 64–5, 281–2.

[193] ILC, *ARSIWA* (n 13) Art 27; *Gabčíkovo-Nagymaros Project (Hungary/Slovakia)* (n 29) [48].

[194] ILC, *ARSIWA* (n 13) Art 56.

[195] ILC, Commentary to the ILC Articles on Responsibility of States for Internationally Wrongful Acts, ILC Ybk 2001/II(2) 31 ('*ARSIWA Commentary*') Art 56 [1].

[196] ILC, *ARSIWA Commentary* (n 195) Art 56 [3]. Joe Verhoeven, 'The Law of Responsibility and the Law of Treaties' in James Crawford, Alain Pellet, and Simon Olleson (eds), *The Law of International Responsibility* (OUP 2010) 107.

UN Charter,[197] or the WTO DSU[198] and they may well allow for the possibility of legal dilemmas.

Even when the ARSIWA apply, however, the ARSIWA's ability to accommodate norm conflicts is not unlimited. Their applicability is naturally conditioned by the prior satisfaction of the specific requirements of a potentially applicable circumstance precluding wrongfulness. For the purposes of this part's thesis concerning the possibility of legal dilemmas, it is particularly noteworthy that the circumstance of distress (Article 24, ARSIWA) cannot be invoked to preclude the wrongfulness of actions that are 'likely to create a comparable or greater peril'.[199] Thus, where 'the author of the act in question has no other reasonable way ... of saving the author's life or the lives of other persons entrusted to the author's care'[200] but by engaging in an act, that creates 'more or comparable peril',[201] distress cannot be invoked. By virtue of this limitation the ARSIWA, almost explicitly, allow for the possibility of dilemmatic conflicts between norms related to the right to life. An actor having to choose between two rights to life in the *Distress at Sea* scenario, for example, could not hope that the potential wrongfulness of the actor's non-compliance with the norm obliging the actor to save that person's life whose life the actor failed to rescue could be precluded. In this regard, distress operates to preclude wrongfulness only in situations when there actually is a 'lesser evil'. It cannot preclude the possibility of dilemmas when the 'evils' concerned are of equal or unknown magnitude.

Similarly, necessity (Article 25, ARSIWA) cannot be invoked where a State's wrongful act 'seriously impair[s] an essential interest of the State or States towards which the obligation exists, or of the international community as a whole'.[202] Thus, while necessity can preclude wrongfulness in situations where 'there is an irresolvable conflict between an essential interest on the one hand and an obligation of the State invoking necessity on the other',[203] it cannot do so when there is an irresolvable conflict between an essential interest and an obligation of the State invoking necessity on the one hand, and an essential interest of the State or the international community to which the obligation is owed on the other. Indeed, the essential interest the State invoking necessity relies on 'must outweigh all other considerations'.[204] In other words, necessity cannot be invoked when the weight of the considerations involved is equal or unknown.

In any case, the ARSIWA's circumstances precluding wrongfulness cannot accommodate conflicts that arise between two *ius cogens* norms.[205] According to Article 26 of the ARSIWA

[197] Vera Gowlland-Debbas, 'Responsibility and the United Nations Charter' in James Crawford, Alain Pellet, and Simon Olleson (eds), *The Law of International Responsibility* (OUP 2010) 117.

[198] Joanna Gomula, 'Responsibility and the World Trade Organization' in James Crawford, Alain Pellet, and Simon Olleson (eds), *The Law of International Responsibility* (OUP 2010) 793.

[199] ILC, *ARSIWA* (n 13) Art 24(2)(b).

[200] ILC, *ARSIWA* (n 13) Art 24(1).

[201] ILC, *ARSIWA* (n 13) Art 24(2)(b).

[202] ILC, *ARSIWA* (n 13) Art 25(1)(b).

[203] ILC, *ARSIWA Commentary* (n 195) Art 25 [2].

[204] ILC, *ARSIWA Commentary* (n 195) Art 25 [17].

[205] See also Part I.B.3.

> [n]othing in this chapter [on circumstances precluding wrongfulness] precludes the wrongfulness of any act of a State which is not in conformity with an obligation arising under a peremptory norm of general international law.[206]

To illustrate, the ILC Commentary explains: 'a genocide cannot justify a counter-genocide'.[207] By analogy, an attacking State's violation of intransgressible humanitarian principles in the *Nuclear Weapons* scenario,[208] for example, cannot preclude the wrongfulness of an attacked State's response by indiscriminate means causing unnecessary suffering and breaching the same principles that the attacking State breached first.[209] Thus, conflicting *ius cogens* norms do not 'cancel one another out'.[210]

To the contrary, the ARSIWA leave the status of conflicting *ius cogens* norms entirely unaffected by excluding the possibility of invoking any of the circumstances precluding wrongfulness in situations involving conflicts between *ius cogens* norms. The ARSIWA's circumstances precluding wrongfulness are unable to sanction an actor's decision in favour of either conflicting norm in situations where an actor must choose between two courses of conduct, each involving the impairment of a *ius cogens* norm. As established previously,[211] the ILC by no means overlooked this possibility when drafting the ARSIWA. The ILC consciously decided not to address the possibility of conflicts between *ius cogens* norms beyond the reference to genocides in the ILC's Commentary.

It follows, overall, that, although the ARSIWA's circumstances precluding wrongfulness can provide indirect relief in some norm conflict scenarios by precluding the wrongfulness of certain acts, their ability to do so is limited by the ARSIWA's scope, by the necessity to satisfy the conditions of each circumstance precluding wrongfulness, and by the requirement that at least one of the conflicting norms must not be of peremptory character.

2. The VCLT

Customary treaty law as reflected in parts of the 1969 Vienna Convention on the Law of Treaties[212] could also be considered to offer certain mechanisms to accommodate particular irresolvable norm conflicts. Indeed, it has been observed that the VCLT provides a normative 'tool-box'[213] for dealing with legal

206 ILC, *ARSIWA* (n 13) Art 26.

207 ILC, *ARSIWA Commentary* (n 195) Art 26 [4]; *Application of the Convention on the Prevention and Punishment of the Crime of Genocide (Bosnia and Herzegovina v Yugoslavia)* (Counter-Claims: Order) [1997] ICJ Rep 243 [35].

208 *Nuclear Weapons Advisory Opinion* (n 42) [79].

209 *Nuclear Weapons Advisory Opinion* (n 42), Separate Opinion of Judge Fleischhauer [3].

210 Contrary to the argument developed here, Kohen maintains that *ius cogens* norms do 'cancel one another out'. See Marcelo G Kohen, 'The Notion of "State Survival" in International Law' in Laurence Boisson de Chazournes and Philippe Sands (eds), *International Law, the International Court of Justice and Nuclear Weapons* (CUP 1999) 307.

211 See Part II.A.1. 212 VCLT (n 13).

213 ILC, *Fragmentation Report* (n 1) para 492.

norm conflicts. In addition to the VCLT's provisions previously considered (for example, concerning interpretation,[214] *lex posterior*, and *lex specialis*)[215] two provisions are particularly relevant for the purposes of this part: first, Article 61, VCLT, concerning the impossibility of the performance of a certain action; and, second, Article 62, VCLT, concerning a fundamental change of circumstance. It will be shown, however, that the legal impossibility of complying with or applying two norms simultaneously, as such, does not engage either one of the two articles.

First, Article 61 of the VCLT sanctions a party's termination or withdrawal from a treaty in cases when the performance of a treaty has become impossible due to the 'permanent disappearance or destruction of an object indispensable for the execution of the treaty'.[216] At least *prima facie* Article 61 of the VCLT sanctions a party's termination of or withdrawal from a treaty in cases where a conflict between two norms renders the lawful compliance with at least one norm impossible. However, the applicability of the VCLT's Article 61 is strictly limited to cases where the performance is physically, rather than legally, impossible.[217] Legal impossibility—the impossibility of complying with or applying two norms simultaneously, for example, due to 'the emergence for a contracting party of a legal obligation, which renders the execution of a treaty illegal (but not materially impossible), is ... not covered by Art. 61'.[218] Similarly, it has been observed that 'a situation in which a State finds itself ... to have undertaken mutually incompatible obligations will not be considered as an impossibility of performance'.[219] Thus, Article 61 could explicitly not be utilized with respect to the norm conflict in the *Canal Treaties* scenario.

Instead, Article 61 of the VCLT covers instances where the performance of one particular norm is itself impossible: *ad impossibilia nemo tenetur*. But as will be established in detail further below,[220] the impossibility of compliance with all norms in dilemmatic circumstances is the result of the simultaneous existence and validity of two norms; not the existence of one norm that itself cannot be complied with, even in the absence of a competing norm. Article 61 of the VCLT was designed to cover scenarios of the latter kind, where actors are confronted with norms that impose 'absurd, inappropriate and meaningless'[221] obligations,

[214] See Part I.A.2.c. [215] See Part II.A.1. [216] VCLT (n 13) Art 61.

[217] Malgosia Fitzmaurice, 'Exceptional Circumstances and Treaty Commitments' in Duncan Hollis (ed), *The Oxford Guide to Treaties* (OUP 2012), 607–8; Thomas Giegerich, 'Article 61' in Oliver Dörr and Kirsten Schmalenbach (eds), *Vienna Convention on the Law of Treaties: A Commentary* (Springer 2012) 1056; Christina Binder, *Die Grenzen der Vertragstreue im Völkerrecht: am Beispiel der nachträglichen Änderung der Umstände* (Springer-Verlag 2013) 182.

[218] Giegerich (n 217) 1056. See also Binder (n 217) 191–2; Mark Eugen Villiger, *Commentary on the 1969 Vienna Convention on the Law of Treaties* (Brill 2009) 755.

[219] Pierre Bodeau-Livinec and Jason Morgan-Foster, 'Article 61' in Olivier Corten and Pierre Klein (eds), *The Vienna Conventions on the Law of Treaties* (OUP 2011) 1390.

[220] See the detailed discussion concerning the 'ought implies can' maxim in Part III.B.2.

[221] Gerald Fitzmaurice, Second Report on the Law of Treaties, ILC Ybk 1958/II, 28 ('*Second Report*') 101.

such as the obligation to return a lighthouse that has been destroyed[222] or the obligation to repair a non-existent house.[223] In contrast, where each prong of a legal dilemma can materially, albeit separately, be complied with, Article 61 does not apply and the article cannot, therefore, accommodate otherwise irresolvable norm conflicts.

Similarly, Article 62 of the same convention is not triggered by the legal impossibility of simultaneous compliance with two conflicting norms. Article 62 concerns a party's right to invoke a fundamental change of circumstance 'as ground for terminating or withdrawing from' a treaty. Since the article refers to a 'change of circumstances',[224] intrinsic norm conflicts, which are non-contingent upon the existence of certain circumstances,[225] are already by definition excluded. Thus, Article 62 would be of no assistance with respect to the intrinsic conflicts in the *Submarine Warfare* and the *Canal Treaties* scenario. However, Article 62 is even unable to accommodate contingent norm conflicts. Admittedly, the ICJ noted that 'changes in the law', as opposed to material impossibility, may in principle 'constitute valid grounds for invoking a change of circumstances'.[226] But with respect to norm conflicts it was observed that 'the fact that a party realizes the incompatibility of a treaty with another treaty concluded with one or more third parties is not considered as a fundamental change of circumstances'.[227] Thus, akin to the limitation of the traditional norm conflict principles discussed above, it is not possible to play off one obligation owed to party A against a different obligation owed to party B. Even if Article 62 could respond to specific forms of legal impossibility in a bilateral context,[228] its applicability is significantly constrained by the article's very restrictive[229] requirements.[230] Against this background it is difficult to imagine a dilemmatic scenario in which Article 62 of the VCLT could provide meaningful relief for the decision-maker facing the dilemma.

Overall, therefore, the capability of the VCLT to accommodate norm conflicts is limited. Article 61 of the VCLT is entirely unsuitable to accommodate norm conflicts and Article 62 of the same convention applies only in very limited circumstances. Additionally, just like the ARSIWA, the VCLT is unable to accommodate otherwise irresolvable norm conflicts between *ius cogens* norms.[231]

[222] *Ottoman Empire Lighthouses Concession (Greece/France)* (1956) 12 RIAA 155, 219–20. See also Part III.C.3.

[223] *Paradine v Jane* 82 Eng Rep 897 (KB 1647) (King's Bench, England and Wales). See also Part III.B.2.

[224] Giegerich (n 217) 1083–4.

[225] See Part I.A.2.d.

[226] *Fisheries Jurisdiction (United Kingdom v Iceland)* (Jurisdiction of the Court: Judgment) [1973] ICJ Rep 3 [32]. See also Giegerich (n 217) 1082.

[227] Malcolm N Shaw and Caroline Fournet, 'Article 62' in Olivier Corten and Pierre Klein (eds), *The Vienna Conventions on the Law of Treaties* (OUP 2011) 1431.

[228] Indeed, it has been observed that Article 62, VCLT, was, at least initially, intended to apply 'mainly in the field of bilateral treaties'. See Fitzmaurice, *Second Report* (n 221) 32.

[229] Fitzmaurice (n 217) 618.

[230] See, eg, Villiger who illustrates the nine parameters conditioning the applicability of Article 62, VCLT, by means of a questionnaire: Villiger (n 218) 778–9.

[231] See above Part II.A.1, and see generally Part I.B.3.

3. The ICCPR

This sub-section briefly highlights, by way of example, the limitations of the specialized norm conflict accommodation mechanism of the 1966 ICCPR.[232] The ICCPR's public emergency provision was chosen as an example, as '[m]any of the substantive and procedural elements [of the ICCPR] are also present in ... other international human rights treaties'.[233]

The ICCPR's Article 4 sanctions a State's derogation from the provisions of the ICCPR at times of a public emergency. In principle, and in a similar manner to the ARSIWA's circumstances precluding wrongfulness, this clause, representing a 'necessary evil',[234] could accommodate a legal dilemma in a situation where a State faces two simultaneous and mutually exclusive conduct norms, by excusing a State's non-compliance with one of the two norms. However, just like the ARSIWA's circumstances, Article 4 of the ICCPR does not respond to legal impossibility per se. Derogations are permissible only '[i]n time of a public emergency which threatens the life of the nation'[235] and to the extent that the excused conduct is 'not inconsistent with [the State's] other obligations under international law'.[236] A mere conflict between two legal norms will not entitle a State to invoke Article 4, ICCPR, unless the conflict arises specifically within the context of a public emergency threatening the life of the nation. Therefore, the ICCPR's utility to accommodate irresolvable norm conflicts is of very limited scope.

Article 4's utility in accommodating a legal dilemma is further constrained by a list of non-derogable articles, whose violation Article 4 cannot excuse. Non-derogable provisions include *inter alia*,[237] the right to life,[238] the prohibition of torture,[239] and the prohibition of slavery.[240] The list of non-derogable articles to which Article 4(2), ICCPR, refers is considered to be non-exhaustive. It has been argued, for example, that Article 10, ICCPR (concerning the rights of detainees),

[232] ICCPR (n 136).

[233] Desierto (n 174) 243–4. See, eg, Convention for the Protection of Human Rights and Fundamental Freedoms (signed 4 November 1950, entered into force 3 September 1953) 213 UNTS 221 Art 15; American Convention on Human Rights (concluded 21 November 1969, entered into force 18 July 1978) 1144 UNTS 123 Art 27. However, numerous human rights treaties, including the Convention on the Elimination of All Forms of Racial Discrimination (adopted 21 December 1965, entered into force 4 January 1969) 660 UNTS 195, the Convention on the Elimination of All Forms of Discrimination against Women (adopted 18 December 1979, entered into force 3 September 1981) 1249 UNTS 13, or the Convention against Torture and Other Cruel, Inhuman or Degrading Treatment or Punishment (adopted 10 December 1984, entered into force 26 June 1987) 1465 UNTS 113, do not contain derogation clauses (cf Desierto (n 174) 248–9) and are therefore unable to accommodate norm conflicts in principle.

[234] Joseph and Castan (n 174) 910; Desierto (n 174) 252; Higgins (n 174) 281. McGoldrick questions the characterization of Art 4, ICCPR (n 136), as a 'necessary evil'. He argues that derogation involves the 'complete or partial elimination' of the obligation in question. See McGoldrick (n 174) 383.

[235] ICCPR (n 136) Art 4(1). [236] ICCPR (n 136) Art 4(1).

[237] In addition, ICCPR (n 136) Art 4(2), identifies as non-derogable the ICCPR's Arts 11, 15, 16, 18.

[238] ICCPR (n 136) Art 6. [239] ICCPR (n 136) Art 7.

[240] ICCPR (n 136) Art 8.

as well as other norms of general international law, such as the prohibition of taking hostages or the prohibition of forced displacement, are non-derogable.[241] Thus, even if the first condition of Article 4, ICCPR, is satisfied and the existence of a public emergency can be established, a State can only invoke the article to excuse the violation of a particular norm if that norm is derogable. This means that Article 4, ICCPR, will not be able to identify a 'less evil' option when a conflict arises between the non-derogable prohibition of torture and the non-derogable right to life, for example.[242] Similarly, Article 4, ICCPR, will be of no use when a contingent conflict arises between non-derogable twin norms. Thus, the ICCPR's Article 4 could not be invoked to assist with the accommodation of the norm conflicts in the *Distress at Sea, Hijacked Airplane*, or *Conjoined Twins* scenarios.

Therefore, the ICCPR's derogation mechanism can accommodate only legal dilemmas that arise with respect to conduct norms of the ICCPR in times of public emergency and only to the extent that the norm, that the State seeks to violate, is derogable. In all other situations, legal norm conflicts will remain irresolvable and, given that the ICCPR mechanism would constitute *lex specialis* for the purposes of Article 55, ARSIWA, a fall-back on the general ARSIWA mechanisms will not be possible.[243]

In light of the very limited applicability of norm conflict accommodation devices to dilemmatic norm conflicts, the existence of these mechanisms does not preclude the possibility of legal dilemmas.

C. Measures of Last Resort

If the previously discussed methods fail to resolve a given norm conflict, measures of last resort include the application of residual rules and the utilization of *non liquet* declarations. If it could be shown that dilemmatic norm conflicts could be satisfactorily addressed by means of such measures, they may still preclude the possibility of the existence of legal dilemmas. This section shows, however, that neither residual rules nor *non liquet* declarations are able to address the problems posed by legal dilemmas. This is so for two related reasons. First, both mechanisms respond to gaps, whereas legal dilemmas respond to legal superpositions[244] and second, because both mechanisms could result in an unwarranted prioritization of either one of two conflicting norms. Both reasons will be discussed in turn with respect to the two mechanisms.

[241] UNHRC (n 118) paras 8, 6, 11; Desierto (n 174) 255.

[242] This limitation mirrors the problem of resolving or accommodating conflicts between *ius cogens* norms, discussed previously. See Parts I.B.3 and II.A.1.

[243] Desierto (n 174) 252–3, 263, 281; McGoldrick (n 174) 385–6. In a very limited number of circumstances, however, and to the extent that general international law recognizes a doctrine of necessity, a State might be able to rely on such a doctrine in an attempt to excuse a violation of an ICCPR article. See Desierto (n 174) 252–3, 263, 281.

[244] See generally Part I.A.3.d.

Residual or closure rules provide for default consequences when confronted with the 'absence of rules or other principles' [245] to govern a particular legal question. International law's most important residual rule is the '*Lotus* Principle',[246] also known as the 'residual negative principle'.[247] The principle is conventionally taken to state that '[w]hatever is not expressly prohibited by international law is permitted'.[248] The reverse of the *Lotus* Principle, that what is not permitted is prohibited,[249] constitutes another example of a residual rule. A further variant is the concept of a casting vote used to decide an equality of votes among judges. For instance, Article 55, ICJ Statute, provides that '[i]n the event of an equality of votes, the President or the judge who acts in his place shall have a casting vote'.[250] Both the *Nuclear Weapons Advisory Opinion* and the PCIJ's *Lotus Case*[251] are striking illustrations of the application of this mechanism. An alternative way to decide an equality of votes by judges in appeals proceedings is to stipulate that a split court affirms the status quo.[252]

Against that background, it could be argued that judicial actors, who are unable to identify a priority between conflicting norms after international law's norm conflict resolution devices and accommodation mechanisms have been exhausted, could resort to a residual rule in order to identify the impairment of one or other norm as being, by default, permitted (or, if the reverse principle is applied, prohibited).

[245] Ole Spiermann, 'Lotus and the Double Structure of International Legal Argument' in Laurence Boisson de Chazournes and Philippe Sands (eds), *International Law, the International Court of Justice and Nuclear Weapons* (CUP 1999) 132.

[246] *The Case of the SS 'Lotus' (France v Turkey)* (Judgment) [1927] PCIJ Series A No 10 ('*SS Lotus*') 18. For a contemporary analysis of the status of the *Lotus* Principle, see Gleider Hernandez, *The International Court of Justice and the Judicial Function* (OUP 2014) 265–6. For criticism of the principle, see, *inter alia*, Pauwelyn (n 1) 154; Juliane Kokott, *The Burden of Proof in Comparative and International Human Rights Law: Civil and Common Law Approaches With Special Reference to the American and German Legal Systems* (Martinus Nijhoff 1998) 168; Julius Stone, 'Non Liquet and the Function of Law in the International Community' (1959) 35 BYIL 124, 136.

[247] Stone (n 246) 135.

[248] Daniel Bodansky, 'Non Liquet and the Incompleteness of International Law' in Laurence Boisson de Chazournes and Philippe Sands (eds), *International Law, the International Court of Justice and Nuclear Weapons* (CUP 1999) 161; Stone (n 246) 135; Hans Kelsen, *Principles of International Law* (Robert W Tucker ed, 2nd edn, Holt, Rinehart and Winston 1966) 438–9; CF Amerasinghe, 'The Legality of the Use of or Threat to Use Nuclear Weapons' (1999) X Finnish Yearbook of International Law 5, 7–8.

[249] See Jan Anne Vos, *The Function of Public International Law* (Springer 2013) 13. On the distinction between the principle of prohibition and the principle of authorization, see also *Nuclear Weapons Advisory Opinion* (n 42), Dissenting Opinion of Judge Shahabuddeen, 377, 389–90.

[250] ICJ Statute (n 13) Art 55. The same statute contains a similar provision concerning the election of ICJ judges, ICJ Statute (n 13) Art 12.

[251] Article 55 of the ICJ Statute mirrors Article 55 of its predecessor's statute. See Statute of the Permanent Court of International Justice (adopted 16 December 1920, entered into force 20 August 1921) 6 LNTS 389 Art 55.

[252] The United States Supreme Court uses this mechanism. For a fictional employment of this method, see Lon L Fuller, 'The Case of the Speluncean Explorers' (1949) 62 Harvard Law Review 616, 645. Note that there are both Jewish as well as Islamic schools of jurisprudence which reject the application of residual rules in such situations and that instead prefer the consultation of additional judges, see Alfredo Mordechai Rabello, 'Non Liquet: From Modern Law to Roman Law' (2004) 10 Annual Survey of International & Comparative Law 1, 20, 24.

One could argue, for example, that a judicial actor asked to establish a priority between the competing norms in the *Nuclear Weapons* scenario could apply the *Lotus* Principle in order to conclude that the threat or use of nuclear weapons is permitted or *vice versa*. However, as argued previously,[253] legal dilemmas do not respond to gaps or the 'absence of rules or other principles'.[254] Nor would it be correct to describe dilemmatic norm conflicts as situations lacking express prescriptive norms in the sense that one could validly conclude that '[w]hatever is not expressly prohibited by international law is permitted'.[255]

In the *Lotus Case* itself, it might have been justified to observe that Turkey was permitted to exercise jurisdiction with respect to the collision of the Boz-Kurt and the SS Lotus in the absence of a 'general prohibition to the effect that States may not extend the application of their laws and the jurisdiction of their courts to persons, property and acts outside their territory'.[256] In that case and at that time, international law left States a 'wide measure of discretion'[257] in this regard. However, the situation in dilemmatic circumstances is quite different.[258] Dilemmatic situations do not concern conflicts where there is an absence of a prohibition on the one hand and a 'wide margin of discretion' on the other. Indeed, in such situations there would not be a norm conflict at all.[259] Instead, actors in legal dilemmas are confronted with two incompatible norms (for example, two prescriptions or one prescriptive and one permissive norm).[260]

Therefore, in dilemmatic situations, it would be inaccurate to state in an unqualified manner that any one of the two acts in question is singularly 'not prohibited' or 'permitted'. There is no regulatory gap that a default rule could fill by stipulating that a given conduct is permitted or prohibited.[261] The *Lotus* Principle may potentially be able to address the problem of legal gaps in the international sphere, but it is unsuitable to address the problem of irresolvable norm conflicts.

Similarly, suggestions[262] that judicial actors facing irresolvable norm conflicts should issue *non liquet* declarations are misplaced. In international law,[263] the term *non liquet* is used to refer to a legal gap, an absence of legal rules applicable to a given situation.[264] Compared to related notions such as

253 See Part I.A.3.d. 254 Spiermann (n 245) 132.

255 Bodansky (n 248) 161; Stone (n 246) 135; Kelsen (n 248) 438–9; Amerasinghe (n 248) 7–8.

256 *SS Lotus* (n 246) 19. 257 *SS Lotus* (n 246) 40.

258 Note once more the difference between Quadrants II and IV of Figure 1 in the Introduction and the discussion in Part I.A.3.d.

259 See Figure I.2 in Part I.

260 For a consideration of the difference between permissive norms, rights, and a 'wide margin of appreciation', see Part I.A.2.d.

261 See Figure 1 in the Introduction and Part I.A.3.d.

262 Pauwelyn (n 1) 152, 419; Jochen von Bernstorff, 'Hans Kelsen on Judicial Law-Making by International Courts and Tribunals: A Theory of Global Judicial Imperialism?' (2015) 14 The Law and Practice of International Courts and Tribunals 35, 49–50.

263 The term originates from Roman law and literally means 'not clear'. See Rabello (n 252) 1–2.

264 Hersch Lauterpacht, 'Some Observations on the Prohibition of "Non Liquet" And The Completeness of the Law' in Elihu Lauterpacht (ed), *International Law—Collected Papers*, vol 2 (CUP 1975) 216–17; Shaw (n 44) 70; Bodansky (n 248) 154; Daniel Bodansky, 'Non Liquet' in Rüdiger Wolfrum (ed), *Max Planck Encyclopedia of Public International Law* (Online ed, Max Planck Institute

'obscurities'[265] or 'deficiencies',[266] a finding of *non liquet* responds to 'genuine gaps in the [positive] law',[267] to a lack of norms governing matters law 'ought to govern'.[268] The fact that 'the principle affirming the completeness of the international legal order'[269] is the 'positive formulation of the prohibition of *non liquet*'[270] confirms that the concept is inherently concerned with gaps.

Again,[271] however, legal dilemmas are not legal gaps, in the sense of being 'non-norm-governed'[272] territory. Legal dilemmas respond to a superposition—not an absence—of norms.[273] Irresolvable norm conflicts are, to that extent, the opposite of legal gaps, the opposite of a state of affairs 'about which the norms say nothing at all'.[274] Thus, if the ICJ's inability to reach a definitive conclusion concerning the question whether the use of nuclear weapons is 'in any circumstance permitted under international law'[275] was due to a 'head-on collision of fundamental principles, neither one of which can be reduced to the other'[276] rather than the fact that 'no … rule of international law exists'[277] that would govern the question, then it would be misleading to characterize paragraph 105(2)(E) of the *Nuclear Weapons Advisory Opinion* as a finding of *non liquet*.

Even if one accepted the suggestion[278] that, although legal dilemmas do not respond to gaps in the sense of an absence of applicable primary rules, they respond to the absence of a secondary norm governing the relationship of the two conflicting norms (*Kollisionslücken*),[279] it is questionable whether *non liquet* declarations, normally responding to 'non-existent, or controversial, or uncertain'[280] conduct norms, could be issued in response to such kinds of gaps. In that regard,

for Comparative Public Law and International Law 2006) para 1; Jean Salmon, *Dictionnaire de Droit International Public* (Bruylant 2001) 747.

[265] See Lucien Siorat, *Le problème des lacunes en droit international: Contribution à l'étude des sources du droit et de la fonction judiciaire* (Pichon & Durant-Auzias 1958) 63 and the corresponding discussion in Hernandez (n 246) 247.

[266] See Siorat (n 265) 85; Hernandez (n 246) 248.

[267] Hernandez (n 246) 249.

[268] Ilmar Tammelo, 'On the Logical Openness of Legal Orders: A Modal Analysis of Law with Special Reference to the Logical Status of Non Liquet in International Law' (1959) 8 American Journal of Comparative Law 187, 192. See also Helen Quane, 'Silence in International Law' (2014) 84 BYIL 243.

[269] Lauterpacht (n 264) 216.

[270] Lauterpacht (n 264) 216.

[271] Part I.A.3.d.

[272] Julius Stone, 'Non Liquet and the International Judicial Function' in Chaim Perelman (ed), *Le problème des lacunes en droit* (Bruylant 1968) 309.

[273] See also Christófolo (n 54) 51–2, 244–5.

[274] Stone (n 272) 305. See also Gerald Fitzmaurice, 'The Problem of Non-Liquet: Prolegomena to a Restatement' in Charles Rousseau (ed), *Mélanges offerts à Charles Rousseau: la communauté internationale* (A Pedone 1974) 97–8.

[275] UNGA Res 49/75 K (15 December 1994) UN Doc A/RES/49/75 K [11].

[276] *Nuclear Weapons Advisory Opinion* (n 42), Declaration of President Bedjaoui [22].

[277] *SS Lotus* (n 246) 23.

[278] Ulrich Fastenrath, *Lücken im Völkerrecht: zu Rechtscharakter, Quellen, Systemzusammenhang, Methodenlehre und Funktionen des Völkerrechts* (Duncker & Humblot 1991) 227; Pauwelyn (n 1) 152, 419.

[279] See also Part I.A.3.d.

[280] Lauterpacht (n 264) 216.

it might be instructive to observe that the cases in which the ICJ is sometimes seen[281] to have come closest to issuing a *non liquet* declaration in the past have not concerned the relationship between secondary norms. For example, in the *Haya de la Torre Case*, the ICJ felt unable to choose 'amongst … various courses by which … asylum may be terminated'[282] where that choice was 'conditioned by facts and possibilities'[283] that the ICJ did not possess.[284] Similarly, in *Maritime Delimitation (Qatar* v *Bahrain)*, the ICJ faced a silence of international law 'on the question whether low-tide elevations can be considered to be "territory" '.[285] In the *Kosovo Advisory Opinion*, the ICJ dealt with the absence of a 'prohibition of declarations of independence'[286] and, in the *Northern Cameroons Case*, the ICJ's refusal to provide an answer was based on the absence of 'an actual controversy … between the parties'.[287] Accordingly, it would at the least be unusual and, in light of the foregoing, unwarranted to issue a *non liquet* declaration in response to an irresolvable norm conflict.[288]

Further, *non liquet* declarations issued in response to secondary norm conflicts would also be problematic to the extent that the *Lotus* Principle, discussed above, can transform seemingly content-neutral *non liquet* declarations into permissions. For example, the view that the ICJ issued a *non liquet* declaration in the *Nuclear Weapons Advisory Opinion* would entail the conclusion that 'States remain free to act as they intend'.[289] Indeed, in accordance with the 'received view'[290] of the *Lotus* Principle, 'the meaning of the [ICJ's] position would be that States have a right in law to use nuclear weapons'.[291] However, if the state of the

[281] Shabtai Rosenne, *The Law and Practice of the International Court, 1920-2005* (4th edn, Martinus Nijhoff 2006) 172–4. For further potential candidates for *non liquet* declarations, see Lauterpacht, (n 264) 217–22.

[282] *Haya De La Torre (Colombia/Peru)* (Judgment) [1951] ICJ Rep 71 ('*Haya De La Torre*') 79.

[283] *Haya De La Torre*' (n 282) 79.

[284] *Haya De La Torre*' (n 282) 79.

[285] *Maritime Delimitation and Territorial Questions between Qatar and Bahrain (Qatar v Bahrain)* (Merits) [2001] ICJ Rep 40 [205].

[286] *Accordance with International Law of the Unilateral Declaration of Independence in Respect of Kosovo (Advisory Opinion)* [2010] ICJ Rep 403 [84].

[287] *Northern Cameroons (Cameroon v United Kingdom)* (Preliminary Objections) [1963] ICJ Rep 15, 33–4.

[288] However, note the observation of the ICJ in the *Reparation for Injuries Case* that, in the event that a State's right to exercise diplomatic protection conflicts with an organization's right of functional protection, 'there is no rule of law which assigns priority to the one or to the other'. See *Reparation for Injuries Suffered in the Service of the United Nations (Advisory Opinion)* [1949] ICJ Rep 174, 185.

[289] *Nuclear Weapons Advisory Opinion* (n 42), Separate Opinion of Judge Guillaume [9].

[290] *Nuclear Weapons Advisory Opinion* (n 42), Dissenting Opinion of Judge Shahabuddeen, 376, 390.

[291] *Nuclear Weapons Advisory Opinion* (n 42), Dissenting Opinion of Judge Shahabuddeen, 426, 376. See also Dapo Akande, 'Nuclear Weapons, Unclear Law? Deciphering the Nuclear Weapons Advisory Opinion of the International Court' (1998) 68 BYIL 165, 216; Amerasinghe (n 248) 44; *Nuclear Weapons Advisory Opinion* (n 42), Dissenting Opinion of Judge Koroma, 558, 581; Kokott (n 246) 160–1. This view directly contradicts the Court's explicit rejection of the contention that 'the present corpus juris is devoid of relevant rules in this matter'. See *Nuclear Weapons Advisory Opinion* (n 42) [18]–[19]. Later, the ICJ did attribute its inability to provide a 'definitive conclusion' to the 'present state of international law' and to the 'elements of fact at its disposal' (*Nuclear Weapons Advisory Opinion* (n 42) [97]). However, the ICJ states nowhere that it was a *lack* of facts or law, rather than

law is such that it is impossible to establish a priority between the right to use nuclear weapons and the prohibition to do so, then the unqualified conclusion that States are entitled to use nuclear weapons constitutes a *non sequitur*. In that sense the combined effect of *non liquet* declarations and default rules risks obscuring the original relationship between the two conflicting norms by transforming normatively contested territory into the providence of permissive rules. This is why, contrary to the view of some,[292] the ICJ's *Nuclear Weapons Advisory Opinion* should not be construed as a case of *non liquet*. Thus, *non liquet* declarations and residual rules do not preclude the possibility of legal dilemmas, since they are conceptually inadequate devices to address irresolvable norm conflicts.

The discussion in this part aimed to demonstrate that contemporary international law's norm conflict resolution devices and accommodation mechanisms are not omnipotent and that they do not preclude, as such, the possibility of legal dilemmas. Table II.1 below provides a concise overview of the limitations discussed in this section. Ultimately, the possibility of resolving a norm conflict rests on the ability to distinguish and to rank two norms. However, there are situations when such distinctions are impossible because particular norms might be incommensurable, incomparable, or simply mirror images of each other. If it is accepted that such situations can exist in principle, then no device will be able to distinguish the indistinguishable, or to dispose of the fact that the application of any norm conflict resolution mechanism necessarily leads to the undue impairment of at least one norm. It is these situations which the concept of a legal dilemma seeks to address.

Despite the limitations established above, it is evidently the case that the international legal order does not grind to a halt whenever it confronts an irresolvable norm conflict. Indeed, in a legal order that does not acknowledge the possibility of legal dilemmas, irresolvable conflicts of norms may often be 'overcome operationally'.[293] Judicial actors may, for example, utilize residual rules, *non liquet* declarations, or judicial legislation in pursuit of the belief that courts must 'make a decision even where there is no particularly good reason for deciding one way rather than another'.[294]

their contradictory nature that caused its problems. Indeed, the judges interpreted this passage very differently. See text to notes 16–22 in the Introduction and compare, eg, *Nuclear Weapons Advisory Opinion* (n 42), Dissenting Opinion of Judge Koroma 557–8; *Nuclear Weapons Advisory Opinion* (n 42), Dissenting Opinion of Judge Higgins [31]–[32]; *Nuclear Weapons Advisory Opinion* (n 42), Declaration of Judge Vereshchetin 280; *Nuclear Weapons Advisory Opinion* (n 42), Declaration of President Bedjaoui [14].

[292] See, eg, Akande (n 291) 212; Shabtai Rosenne, *Rosenne's the World Court: What It Is and How It Works* (Terry D Gill ed, 6th edn, Martinus Nijhoff 2003) 210; Richard A Falk, 'Nuclear Weapons, International Law and the World Court: A Historic Encounter' (1997) 91 AJIL 64, 68; Amerasinghe (n 248) 44; Vaughan Lowe, 'Shock Verdict: Nuclear War May or May Not Be Unlawful' (1996) 55 The Cambridge Law Journal 415, 417; Bodansky (n 248) 151.

[293] Richard Nobles and David Schiff, 'Review of Paradoxes and Inconsistencies in the Law by Oren Perez; Gunther Teubner' (2007) 70 MLR 505, 509.

[294] Nobles and Schiff (n 293) 509. Similarly, Lauterpacht observes that, even in situations when a court's decision 'might well have gone the other way … [a] decision, final and authoritative, there must be'. See Lauterpacht (n 264) 235.

Table II.1. The table supplements Figure I.3 with a summary of the limitations of contemporary international law's norm conflict resolution devices and accommodation mechanisms.

	Different Norms				Twin Norms
	Same Author(s)		Different Authors		Same Author(s)
	Contingent	Intrinsic	Contingent	Intrinsic	Contingent
Traditional Resolution Principles	Same, unknown, or irrelevant value?	Same, unknown, or irrelevant value?	x	x	x
Conflict-of-Laws Approaches	Same regime?	Same regime?	Judicial lawmaking?	Judicial lawmaking?	x
Proportionality	Legally absolute, factually indivisible, incommensurable, or stalemate?	Legally absolute, factually indivisible, incommensurable, or stalemate?	Legally absolute, factually indivisible, incommensurable, or stalemate?	Legally absolute, factually indivisible, incommensurable, or stalemate?	x
Accommodation	Outside scope, requirements not met, or conflict with *ius cogens*?	Outside scope, requirements not met, or conflict with *ius cogens*?	Outside scope, requirements not met, or conflict with *ius cogens*?	Outside scope, requirements not met, or conflict with *ius cogens*?	Outside scope, requirements not met, or conflict with *ius cogens*?
Default	x	x	x	x	x
Non liquet	x	x	x	x	x
Example Type	*Nuclear Weapons*	*Submarine Treaty*	*Military Alliances*	*Canal Treaties*	*Distress at Sea*
Norm 1	Art 51, UN Charter, customary right to self-defence	Art 1(1), 1922 Submarine Treaty	Art 2, 1950 Joint Defence Treaty	Art 8, 1858 Cañas–Jerez Treaty	Reg 33, ch V, SOLAS
Norm 2	Arts 23, 25, 1907 Hague Convention and Arts 35, 48, 51, 52, 1949 Geneva Conventions (AP I)	Arts 1(2), 4, 1922 Submarine Treaty	Art 3(1)c, 1979 Peace Treaty	Art 1, 1914 Bryan-Chamorro Treaty	Reg 33, ch V, SOLAS
Contingency?	Extreme situation where nuclear weapon is only means of State survival	N/A	Attack of Arab League member by Israel	N/A	Simultaneous rescue impossible

However, this book argues that the mere fact that contemporary international law has developed certain coping strategies to deal with irresolvable norm conflict does not mean that irresolvable norm conflicts are currently being dealt with in the most methodologically accurate and optimal manner. Against that background, the next and final part develops a three-step procedure to address legal dilemmas which aims to ensure that irresolvable norm conflicts are dealt with by competent and accountable decision-makers in a manner that is methodologically accurate.

Part III

The Decision of a Legal Dilemma

The second part established that legal dilemmas are possible in international law and that the contemporary international legal framework does not preclude their existence. Thus, the second of the three questions, 'Can legal dilemmas exist in contemporary international law?', has been answered in the affirmative. This part addresses the third question; namely by whom and how should a legal dilemma be decided? The first section of this part focuses mainly on the introduction and description of the proposal's three elements. The second and third section will then defend the proposal against various theoretical and practical objections.

A. Proposal

Beyond the analysis concerning the possibility of the emergence of legal dilemmas in the previous part, it is crucial to address the question how dilemmas, when and if they arise, should be dealt with by judicial actors since the merit of the concept of a dilemma itself depends significantly on the way in which a legal order responds to legal dilemmas. If it were the case, for example, that the acknowledgement of a true legal contradiction leads to the collapse of the entire legal order, one might be inclined to favour the systematic preclusion of the possibility of irresolvable norm conflicts. If, on the other hand, it can be shown that the potential destabilizing effect of legal dilemmas can be contained and that the acknowledgement of dilemmas can in fact enhance respect for the rule of law, the concept of a dilemma itself may be less difficult to accept. Against this background, it is proposed that legal dilemmas should be addressed in three successive steps. First, before a dilemma is decided, a court should issue a declaration that a legal dilemma exists (Section 1). Second, the sovereign facing the dilemma should decide in accordance with which of the conflicting norms the sovereign wishes to act (Section 2). Third, a court should enforce any prescriptive norm with which a sovereign elected not to comply (Section 3).[1]

[1] There will be no need for judicial enforcement if a sovereign, faced with a dilemma involving permissive norms, decides not to exercise that permissive norm in favour of a prescriptive norm. See Part III.A.3.a.

1. Dilemmatic declaration

The first element of the proposed procedure for dealing with legal dilemmas consists of a 'dilemmatic declaration'. The term 'dilemmatic declaration' is used as a term of art. It refers to a judicial declaration that acknowledges the existence of a legal dilemma and that delegates[2] the decision-making competence to decide the dilemma to the legal actor facing it. By identifying the norms constituting the dilemma, the dilemmatic declaration demarcates the normative perimeter within which sovereigns may subsequently,[3] being fully aware that legal wrongdoing is unavoidable, determine how to decide the dilemma. In this way, the dilemmatic declaration communicates the existence of a legal superposition state to the relevant actors, bringing to life a legal 'Garden of Forking Paths'[4] within which each course of action is 'burdened with an alternative'.[5] This sub-section will first set out the characteristics of a dilemmatic declaration before proceeding to consider the reasons that favour the proposal's first element.

According to the proposal, judicial actors may only issue a dilemmatic declaration if they encounter a legal dilemma in proceedings concerning a dilemma that has not yet been decided by means of a sovereign decision.[6] Further, and crucially, a dilemmatic declaration may be issued in the course of such proceedings only once a most rigorous and stringent application of contemporary international law's norm conflict resolution and accommodation devices[7] has been unable to decide a given norm conflict. Only once all norm conflict resolution devices have proved unsuitable, or have failed to produce an answer, when 'legal statements ... oscillate between contradictions that cannot be accounted for through further refinement',[8] do any dilemmatic considerations arise.

[2] In this context, the term 'delegation' refers to the judicial entrustment of the actor facing the dilemma with the responsibility of deciding it. The term 'delegation' is not used in the strict legal sense—a transfer of competence—since judicial actors at do not posses the legal competence to decide dilemmas which they could subsequently transfer.

[3] See Part III.A.2.

[4] Jorge Luis Borges, 'The Garden of Forking Paths' in Anthony Kerrigan (ed), *Ficciones* (Grove Press 1994). See also Michael McKenna and D Justin Coates, 'Compatibilism' in Edward N Zalta (ed), *The Stanford Encyclopedia of Philosophy* (Summer edn, 2015) <http://plato.stanford.edu/archives/sum2015/entries/compatibilism/> accessed 4 November 2016.

[5] Heinrich Popitz, 'Soziale Normen' (1961) 2 European Journal of Sociology / Archives Européennes de Sociologie 185, 185 (tr by author).

[6] With respect to the judicial treatment of dilemmas that have been decided by means of a sovereign decision, see Part III.A.3.

[7] See Part II.

[8] Richard Nobles and David Schiff, 'Review of Paradoxes and Inconsistencies in the Law by Oren Perez; Gunther Teubner' (2007) 70 MLR 505, 509. A good (albeit fictional) description of such a situation is provided by Tatting J in the Case of the Speluncean Explorers, where he struggles to decide which side he favours, stating that '[t]he more I examine this case and think about it, the more deeply I become involved. My mind becomes entangled in the meshes of the very nets I throw out for my own rescue. I find that almost every consideration that bears on the decision of the case is counterbalanced by an opposing consideration leading in the opposite direction.' See Lon L Fuller, 'The Case of the Speluncean Explorers' (1949) 62 Harvard Law Review 616, 631.

This means that judicial actors confronted with hard cases[9] cannot resort to dilemmatic declarations as an 'easy way out'.[10] It also means that the judicial awareness and acceptability of finding dilemmas could not lead judges to identify legal dilemmas where none exist.[11] Legal dilemmas are not identified based on 'first, nonreflective impressions'[12] and they 'do not occur in a legal vacuum, but in a space to which international law is'[13] centrally relevant. There is a distinction between the mere pronouncement of an unequivocal decision, and the most conscientious participation in the judicial process that precedes any pronouncement of that kind.[14] While legal dilemmas may not require judges to identify an unequivocal solution, they do not relieve them from the general duty to participate most conscientiously in the deliberative judicial process. In this sense, dilemmatic declarations are the result of and presuppose a rigorous judicial analysis of a given set of conflicting norms.

Consider, for example, the *Nuclear Weapons* scenario. A court confronting a potential norm conflict related to the reconcilability of a State's right to self-defence and the prohibition of nuclear weapons should in the first instance, and in accordance with the proposed procedure for dealing with legal dilemmas, engage in a most comprehensive application of contemporary international law's norm conflict resolution and accommodation mechanisms in order to attempt to resolve the conflict. This is what the ICJ did in its proceedings concerning the *Nuclear Weapons Advisory Opinion*. Once such attempts have proved unable to establish a hierarchy or compromise between the norms concerned, the court should proceed to declare the legal impossibility of reconciling the conflicting norms. Arguably, paragraph 105(2)E of the *Nuclear Weapons Advisory Opinion* can be read as doing exactly this by acknowledging that 'the Court cannot conclude definitively whether the threat or use of nuclear weapons would be lawful or unlawful in an extreme circumstance of self-defence'.[15] Indeed, in the words of the ICJ's President, paragraph 105(2)E provides that there is 'a head-on collision of fundamental principles, neither one of which can be reduced to the other'.[16] Based on the proposal espoused here, a declaration of this kind would burden a State confronting such a dilemmatic conflict with the

[9] See Part I.A.3.g for the distinction between hard cases and legal dilemmas.

[10] Frederick Schauer, 'Instrumental Commensurability' (1998) 146 University of Pennsylvania Law Review 1215, 1226, 1230.

[11] See, eg, Schauer's observations regarding the risks of accepting the incommensurability of norms, Schauer (n 10) 1226; David Wolitz, 'Indeterminacy, Value Pluralism, and Tragic Cases' (2014) 62 Buffalo Law Review 529, 595.

[12] Schauer (n 10) 1226. See also Wolitz (n 11) 533.

[13] MacCormick makes this observation in the context of discussing the distinction between radical pluralism (defended by Rossa Phelan) and soft pluralism (which MacCormick favours) in the European legal order. See Neil MacCormick, 'Risking Constitutional Collision in Europe?' (1998) 18 Oxford Journal of Legal Studies 517, 531.

[14] Alfredo Mordechai Rabello, 'Non Liquet: From Modern Law to Roman Law' (2004) 10 Annual Survey of International & Comparative Law 18–19, 21.

[15] *Legality of the Threat or Use of Nuclear Weapons (Advisory Opinion)* [1996] ICJ Rep 226 ('*Nuclear Weapons Advisory Opinion*') [105(2)E].

[16] *Nuclear Weapons Advisory Opinion* (n 15), Declaration of President Bedjaoui [22].

responsibility of choosing which of the two norms to honour and which to violate, knowing that, irrespective of the choice, one norm would be unduly impaired.[17]

The main reasons supporting the argument in favour of dilemmatic declarations are reasons of conceptual clarity and methodological honesty. If a court is in fact (and *de jure*) confronted with a dilemmatic norm conflict, a judicial declaration that acknowledges as much is the most accurate response. Far from being an 'anti-climatic embarrassment'[18] of the judicial discipline, the acknowledgement that two 'oughts' conflict irreconcilably, when and if they do, is the only accurate representation of such a normative state. It ensures that legal conclusions cohere with the 'facts of experience'[19] in the sense that a dilemmatic legal representation reflects the actual relationship between irreconcilably conflicting norms.

No doubt, the view that every legal state of affairs can be characterized as being either legal or illegal or, at worst, as being unregulated, may be appealing.[20] Some may, on that basis, question the merits of the proposal espoused here and might favour concealing[21] underlying conflicts by means of judicial lawmaking, for example.[22] However, absent any positive authorization to the contrary, judicial pronouncements should represent the law as it stands 'even if the heavens fell'[23]—*fiat*

[17] As argued previously, a permissive norm is unduly impaired if a sovereign decides to comply with a conflicting prescriptive norm. See Part I.A.2.d.

[18] Hersch Lauterpacht, *The Development of International Law by the International Court* (CUP 1982) 146.

[19] Albert Einstein, 'Physik und Realität' (1936) 221 Journal of the Franklin Institute 313, 315–16 (tr by author). In the domestic context, Luhmann also admits that a legal system's consistency and prohibition of contradictions may be upheld 'contra-factually.' See Niklas Luhmann, *Law as a Social System* (Fatima Kastner and others eds, Klaus A Ziegert tr, OUP 2004) 286.

[20] This was the position of Leibniz. See Gottfried Wilhelm Leibniz, 'Inaugural Dissertation on Perplexing Cases in the Law' in Alberto Artosi, Bernardo Pieri, and Giovanni Sartor (eds), *Leibniz: Logico-Philosophical Puzzles in the Law* (Springer 2013); MV Dougherty, *Moral Dilemmas in Medieval Thought: From Gratian to Aquinas* (CUP 2011) 171–2. See also, in the international context, Hersch Lauterpacht, 'Some Observations on the Prohibition of "Non Liquet" and the Completeness of the Law' in Elihu Lauterpacht (ed), *International Law—Collected Papers*, vol 2 (CUP 1975) 235.

[21] With respect to paradoxes in moral philosophy, Nussbaum concludes that '[c]onsistency in conflict is bought at the price of self-deception'. See Martha C Nussbaum, *The Fragility of Goodness: Luck and Ethics in Greek Tragedy and Philosophy* (CUP 2001) 242. Singer applies this insight to property law (Joseph William Singer, *Entitlement: The Paradoxes of Property* (Yale UP 2000) 205–6) and, concerning international law, Lauterpacht in one of his later writings observes that the ICJ's 'apparent indecision' in an advisory opinion 'may … be preferable to a deceptive clarity which fails to give an indication of the inherent complexities of the issue'. See Lauterpacht (n 18) 152. Similarly, Akande observes that 'pointing out deficiencies or gaps in the law (if there are such gaps) might be better than papering over the cracks'. See Dapo Akande, 'Nuclear Weapons, Unclear Law? Deciphering the Nuclear Weapons Advisory Opinion of the International Court' (1998) 68 BYIL 165, 212.

[22] Luhmann suggests, eg, that courts must also decide cases, even if 'valid law is not enough to state the facts of who is in a legal position and who is in an illegal position … [by] … develop[ing] rules of decision-making for their decision'. See Niklas Luhmann, *Law as a Social System* (n 19) 287. In the *Nuclear Weapons Advisory Opinion*, Judge Koroma expresses a similar view, see *Nuclear Weapons Advisory Opinion* (n 15), Dissenting Opinion of Judge Koroma, 559.

[23] An early example of the maxime's invocation by an English court is *R v John Wilkes* (1770) 4 Burr 2527, 98 ER 328 (King's Bench, England and Wales), Lord Mansfield at 2562. More recently, the UK Supreme Court referred to it in *PJS v News Group Newspaper Ltd* [2016] UKSC 26, Lord Mance at 3. For an international legal manifestation of this view, see *Nuclear Weapons Advisory Opinion* (n 15), Dissenting Opinion of Judge Weeramantry, 440.

justitia ruat cælum—and it is improbable that dilemmatic declarations will cause the heavens to descend. Moreover, international affairs, as much as social reality, are shaped by diverse thoughts 'of many minds, that are [at least sometimes] fundamentally contradictory'.[24] A view of law that fails to reflect law's 'occasional obscurity or inconclusiveness'[25] entails the risk that law degenerates into a 'system of self-made concepts which slides a fully-developed jurisprudence in front of society's life-process … [thereby] … presupposing that order'[26] which jurisprudence is supposed to reflect. In this regard, it has been observed that:

> [in] conditions of social complexity, it is pointless to insist on formal unity. A law that would fail to articulate the experienced differences between fact-situations or between the interests or values that appear relevant in particular problem-areas would seem altogether unacceptable, utopian and authoritarian simultaneously.[27]

Dilemmatic declarations, in contrast, admit that 'positive law is no "*ratio scripta*" but a man-made entity shaped by history, which … necessarily contains contradictions and inadequacies'.[28] Under such conditions it should not be surprising that certain normative relationships can only be expressed in dilemmatic terms.[29] To that extent, dilemmatic declarations that acknowledge the presence of an irresolvable norm conflict offer a coherent[30] and conceptually accurate account of the relationship between conflicting norms without attempting to establish hierarchies where none exist.[31]

No doubt, there remain many potential objections to the proposal's first element. However, before addressing them in great detail in the second and third section of this part, it is instructive to consider the proposal's second element: The delegation of the responsibility to decide a dilemma to a sovereign decision-maker.

[24] Robert W Gordon, 'Critical Legal Histories' (1984) 36 Stanford Law Review 57, 114.

[25] Lauterpacht (n 18) 152. See also Hugh Thirlway, 'The Nuclear Weapons Advisory Opinions: The Declarations and Separate and Dissenting Opinions' in Laurence Boisson de Chazournes and Philippe Sands (eds), *International Law, the International Court of Justice and Nuclear Weapons* (CUP 1999) 434.

[26] Theodor Adorno, *Negative Dialektik* (Suhrkamp 1966) 303, 302–3 (tr by author).

[27] See ILC, Report of the Study Group of the International Law Commission finalized by Martti Koskenniemi, *Fragmentation of International Law: Difficulties Arising from the Diversification and Expansion of International Law* (13 April 2006) UN Doc A/CN.4/L.682 ('*Fragmentation Report*') para 16.

[28] Hans Christoph Grigoleit and Jörg Neuner, *Claus-Wilhelm Canaris, Gesammelte Schriften* (Walter de Gruyter 2012) 292 (tr by author).

[29] Singer makes a similar observation regarding property law, noting that 'sometimes the best way to express our values and our social and legal practices is by adopting what seem to be contradictory principles, even though we cannot now, and perhaps never will, be able to reconcile them fully. The truth of our moral situation may sometimes require us to stop trying to reconcile a contradiction.' See Singer (n 21) 204–5.

[30] In the context of incommensurable values, Klabbers observes that a legal order 'in absence of common agreement that the one is superior to the other … [a legal order] … cannot place one value systematically over another one without becoming incoherent'. See Jan Klabbers, *Treaty Conflict and the European Union* (CUP 2009) 46.

[31] In this regard, dilemmas may be compared to Luhmann's understanding of paradoxes, which 'provide grounds for statements despite the absence of grounds'. See Nobles and Schiff (n 8) 510–11.

2. Sovereign decision

Once a court has issued a dilemmatic declaration, it is the declaration's sovereign[32] addressee who 'takes over' by determining how the dilemma thus identified should be decided. The space within which the sovereign decides is encompassed by law, yet it is a space to which law's otherwise specific, deterministic character does not extend. Within this space, law exists but is in a superposition state. As soon as the sovereign has decided the dilemma, the legal superposition state collapses and law continues to govern in the ordinary manner. Again, this sub-section first sets out the characteristics of a sovereign's decision of a dilemma before proceeding to consider three reasons that favour the proposal's second element.

In dilemmatic situations, when law has ceased to offer reasons to act one way to the exclusion of another,[33] the decision of a sovereign is the *ultima ratio*.[34] The sovereign's choice is distinctly sovereign,[35] because the decision is taken, as *princeps ex machina*, from a position above[36] the conflicting norms and unbound by ordinarily applicable legal constraints.[37] The choice[38] is 'originative',[39]

[32] It is, strictly speaking, more appropriate to refer to the decision-maker of a dilemma as a sovereign rather than a State. While States are legal persons, sovereigns can be both legal and natural persons. In dilemmatic circumstances, legal persons, being inherent creatures of law without human qualities, will be unable to overcome the oscillatory legal state that characterizes a legal dilemma. Thus, dilemmatic circumstances call rather for a sovereign judgment than for a decision of a State.

[33] The use of the term *ultima ratio* is particularly fitting, not only because of the term's historical association with a king's final decision of a dispute ('*ultima ratio regis*'), but also because a sovereign's decision furnishes the ultimate reason for acting in the way a sovereign chooses to act in dilemmatic situations.

[34] Bonhoeffer uses the term to describe a situation where human reason does not allow for a variety of choices but rather forces a moral agent to act in a manner that is impermissible and that should not even be considered as a possibility under ordinary circumstances. See Dietrich Bonhoeffer, *Ethik* (Eberhard Bethge ed, 2nd edn, Christian Kaiser Verlag 1953) 185.

[35] Zuleeg's principle of the political decision of irresolvable norm conflicts illustrates this sovereign quality in the context of treaty law. See Manfred Zuleeg, 'Vertragskonkurrenz im Völkerrecht. Teil I: Verträge zwischen souveränen Staaten' (1977) 20 German Yearbook of International Law 246, 268. See also Schmitt's (in)famous observation that it is the sovereign who 'decides on the exception'. See Carl Schmitt, *Political Theology: Four Chapters on the Concept of Sovereignty* (University of Chicago Press 1985) 5. Schmitt's concept of the exception is nonetheless different from a legal dilemma. See Part III.C.2.

[36] The adjective 'sovereign' derives from the Latin words *super* (over/above), *superus* (being above) and the vulgar Latin *superanus* (being above/superios). See Hans Schulz and Otto Basler, *Deutsches Fremdwörterbuch* (De Gruyter 2004) 284–6; Adolf Tobler and Erhard Lommatzsch, 'Soveraineté' *Altfranzösisches Wörterbuch*, vol 9 (Steiner 1973) 1032; Hans Boldt and others, 'Staat und Souveränität' in Otto Brunner, Werner Conze, and Reinhart Koselleck (eds), *Geschichtliche Grundbegriffe*, vol 6 (Klett-Cotta 1990).

[37] Note here the observations concerning the scope of a sovereign's decision-making competence in dilemmatic circumstances in Part III.C.2.

[38] Berlin might have characterized the sovereign's choice as 'radical' (John Gray, *Isaiah Berlin* (Princeton UP 1996) 33) but, given that the term 'decision' already entails the notion of forcefully separating and cutting disentangled options (the term derives from the Latin *decidere*, which in turn derives from *de-* (down/away from) and *caedere* (chop/hew/slaughter)), the attribute 'radical' does not add much that the term decision does not already express. On the inherent undecidability that a decision presupposes, see also Niklas Luhmann, *Law as a Social System* (n 19) 282; Jacques Derrida, 'Force De Loi: Le Fondement Mystique De L'Autorité' (1989) 11 Cardozo Law Review 920, 963.

[39] Gray (n 38) 15.

subjective,[40] and underived from pre-existing principles[41] springing instead directly from the decision-maker's will—*stat pro ratione voluntas*.[42]

The fact that the sovereign's choice is taken from a position above the conflicting norms unbound by otherwise applicable legal constraints does not mean that the sovereignty characterizing this act of decision-making is pre-legal or extra-legal.[43] However, it does mean that a sovereign can decide once the law's decision-making capacities have been exhausted. A sovereign can decide when and what the law cannot. The problem posed by a legal dilemma remains a legal problem despite law's inability to solve it: The sovereign's options remain circumscribed by law, the sovereign's decision has no precedential value whatsoever,[44] and the sovereign is legally responsible for any decision taken.[45]

Further, the fact that a sovereign's decision is subjective—not derived from pre-existing legal principles—does not mean, contrary to what some[46] have argued, that any such decision is irrational or arbitrary. The inconclusiveness of legal reason does not mean that all 'practical and theoretical reason [has] run out',[47] and that sovereigns are asked to make a 'groundless … choice'.[48] Instead, in deciding what to do, sovereigns should still deliberately[49] distinguish and weigh competing reasons for action.[50] This does not preclude self-interested or biased decisions, but it excludes random, arbitrary, insane, or absurd decisions. Throughout the decision-making process, reason still guides the sovereign. It just does not take the sovereign 'all the way' to a uniquely correct solution. While in dilemmatic circumstances, 'no argument can force the decision in favour of one or the other option',[51] arguments supporting each option still exist.[52] Action for a 'reason that [does not] defea[t]

40 See Part III.A.2.a and Part III.A.2.b for a more detailed consideration of the significance and meaning of the subjectivity of the sovereign's decision.

41 Gray (n 38) 62; Karl Jaspers, *Die Atombombe und die Zukunft des Menschen. Politisches Bewußtsein in unserer Zeit* (Piper 1960) 231; John Finnis, *Nuclear Deterrence, Morality and Realism* (Clarendon Press 1987) 256.

42 To Leibniz, this phrase represented the 'motto of a tyrant', Gottfried Wilhelm Leibniz, 'Meditation on the Common Concept of Justice' in Patrick Riley (ed), *Political Writings* (2nd edn, CUP 1988) 46. See also Theo Kobusch, 'Paradoxon und Religiöse Existenz' in Roland Hagenbüchle and Paul Geyer (eds), *Das Paradox: Eine Herausforderung des abendländischen Denkens* (2nd edn, Königshausen & Neumann 2002) 461. Accordingly, it will be argued below that problematic decisions of this kind should, if at all, be taken only by sovereigns and not by judicial actors. See Part III.A.2.

43 Thus Agamben's characterization of the state of exception as a 'space that is neither outside nor inside' of the legal order (Giorgio Agamben, *State of Exception* (University of Chicago Press 2008) 35) could also adequately describe the sphere within which a sovereign decides a legal dilemma. See also Part III.C.2.

44 See also Part III.A.3.a.

45 See Part III.A.3.

46 Bonhoeffer (n 34) 185–6; Gray (n 38) 71.

47 Gray (n 38) 71.

48 Gray (n 38) 71.

49 Jaspers (n 41) 231; HE Mason, 'Responsibilities and Principles: Reflections on the Sources of Moral Dilemmas' in HE Mason (ed), *Moral Dilemmas and Moral Theory* (OUP 1996) 233.

50 Finnis (n 41) 258–9.

51 Jaspers (n 41) 231 (tr by author).

52 A decision-maker's choice would arguably still comply with Linderfalk's 'Principle of Rational Decision Making' which provides that 'observers should always be able to reconstruct [a legal actor's decision] as a conclusion inferred from sound premises according to the accepted rules of inference'. See Ulf Linderfalk, 'The Principle of Rational Decision-Making—As Applied to the Identification of Normative Conflicts in International Law' (2013) Zeitschrift für ausländisches öffentliches Recht und Völkerrecht 591, 592.

all those [reasons] that conflict with it'[53] is still rational action. Thus, a sovereign's choice can be rational, as long as the chosen action is supported by 'reason[s] that [are] reasonably thought to be undefeated',[54] despite the existence of possibly equally valid and equally powerful reasons for acting differently.

Finally, it is still adequate to speak of a sovereign's 'freedom' to decide a legal dilemma, despite the unavailability of a choice that would not unduly impair at least one norm. Unless one believes that every agent's acts are pre-determined,[55] even having a choice between two unlawful actions is an attribute of freedom,[56] rather than constraint.[57] It is the 'freedom of those responsible'[58] for making a decision in times when the law provides no determinative answer. Indeed, only where an agent can choose between two or more reasonable choices does it make sense to speak of a freedom to choose. It would be a very impoverished freedom, indeed, if one had available only one reasonable option.[59]

Ultimately, from a legal point of view, a sovereign's decision may be 'a highly mysterious process'.[60] While experience, a deep understanding of the concrete situation, and certain general principles[61] may aid a decision-maker when deciding how to overcome a particular dilemma,[62] it is distinctly impossible[63] and indeed undesirable[64] to provide a detailed formula regarding the way in which decision-makers should decide dilemmas.

Despite the fact that a sovereign's decision of a given dilemma is still supported by reasons, sovereigns should decide in full appreciation of the fact[65] that, whatever they choose, they will unduly impair at least one norm. Thus, in the moment of the decision, sovereigns should conduct themselves with a sense of humility.[66]

[53] Joseph Raz, *Between Authority and Interpretation: On the Theory of Law and Practical Reason* (OUP 2009) 368; Joseph Raz, *The Morality of Freedom* (Clarendon Press 1986) 334. Similarly, Hart observed that in hard cases judges make decisions that are 'neither arbitrary nor mechanical'. See HLA Hart, *The Concept of Law* (2nd edn, Clarendon Press 1994) 204–5.

[54] Raz, *Between Authority and Interpretation* (n 53) 368; Raz, *The Morality of Freedom* (n 53) 334.

[55] Gray (n 38) 15, 80.

[56] Isaiah Berlin, *Liberty* (OUP 2002) 214; Gray (n 38) 62–3.

[57] Gray (n 38) 19.

[58] Bonhoeffer uses the term '*Freiheit der Verantwortlichen*'. See Bonhoeffer (n 34) 186 (tr by author).

[59] John Finnis, 'Natural Law and Legal Reasoning' in Robert P George (ed), *Natural Law Theory: Contemporary Essays* (Clarendon Press 1992) 136; Finnis (n 41) 256.

[60] Hannah Arendt in an interview with Günter Gaus. See Günter Gaus, Interview with Hannah Arendt (28 October 1964) <http://www.rbb-online.de/zurperson/interview_archiv/arendt_hannah.html> accessed 27 January 2016 (tr by author).

[61] Such as Hans Jonas' 'Imperative of Responsibility' ['Schließe in deine gegenwärtige Wahl die zukünftige Integrität des Menschen als Mit-Gegenstand deines Wollens ein'], for example. See Hans Jonas, *Das Prinzip der Verantwortung—Versuch einer Ethik für die technologische Zivilisation* (Suhrkamp 1984) 36 (tr by author).

[62] See, in particular, the discussion concerning moral and empirical competence in Part III.A.2.a.

[63] Wolitz (n 11) 589.

[64] See Part III.C.3. See also Isaiah Berlin, 'On Political Judgment' [1996] *The New York Review of Books* 29 <http://www.nybooks.com/articles/archives/1996/oct/03/on-political-judgment> accessed 1 June 2017.

[65] See also Bonhoeffer (n 34) 186.

[66] Ronald Dworkin, *Taking Rights Seriously* (A&C Black 2013) 159. The ascription of personal qualities like humility to the sovereign is based on the assumption that the 'acts of states are also the acts of persons'. See Karl Jaspers, *The Question of German Guilt* (EB Ashton tr, OUP 1947) 49. See also

Their conduct should reflect both a consciousness of their own inability[67] to solve the legal dilemma[68] and an acute awareness of the fact that the virtue of their decision can often be assessed only retrospectively and not at the moment of choice.[69] In making the decision and being unable to shelter behind any exclusively non-defeasible reasons, the responsible decision-maker surrenders to the eventual judgment of others.[70] At the same time, recognizing that a sovereign could not but unduly impair at least one norm under dilemmatic circumstances entails an invitation to show mercy when it comes to holding sovereigns accountable for their conduct at the post-decision stage.[71]

The delegation of the decision-making responsibility to the addressee of the dilemmatic declaration is not unproblematic. In a world populated by sovereigns whose competence and/or benevolent intentions may not be beyond doubt, the proposal to entrust sovereigns, rather than judicial actors, with the decision of a legal dilemma might seem, at least *prima facie*, ill-advised, if not irresponsible.

Instead, it could be argued that, once the existence of a legal dilemmas has been identified, judicial actors should respond by means of judicial legislation. That is, judicial actors confronted with a choice between two irreconcilably conflicting norms could create a new norm that allows for the resolution of the conflict either in favour of one of the conflicting norms or in favour of an altogether different norm.[72] Specifically, judges could create a new primary norm, or they could craft a new collision norm, or both. For example, the judges in the *Nuclear Weapons* scenario could determine *de lege ferenda* that the necessity to protect the survival of a State justifies violating intransgressible principles of humanitarian law. Conversely, the judges could decide that, if in doubt, safeguarding norms of humanitarian law must prevail of a State's desire to survive. Further still, the judges could determine that nuclear weapons are prohibited per se so that there is no question that nuclear weapons could possibly be used in circumstances of self-defence.

Indeed, at least with respect to conflicts between norms belonging to different regimes, for example, it has been suggested that judicial actors should overcome such conflicts by creating novel 'substantive rules'[73] and 'substantive

Jurisdictional Immunities of the State (Germany v Italy: Greece Intervening) (Judgment) [2012] ICJ Rep 99 ('*Jurisdictional Immunities*'), Dissenting Opinion of Judge Cançado Trindade [236].

67 This acknowledgement is appropriate irrespective of the cause (epistemic or metaphysical, see Part I.C) of a given dilemma's undecidability. If a dilemma's undecidability was caused by legal imperfections, sovereigns should acknowledge their failure to craft non-dilemmatic legal norms. If a dilemma's undecidability was caused by metaphysical disagreement, sovereigns should acknowledge their inability to overcome entrenched metaphysical disagreement.

68 Dan M Kahan, 'The Supreme Court 2010 Term—Foreword: Neutral Principles, Motivated Cognition, and Some Problems for Constitutional Law' (2011) 125 Harvard Law Review 1, 62 fn 347.

69 Søren Kierkegaard, *Fear and Trembling/Repetition* (Howard Vincent Hong and Edna Hatlestad Hong trs, Princeton UP 1983) 63.

70 See also Bonhoeffer (n 34) 186.

71 Wolitz (n 11) 587–8.

72 João Ernesto Christófolo, *Solving Antinomies between Peremptory Norms in Public International Law* (Schulthess 2016) 244–5.

73 Andreas Fischer-Lescano and Gunther Teubner, 'Regime-Collisions: The Vain Search for Legal Unity in the Fragmentation of Global Law' (2004) 25 Michigan Journal of International Law 999, 1022.

norms'.[74] Focussing on the ICJ, the book argues, however, that it is preferable to provide for the decision of legal dilemmas by sovereigns for three reasons. The three reasons relate, respectively, to the legal and moral competence of judicial actors, and to their accountability. They will be considered in turn.

a) Legal competence

Before considering the legal competence of judicial actors to decide legal dilemmas, it is instructive to recall what kind of decision dilemmatic norm conflicts require. Legal dilemmas require creative, originative decisions that cannot be derived from precedents, statutes, analogous situations, or indefeasible legal reasons.[75] Thus, the decision of a legal dilemma by judicial actors would explicitly entail judicial law-making. It is against this background that this section argues that, by comparison with judicial actors, sovereign decision-makers are better placed to decide such dilemmatic conflicts.[76]

At the outset, it should be acknowledged that the judicial function by international judicial actors can, undoubtedly, be a creative exercise in the sense that it goes beyond the mere technical application of legal norms to facts. Decisions of international courts and tribunals, in particular those of the ICJ, shape, influence, and develop international law.[77] The default rule remains,[78] however, that, unless explicitly authorized to do otherwise,[79] the ICJ applies the law and does not make it. In the eyes of the ICJ itself, 'the Court is not a legislative body'.[80] This 'truism'[81] derives directly from the ICJ Statute's Article 38(1) that expressly mandates the ICJ to 'apply' the law based on the various sources listed in Articles 38(1)(a)–(d). The ICJ itself observed that it 'is clear that the Court cannot legislate'[82] and that 'the Court, as court of law, cannot render judgment *sub specie legis ferendae*, or anticipate the law before the legislator has laid it down'.[83] Thus, being fully aware of the

[74] Andreas Fischer-Lescano and Gunther Teubner (n 73) 1022.

[75] See Part III.A.2.

[76] The claim of this section is no stronger than that. The argument is merely that sovereigns are comparatively better suited to decide legal dilemmas than judicial actors.

[77] See generally Christian J Tams and James Sloan, *The Development of International Law by the International Court of Justice* (OUP 2013).

[78] See also Shabtai Rosenne, *The Law and Practice of the International Court, 1920-2005* (4th edn, Martinus Nijhoff 2006) vol I, 169; Franklin Berman, 'The International Court of Justice as an "Agent" of Legal Development?' in Christian J Tams and James Sloan (eds), *The Development of International Law by the International Court of Justice* (OUP 2013) 11; Gleider Hernandez, *The International Court of Justice and the Judicial Function* (OUP 2014) 85.

[79] According to the ICJ Statute, the ICJ may decide cases *ex aequo et bono* 'if the parties agree thereto.' Statute of the International Court of Justice (adopted 26 June 1945, entered into force 24 October 1945) 1946 UKTS 67 ('ICJ Statute') Art 38(2). See also Alain Pellet, 'Article 38' in Andreas Zimmermann and others (eds), *The Statute of the International Court of Justice: A Commentary* (OUP 2012) 731.

[80] *South West Africa (Ethiopia v South Africa; Liberia v South Africa)* (Second Phase) [1966] ICJ Rep 6 ('*South West Africa*') [89]. See also Pellet (n 79) 788.

[81] Robert Yewdall Jennings, 'Treaties as "Legislation"' in Gabriel M Wilner (ed), *Jus et Societas: Essays in Tribute to Wolfgang Friedmann* (Martinus Nijhoff 1979) 159.

[82] *Nuclear Weapons Advisory Opinion* (n 15) [18].

[83] *Fisheries Jurisdiction (United Kingdom v Iceland)* (Merits) [1974] ICJ Rep 3 ('*Fisheries Jurisdiction (United Kingdom v Iceland)*') [53].

difficulty, if not impossibility, of drawing a clear line between *ultra vires* judicial legislation and the warranted progressive development of international law,[84] the book argues that the ICJ should not exceed 'the parameters of permissible interpretation'[85] in pursuit of the exercise of its judicial function.

The creation of new primary or secondary norms by judicial actors in response to an irresolvable norm conflict, however, clearly exceeds the 'parameters of permissible interpretation' or the bounds of the judicial function. In particular, when a norm conflict concerns *ius cogens* norms, which can be modified only 'by the international community of states as a whole',[86] any creative judicial legislation would be impermissible.[87] Were it otherwise, the legitimacy of the international judicial process could be called into question very quickly.

To recall, the state of the law in dilemmatic circumstances is clear, settled, certain. It is not a situation where judicial lawmaking would be used to extend the law to previously unregulated areas, or for the purpose of settling previously unsettled legal questions. It is not a situation where there is a small 'margin of preference for giving a priority to one principle over another'[88] upon which a court could rely in order to establish a precarious priority of one norm over another. Rather, it is a situation where there is no judicial margin of preference at all. It might be an exaggeration to observe that States let judicial actors settle their disputes because they 'know the law' and not 'because they are wise or statesmanlike—very often they are manifestly neither'.[89] In principle, however, it is entirely correct, as the ICJ itself has pointed out repeatedly,[90] that it is the core and the distinct function of judicial actors to apply the law and not to serve as a council of wise statesmen that can create new norms. Indeed, it would be difficult to conceive of an international tribunal that, in absence of an express authorization to do so, would resolve the norm conflict in the *Military Alliances* scenario in favour of one or the other norm by modifying one of Egypt's obligations or by creating an entirely new prescriptive norm. Similarly, it would have been inappropriate for the judges in the *Nuclear Weapons Advisory Opinion* to establish a hierarchy between the conflicting norms or to create an altogether new norm when States themselves had apparently not yet done so.

[84] Along the same lines, Currie remarks that, despite the difficulty of drawing a precise line between permissible and impermissible 'judicial legislation', the 'assessment of the respective values of the competing legitimate interests of two sovereign states ...is a political function of a very high order ...[,] a function which should not be committed to courts ... [and] ... a function which the courts cannot perform effectively, for they lack the necessary resources'. See Brainerd Currie, 'Notes on Methods and Objectives in the Conflict of Laws' [1959] Duke Law Journal 171, 176.

[85] Robert Yewdall Jennings, 'The Judiciary, International and National, and the Development of International Law' (1996) 45 International and Comparative Law Quarterly 1, 3.

[86] Vienna Convention on the Law of Treaties (opened for signature 23 May 1969, entered into force 27 January 1980) 1155 UNTS 331 ('VCLT') Art 53.

[87] Christófolo (n 72) 244–5.

[88] *Nuclear Weapons Advisory Opinion* (n 15), Dissenting Opinion of Judge Koroma, 559.

[89] Jennings (n 85) 3.

[90] In *Burkina Faso v Mali*, eg, the ICJ noted that, since 'the Parties have not entrusted it with the task of carrying out an adjustment of their respective interests, it must also dismiss any possibility of resorting to equity *contra legem*'. See *Frontier Dispute Case (Burkina Faso v Republic of Mali)* [1985] ICJ Rep 6 [28].

Therefore, *de lege lata*, judicial actors confronted with a legal dilemma do not possess the judicial competence to respond to legal dilemmas by means of judicial legislation. That does not necessarily mean that judicial actors should not possess the competence to preclude the possibility of legal dilemmas. One could certainly argue that judicial actors should avoid the acknowledgement of legal superposition states at all costs. Indeed, some have argued that judicial actors should avoid the acknowledgement of legal gaps if at all possible. However, this would entail the delegation of a political, sovereign function of the highest order to judicial actors. It could eventually amount to the installation of sovereign judges at the apex of the international legal order. The next section considers why this would be undesirable.

b) Moral competence

Beyond a decision-maker's legal competence, competence can be measured in empirical and moral terms.[91] Empirical competence relates to a decision-maker's access to and comprehension of information relevant to making a decision. A decision-maker's moral competence relates to the ability to order the available information acquired by means of empirical competence[92] in a particular manner. In principle, and in almost all cases, the empirical and moral competence of judicial actors matches, if not surpasses, that of sovereign decision-makers.[93] However, given the uniqueness of the problem posed by dilemmatic norm conflicts, the situation is slightly different in this context. While judicial actors may still have a sufficient level of empirical competence in dilemmatic scenarios, they are, compared to sovereign decision-makers, not as well positioned to acquire the required moral competence.

The empirical competence required to decide a dilemma consists of an awareness of the objective factors that could influence a decision either way. Such factors may include legal considerations.[94] However, in dilemmatic circumstances legal considerations will not be sufficient to determine what to do. Rather, unique policy objectives, interests, and long-term strategies of the affected actors will be more determinative. In the context of a dilemmatic water dispute,[95] for example, empirical expertise will be acquired by ascertaining the existence of certain irrigation projects or proposals to construct hydroelectric power plants. Further, empirical expertise will be acquired by ascertaining the overall volume of available water, determining the water consumption of a particular country, studying the climatic circumstances as they relate to the availability of water resources, or by analysing the effectiveness of a dam-building project to produce energy. Moreover, empirical competence might be used to identify specific values or principles that a country

[91] Kai Möller, *The Global Model of Constitutional Rights* (OUP 2012) 130.

[92] Möller (n 91) 130–1.

[93] This is particularly the case concerning the judicial review of decisions rather than the judicial making of decisions.

[94] MacCormick (n 13) 531.

[95] See Part II.A.1.

treasures, relating, for example, to a cultural affinity to protect nature or an attachment to a specific natural phenomenon. In the *Military Alliances* scenario, where Egypt contracted to assist two opposing parties in an armed conflict, empirical expertise may be acquired by ascertaining whether the country facing the dilemma has particularly strong (historic, cultural, economic) ties with either of the two warring parties, whether there are certain domestic pressures that militate in favour of siding with a particular country, or whether siding with one or the other country could have far-reaching impact on other bilateral agreements *et cetera*.

Judicial actors can determine the existence of these facts and, in ordinary proceedings, they do so on a regular basis in a most competent manner. Judicial actors can ask parties to provide all relevant information and, depending on the judicial forum, it may also be possible to enlist and question experts or to establish a fact-finding commission.[96] It will become apparent, however, that, compared to sovereign decision-makers, it is much more difficult for judicial actors to acquire the kind of moral competence that would be required to identify how a specific legal dilemma should be decided.

In dilemmatic circumstances, moral competence is required to determine the relative weight of each of the factors relevant to the decision. This necessitates the assumption of a comprehensive perspective that balances and considers all relevant factors from a decidedly subjective[97] point of view. In a dilemmatic self-defence scenario, for example, moral competence is needed to determine whether, from the sovereign's point of view, it is the survival of a State or the prohibition of the use of force that should take priority. In a dilemmatic water law scenario, actors would need to decide whether, all things considered, it is the population of the upstream or the downstream State that should deal with severe water shortages.[98] These are decisions that judicial actors are in principle competent to make but, in dilemmatic circumstances, two factors limit the moral competence of judicial actors (compared to that of sovereigns) in this regard.

[96] ICJ Statute (n 79) Arts 50, 51; ICSID Rules of Procedure for Conciliation Proceedings (2006) Doc ICSID/15 81 rule 28; WTO Understanding on Rules and Procedures Governing the Settlement of Disputes (Annex 2 of the WTO Agreement (adopted 15 April 1994, entered into force 1 January 1995) 1869 UNTS 401) Art 13.

[97] The term 'subjective' here means not only that a decision-maker should take the subjective considerations of other affected stakeholders into account (which is something judges are regularly asked to do, of course, when determining the best interest of a child in family law cases, for example) but also that a decision is coloured and shaped by the decision-maker's own preferences to an extent that goes beyond that which would be acceptable for judicial actors. In other words, the metric used to determine the relative weight of the competing factors is decidedly non-legal, non-judicial, and markedly political and subjective.

[98] Referring to import restrictions in the context of a trade dispute within the framework of the WTO, Howse et al point out, that moral competence would be required to determine, eg, whether a Jewish State could justify 'an import ban on non-kosher products' based on the Torah or whether an Islamic State could 'ban alcohol imports' based on the Quran. See Robert L Howse, Joanna Langille, and Katie Sykes, 'Pluralism in Practice: Moral Legislation and the Law of the WTO After *Seal Products*' (2015) 48 The George Washington International Law Review 81, 100–1. The authors go on to observe that to expect a WTO panel to pass judgment on such questions would be 'ridiculous, and it would undermine the WTO's legitimacy' (ibid 147–8).

The first limitation derives from the judicial discipline itself. In their attempt to decide a dilemma, judicial actors are, by virtue of being judicial actors, more constrained than sovereigns, by the necessity to arrive at conclusions based on legal reasons.[99] Judicial actors must ground their decisions on, and must construct their arguments with reference to, legal precedents, legal texts,[100] or any other applicable source of law. Thus, it was pointed out by several judges[101] in the *Nuclear Weapons Advisory Opinion* that the views of the citizens of the world, communicated to the Court in 'thousands of letters',[102] could only be relevant to the extent that positive law identified them as being legally relevant.[103]

These otherwise unproblematic and, indeed, desirable characteristics of the judicial process undermine the suitability of judicial actors to decide legal dilemmas, since legal reasons are inconclusive in dilemma situations and because the examination of legal precedents, agreements, or *travaux préparatoires* will yield inconclusive results. Legal reasons and texts are, as such, unable to assist with the final decision of a legal dilemma.[104] Thus, in dilemmatic situations judicial actors would need to rely on subjective, political, social, or economic reasons.[105] However, this would exceed the competence of judicial actors whose key skill is to analyse and categorize specific situations in general,[106] 'apolitical and technical terms'.[107]

[99] This does not mean that judicial actors may not enjoy a certain degree of flexibility in this regard and that decisions of judicial actors may not or should not also be influenced by non-legal reasons. However, by comparison to sovereign decision-makers, judicial actors are usually expected to rely on and to conform to particular legal reasons to a much greater extent. Note, also, that the difference between legal and non-legal norms is not necessarily one of content but refers rather to the way in which norms are used. The norm 'do not lie' could be both a legal and moral norm, eg, but its existence and operation as a legal norm is governed by the rules of a given legal system. Kratochwil observes in this regard that legal norms are not a special 'type of norms', but that legal norms are norms used in a specific manner. See Friedrich V Kratochwil, *Rules, Norms, and Decisions: On the Conditions of Practical and Legal Reasoning in International Relations and Domestic Affairs* (CUP 1989) 205, 205–10.

[100] Isabelle Ley, *Opposition im Völkerrecht—Ein Beitrag zur Legitimation internationaler Rechtserzeugung* (Springer 2015) 261–2; Armin von Bogdandy and Ingo Venzke, *In Whose Name? A Public Law Theory of International Adjudication* (OUP 2014) 110.

[101] *Nuclear Weapons Advisory Opinion* (n 15), Separate Opinion of Judge Guillaume [2]; *Nuclear Weapons Advisory Opinion* (n 15), Dissenting Opinion of Judge Shahabuddeen, 409.

[102] *Nuclear Weapons Advisory Opinion* (n 15), Separate Opinion of Judge Guillaume [2].

[103] *Nuclear Weapons Advisory Opinion* (n 15), Dissenting Opinion of Judge Shahabuddeen, 409. In the domestic context, Dicey similarly observed that the 'judges know nothing about any will of the people except in so far as that will is expressed by an Act of Parliament' (AV Dicey, *An Introduction to the Law of the Constitution* (8th edn, Macmillan 1915) 57, 72). This position was recently confirmed by the English High Court in *R (Miller) v Secretary of State for Exiting the European Union* [2016] EWHC 2768 (Admin) [22] (Queen's Bench, England and Wales).

[104] This is not to say, however, that legal reasons or texts are altogether irrelevant. They are extremely important and guide the decision-making process throughout; they merely do not guide actors 'all the way' to a final decision of a dilemma. See Part III.A.2.

[105] Priest, *In Contradiction* (OUP 2006) 187–8.

[106] Raz, *Between Authority and Interpretation* (n 53) 368–9. Similarly, Kratochwil observes that '"legality" requires the evenhanded application of rules in "like" situations in the future.' See Kratochwil (n 99) 208.

[107] Martti Koskenniemi, 'The Fate of Public International Law: Between Technique and Politics' (2007) 70 MLR 1, 29.

The ICJ itself observed that it can 'take account' of non-legal principles 'only in so far as these are given a sufficient expression in legal form'.[108] 'Law exists', the ICJ continued, 'to serve a social need; but precisely for that reason, it can do so only through and within the limits of its own discipline. Otherwise, it is not a legal service that would be rendered.'[109] While the view that judges can legitimately refer to certain non-legal factors when making legal decisions might be defensible in ordinary legal proceedings,[110] in dilemmatic circumstances non-legal factors would not simply inform a legal decision. As argued above, in dilemmatic situations it is the decision-maker's will (*stat pro ratione voluntas*) and not legal reason that determines how an irresolvable conflict is decided. Non-legal, political factors would be decisive.[111] However, the subjective will of judges and 'openly political justification[s]'[112] cannot form the basis of a judicial decision.[113] It would lead to an 'über-politicisation'[114] of the judicial process and could, as a result, undermine the authority and integrity of international law.

By comparison and given these limitations, sovereigns are better placed to acquire the specific kind of moral competence that dilemmas require. Since sovereigns are, as political actors, unrestrained by the inherent procedural requirements of the legal discipline, they enjoy more methodological flexibility[115] and do not need to analogize or search for acceptable precedents to the same extent as judicial actors.[116] Thus, sovereigns can engage in a comparatively more groundbreaking and distinctly forward-looking[117] analysis of non-legal and legal factors. For example, sovereigns may take into account the potentially different sanctions that attach to the non-compliance with one or the other norm—just because two norms may conflict irreconcilably, they are not necessarily protected by sanctions of the same severity. While deontic legal reasoning cannot take these differences

108 *South West Africa* (n 80) [49]–[50].

109 *South West Africa* (n 80) [49]–[50].

110 Ordinarily, however, most international courts and tribunals are bound to apply the law as it stands based on clearly identified legal sources (eg ICJ Statue (n 79) Art 38). See *Nuclear Weapons Advisory Opinion* (n 15), Declaration of Judge Vereshchetin, 280; Julius Stone, 'Non Liquet and the Function of Law in the International Community' (1959) 35 BYIL 124, 133. In this regard, the position of the international judge contrasts with that of numerous domestic systems where judges are at times authorized to reach beyond the law in an attempt to avoid gaps or inconsistencies, Rabello (n 14) 9. Indeed, the French Civil Code provided, eg, that a 'judge who refuses to decide a case, on the pretext that the law is silent, obscure or insufficient, may be prosecuted as being guilty of denial of justice'. See Code Civil 1804 Art 4 (France).

111 See also Claus-Wilhelm Canaris, *Systemdenken und Systembegriff in der Jurisprudenz: Entwickelt am Beispiel des deutschen Privatrechts* (Duncker & Humblot 1969) 46; Bruno Simma and Dirk Pulkowski, 'Of Planets and the Universe: Self-Contained Regimes in International Law' (2006) 17 EJIL 483, 498.

112 Bogdandy and Venzke (n 100) 109.

113 In the *Nuclear Weapons Advisory Opinion*, Judge Guillaume explicitly noted in this regard that 'it is not the role of the judge to take the place of the legislator ... [It] must limit itself to recording the state of the law without being able to substitute its assessment for the will of sovereign States.' See *Nuclear Weapons Advisory Opinion* (n 15), Separate Opinion of Judge Guillaume [14].

114 Ley (n 100) 260 (tr by author).

115 Berlin (n 64) 27. See also Ley (n 100) 261–2.

116 Berlin (n 64) 27–8.

117 The ICJ has noted, eg, that 'as a court of law, [it] cannot render judgment *sub specie legis ferendae* or anticipate the law before the legislator has laid it down'. See *Fisheries Jurisdiction (United Kingdom v Iceland)* (n 83) [53].

into account, sovereign decision-makers may let themselves be guided by them. They are comparatively better suited to make the political judgments that legal dilemmas call for in order to identify the solution that, though sub-optimal, still fits a sovereign's situation best.

The second limitation on judicial actors' ability to acquire and utilize moral competence in dilemmatic circumstances relates to their specific experience and personal backgrounds. In order to decide a legal dilemma in a morally competent manner, decision-makers need to order the available information acquired by means of empirical competence[118] in accordance with the best interests of those affected by the decision. An understanding of the best interests of those affected by the decision in turn presupposes that decision-makers are integrated within the society affected by a given dilemma.[119] That way, they are able to 'understand a particular situation in its full uniqueness ... [and] the particular hopes and fears'[120] of those affected by the consequences of their decision.[121] However, the problem is that international judges are often, and by design, 'far removed from the ideas, interests, and values'[122] of the people and societies which are affected by legal dilemmas.[123]

The fact that judicial actors are 'far removed' from the people affected by their decision[124] manifests itself in a variety of ways, including judicial actors' membership of a specific socio-economic class, nationality, and their highly specialized and increasingly narrow expertise. With respect to the composition of the WTO Appellate Body it has been observed, for example, that '[h]egemonial structures are more than evident'.[125] Of all ICSID arbitrators nearly 70 per cent are either from North America or the EU (33 per cent are from the US, France, and the UK alone).[126] Seventy-five per cent of UN member States have never been represented

[118] Möller (n 91) 130–1.

[119] Gray (n 38) 74, 158; Wolitz (n 11) 586. Timmermann observes although 'moral conflicts always have one solution ... [w]ithin Kant's Ethics', this solution is not found in ethics but in 'moral practice'. See Jens Timmermann, 'Kant und die Lüge aus Pflicht: Zur Auflösung moralischer Dilemmata in einer kantischen Ethik' (2000) 107 Philosophisches Jahrbuch 267, 283. If this is the case, then the resolution of moral conflicts requires not only an understanding of the underlying ethical questions in the abstract, but also a fine sense of the practical parameters of ordinary life.

[120] Berlin (n 64) 27.

[121] Gray (n 38) 158; Jaspers (n 41) 231.

[122] Bogdandy and Venzke (n 100) 158. See also James Crawford, *Chance, Order, Change: The Course of International Law, General Course on Public International Law* (Brill—Nijhoff 2014) 152–3; Michael Waibel, 'Interpretive Communities in International Law' in Andrea Bianchi, Daniel Peat, and Matthew Windsor (eds), *Interpretation in International Law* (OUP 2015) 155. In the same spirit, von Bernstorff asks whether 'we really want arbitrators with a commercial background in ICSID-tribunals to define the limits of the right to water of slum dwellers in Nairobi?' See Jochen von Bernstorff, 'Hans Kelsen on Judicial Law-Making by International Courts and Tribunals: A Theory of Global Judicial Imperialism?' (2015) 14 The Law and Practice of International Courts and Tribunals 35, 48.

[123] For an argument questioning the 'superiority of ... judge-made constitutional law' in the domestic context due to '[t]he relatively small number of judges on relevant courts, their limited informational base, their professional homogeneity, and their generalist rather than specialized skills', see Adrian Vermeule, *Law and the Limits of Reason* (OUP 2009) 2–3.

[124] For the implications of this observation on the accountability deficit of judicial actors in dilemmatic circumstances, see Part III.A.2.c.

[125] Bogdandy and Venzke (n 100) 164.

[126] Joost Pauwelyn, 'The Rule of Law without the Rule of Lawyers? Why Investment Arbitrators Are from Mars, Trade Adjudicators from Venus' (2015) 109 AJIL 761, 769–70.

by a judge on the bench of the ICJ.[127] Specifically, with respect to the composition of the ICJ, one ICJ judge observed extra-judicially that:

[w]hen Article 9 of the Statute of the International Court of Justice required that the body of judges as a whole should assure the representation of the 'main forms of civilization and the principal legal systems of the world', there was a clear indication of an expectation that the insights from all these systems would be fed into the developing body of international law. That has not happened thus far in any significant measure, and such input, if any, has been minuscule.[128]

Overall and across categories of nationality or culture, it has been observed that members of the international judiciary can be adequately described as 'mostly white, male, professional, and relatively wealthy. However humble their backgrounds, they are members of a ruling elite'.[129] These characteristics separate judicial actors from the majority of people affected by dilemmatic decisions. They make it difficult for judicial actors to acquire the moral competence required to decide dilemmas in accordance with the best interests of those affected by a dilemmatic decision.

Further, the 'increasingly narrow legal education and subject matter specialization'[130] of international judicial actors and their gradual differentiation into particular 'epistemic communities'[131] contributes to international judicial actors' susceptibility to develop 'tunnel vision'.[132] This 'tunnel vision' of judicial actors is problematic in the context of moral competence, as it makes it difficult for judicial actors to identify and consider all relevant factors. If judicial actors 'for the most part [ignore] what is going on in other unrelated areas of international law [and] believe that the only meaningful practice or the very core business of international law is their own specialization',[133] there is a significant risk that they

[127] The following 49 States were represented by at least one of their citizens on the bench of the ICJ since its inception: Russia/USSR (9), UK (7), US (7), Brazil (5), China (5), France (5), India (4), Italy (4), Mexico (4), Egypt (3), Germany (3), Japan (3), Nigeria (3), Argentina (2), Australia (2), Norway (2), Poland (2), Senegal (2), Syria (2), Uruguay (2), Venezuela (2), Algeria, Belgium, Benin, Canada, Chile, El Salvador, Greece, Guyana, Hungary, Jamaica, Jordan, Lebanon, Madagascar, Morocco, Netherlands, New Zealand, Pakistan, Panama, Peru, Philippines, Sierra Leone, Slovakia, Somalia, Spain, Sri Lanka, Sweden, Uganda, Yugoslavia. See also Eric A Posner, *The Perils of Global Legalism* (University of Chicago Press 2009) 136–7.

[128] CG Weeramantry, 'Cultural and Ideological Pluralism in Public International Law' in Nisuke Ando, Edward McWhinney, and Rüdiger Wolfrum (eds), *Liber Amicorum—Judge Shigeru Oda* (Kluwer Law International 2002) vol 2, 1492.

[129] Paul Brest, 'Interpretation and Interest' (1982) 34 Stanford Law Review 765, 771. Waibel quotes Brest's observation regarding the composition of 'dominant interpretive community' of the US and notes that this observation applies to international law as well. See Waibel (n 122) 161.

[130] Waibel (n 122) 154.

[131] Andrea Bianchi, 'Gazing at the Crystal Ball (again): State Immunity and Jus Cogens beyond Germany v Italy' (2013) 4 Journal of International Dispute Settlement 457, 464; Ley (n 100) 71; Waibel (n 122) 149–51. For an overview of certain parameters shaping the epistemic community of WTO panellists ('faceless bureaucrats') and ICSID arbitrators ('inner mafia of super arbitrators'), see Pauwelyn (n 126).

[132] Waibel (n 122) 159. The CJEU's recent advisory opinion concerning the legality of the European Union's accession to the ECHR constitutes a powerful attempt of one specialized regime (that of EU law) to protect itself against the potential influence of another (that of ECHR law). See Opinion 2/13 *EU Accession to the ECHR* (18 December 2014).

[133] Bianchi (n 131) 464; Ley (n 100) 71–2.

'blank out'[134] considerations that they believe to be irrelevant based on their own 'value judgments'.[135] For example, particular views of individual States[136] or of those not part of a particular epistemic community 'such as indigenous populations in the area of intellectual property rights protection [or] people in conflict zones when the UN Security Council adopts measures under Chapter VII to maintain international peace and security'[137] may not be taken into account and are unable to influence the decision-making process. In ordinary legal proceedings one might reject such views as being irrelevant, but in legal dilemmas the potentially idiosyncratic views of those affected are decisive.

By comparison, and given these observations, sovereign actors are, at least ideally, slightly better placed to acquire and possess the moral competence to decide a legal dilemma. Their geographic proximity, and the fact that many of them are elected[138] agents of the people they represent, means that they are more likely to possess a better understanding of the 'unique combination of characteristics [such as 'economic, political, personal factors'] that constitute'[139] a particular dilemma.[140] They are in that sense better positioned to acquire the moral competence required to arrive at informed 'moral convictions of the people's moral convictions'[141] in an attempt to identify the best answer to a given legal dilemma.[142]

Moreover, unrestricted by legal etiquette and rules of procedure, sovereigns can enter into a dialogue not only with the people they represent, but also with other affected States. This enables sovereigns to acquire the moral competence to identify how a legal dilemma should be decided. As a result of such consultations, existing legal norms might be modified[143] or, in the case of dilemmas caused by metaphysical disagreement,[144] ways of tolerating or accommodating norm conflicts might

[134] Ley (n 100) 71, 257 (tr by author). See also Bogdandy and Venzke (n 100) 134–5.

[135] Frederick Sherwood Dunn, *The Diplomatic Protection of Americans in Mexico* (Columbia UP 1933) 105–7; Ralf Michaels and Joost Pauwelyn, 'Conflict of Norms or Conflict of Laws?: Different Techniques in the Fragmentation of Public International Law' (2012) 22 Duke Journal of Comparative & International Law 349, 368; Waibel (n 122) 160.

[136] Koskenniemi observes, eg, that judicial and arbitral practice indicates that States aim to avoid giving 'outsiders [the power] to decide on what may appear as coordinating difficulties that may have their roots already in the heterogeneous interests represented in national administrations'. See ILC, *Fragmentation Report* (n 27) para 41.

[137] Waibel (n 122) 161.

[138] Even if they are not elected, they are often slightly more accountable than members of the international judiciary. See Part III.A.2.c.

[139] Berlin (n 64) 27.

[140] Approving of Kierkegaard's conceptualization of tragic decisions, Derrida describes the 'moment of decision' as 'madness' which interrupts the 'juridico- or ethico- or politico-cognitive deliberation that precedes it'. See Derrida (n 38) 967. See also Gunther Teubner, 'Dealing with Paradoxes of Law: Derrida, Luhmann, Wiethölter' in Oren Perez and Gunther Teubner (eds), Ian L Fraser (tr), *Paradoxes and Inconsistencies in the Law* (Hart 2006) 56.

[141] Luhmann, *Law as a Social System* (n 19) 288. Luhmann's argument that 'the moral conviction of the judge or, better, his moral convictions of the people's moral convictions' may be a good, if 'unpredictable', guide when deciding norm conflicts by judicial legislation might be valid in the domestic context, but it is less convincing in international legal settings for the reasons set out above.

[142] For a dramatic illustration of this process, consult the short film 'Aporia', Valentin Jeutner, 'Aporia' (1 April 2015) <https://www.youtube.com/watch?v=B9D6LP8wvL0> accessed 16 November 2016.

[143] See Part III.A.3.a.

[144] See Part I.C.

be identified.[145] In the *Nuclear Weapons* scenario, the sovereign actor representing the attacked State might, for example, decide to surrender or to negotiate a truce. The decision to surrender, however, is not something that judicial actors can decree. International law can limit a State's right to self-defence, but absent any previously agreed norm that would authorize international judicial actors to order a sovereign to surrender, they are not competent to do so. It is the ability of sovereign decision-makers to make use of these flexible, political processes taking place, at least partly, outside a legal forum[146] that makes it more likely that sovereign decision-makers are acquainted with and will consider the views of affected stakeholders. An additional factor making it comparatively more likely that sovereign actors know and will consider the views of those they represent is that sovereigns facing dilemmas are accountable for the decisions they make in a way that judicial actors are not.

c) *Accountability*

The accountability of sovereign actors is the third reason that they are comparatively more suitable to decide dilemmas. This section approaches the question of accountability in three steps. It will consider: first, to whom decision-makers should be accountable; second, how accountability is measured; and, finally, why accountability matters in this context.

As argued previously,[147] international judicial actors are often far-removed (both geographically and figuratively) from the places and from the people who feel the consequences of their actions. This circumstance does not only affect the ability of judicial actors to acquire the necessary competence to adequately decide a legal dilemma. In dilemmatic circumstances, it also undermines the accountability of judicial actors, as the disconnect means that affected stakeholders are unable to participate in and to influence the outcome of international judicial decision-making processes. An open-ended,[148] transparent dialogue with all affected stakeholders within the different international legal fora is impossible.[149] Indeed, as noted above, in the *Nuclear Weapons Advisory Opinion* the ICJ strongly rejected any suggestion that the views of the world's public could have had any influence on the ICJ's decision.[150] One judge[151] even pondered whether the mere fact that the proceedings were accompanied by campaigns of international civil society organizations could

[145] Ley (n 100) 268–9.

[146] Stone argues that leaving certain problems of international affairs to be 'worked out in the play of practice, including of course the possibilities of conflict, negotiation and compromise' may be preferable to the extension of the jurisdiction of international tribunals and courts. See Stone (n 110) 149–50.

[147] See Part III.A.2.b. See also Waibel (n 122) 155–6, 161.

[148] Ley (n 100) 268–9; Bogdandy and Venzke (n 100) 134–5.

[149] Bogdandy and Venzke argue, eg, that the undue juridification of political questions entails disenfranchising all non-legal stakeholders of the political process and 'impair[s] democratic generality'. See Bogdandy and Venzke (n 100) 134–5.

[150] *Nuclear Weapons Advisory Opinion* (n 15), Separate Opinion of Judge Guillaume [2]. See also *Nuclear Weapons Advisory Opinion* (n 15), Dissenting Opinion of Judge Shahabuddeen, 409.

[151] *Nuclear Weapons Advisory Opinion* (n 15), Separate Opinion of Judge Guillaume [2].

be a reason to dismiss the case outright.[152] This separation of judicial actors from the stakeholders ultimately affected by their judgments is especially distinct in the context of private international arbitration proceedings, which 'make it impossible for affected populations to criticize the effects of tribunal decisions … [and] … impede a subsequent discursive engagement of relevant expert communities'.[153]

In domestic settings, democratic mechanisms like general elections, for example, ensure that there is at least ideally and in principle a link between the persons affected by the decision and the decision-maker.[154] Even ideally, no such link exists between the affected persons and an international judge. Again, in most judicial contexts, a distance between those affected by a judicial decision and the judicial decision-maker is an objective to achieve, rather than an indicator of an imperfect administration of justice.[155] However, given the high sensitivity of the questions that legal dilemmas are likely to raise and the fact that legal reasoning is inconclusive in such situations, it is all the more important that those who decide such dilemmas possess at least some amount of justifiable trust[156] of those affected by the decision.

One might object that this observation applies similarly to domestic decision-makers (both sovereign and judicial), who are more often than not members of privileged, exclusive social groups seemingly 'out of touch' with the concerns of ordinary persons. There are two differences, however. The first relates to the reviewability and reversibility of decisions by such domestic actors. While in domestic settings questionable decisions by judges or politicians can be corrected (more or less) speedily, for example, by voting political decision-makers out of office or by enacting new laws,[157] the same does not apply to the international sphere, where the interests of a much larger number of stakeholders need to be considered. Here, the primary, if not the only, option to change decisions of judicial actors is by modifying, renegotiating existing, or concluding new treaties.[158] Such processes are very slow[159] and 'often require unanimity or a qualified majority that is difficult to attain'.[160] In the meantime, international judicial decisions would continue to influence[161] the judicial treatment of a dilemmatic question for as long as the issue remains unremedied.[162] Thus, although sovereign decisions may still

[152] Judge Weeramantry, however, left no doubt that the more than three million signatures the ICJ received 'evidence a groundswell of global public opinion which is not without legal relevance'. See *Nuclear Weapons Advisory Opinion* (n 15), Dissenting Opinion of Judge Weeramantry, 438.

[153] von Bernstorff (n 122) 49.

[154] Jaspers (n 41) 231.

[155] In this regard, see particularly Judge Guillaume's comments referred to above (text to n 152) and see *Nuclear Weapons Advisory Opinion* (n 15), Separate Opinion of Judge Guillaume [2].

[156] Jaspers (n 41) 231.

[157] Bogdandy and Venzke (n 100) 124.

[158] Bogdandy and Venzke (n 100) 125.

[159] Bogdandy and Venzke (n 100) 124.

[160] Bogdandy and Venzke (n 100) 125. See also Posner (n 127) 166, 174.

[161] Although international law does not possess a formal system of binding precedents (see ICJ Statue (n 79) Art 59); *Continental Shelf (Libyan Arab Jamahiriya/Malta)* (Application to Intervene: Judgment) [1984] ICJ Rep 3 [42]), in practice, 'a published judicial decision shapes the legal order by establishing a point of reference for subsequent juridical discourses' (Bogdandy and Venzke (n 100) 115) and the ICJ relies on and refers to its own 'settled' (*United States Diplomatic and Consular Staff in Tehran (United States v Iran)* (Judgment) [1980] ICJ Rep 3 [33]) or 'consistent' (*Nuclear Weapons Advisory Opinion* (n 15) [14]) jurisprudence in support of its contentions.

[162] Bogdandy and Venzke (n 100) 115.

be imperfect, they are at least in principle easier to reverse than decisions of international judicial actors.

The second difference concerns the ability of affected stakeholders to participate in the process of choosing or appointing those who decide dilemmatic norm conflicts. This factor is of particular importance in contexts, such as legal dilemmas, where decisions are subjective in as much as the outcome of the decision depends on the personality of the decision-maker. Thus, in principle, the subjectivity of a decision should correspond to the accountability of the actor making the decision (see Figure III.1). While sovereigns are, ideally, elected, the appointment of international judicial actors to the 'invisible college of international lawyers',[163] whose composition and location is difficult to ascertain, does, ideally, not involve any input from ordinary individuals. Given the 'mystery'[164] pertaining to their appointment[165] and their often little-known identity, the accountability of international judicial actors differs, in principle, from that of sovereign decision-makers, even if the degree of accountability of many sovereign actors may still be considered sub-optimal. While the inability of those affected by a decision to influence the identity of the decision-maker may be a fundamental element of the rule of law ensuring the impartial application of legal norms in ordinary legal proceedings, a decision-maker's direct accountability is crucial in dilemmatic circumstances.

This is so, because a decision-maker's accountability increases the likelihood that the views of those affected by a decision (and it is these subjective views rather than rationalized legal thought that should decide dilemmas) are taken into account. Accountability also matters, because it reduces the extent to which decision-makers can use 'distancing devices'[166] (for example, norm conflict resolution devices) that separate them personally from the decisions they make. A judge's utilization of such distancing devices 'allows the abdication of personal responsibility for anything that can be supported by ... [legal] ... technique—and anything can'.[167] It is exactly this ability of judicial actors to absolve themselves of any personal and, usually, also of legal responsibility that means that the judicial process of deliberation and reflection[168] is very different compared to the conditions under which a sovereign

[163] Oscar Schachter, 'Invisible College of International Lawyers' (1977) 72 Northwestern University Law Review 217.

[164] Bogdandy and Venzke (n 100) 163.

[165] Waibel observes that, paradoxically (though understandably in the context of ordinary judicial proceedings), '[t]he influence of interpretive communities is inversely related to their openness: the more accessible an interpretive community, the less influential it is. The higher the barriers to entry, the more weight the members of an interpretive community carry'. See Waibel (n 122) 156.

[166] Raz, *Between Authority and Interpretation* (n 53) 368–9.

[167] Martti Koskenniemi, 'Case Analysis: Faith, Identity, and the Killing of the Innocent: International Lawyers and Nuclear Weapons' (1997) 10 Leiden Journal of International Law 137, 160, 161. In this regard, it could be argued that the ICJ's judges in the *Jurisdictional Immunities Case*, eg, were able to distance themselves from the result of their decision (the denial of compensation to victims of war crimes) by sheltering behind technical and controversial distinctions between procedural and substantive rules. See *Jurisdictional Immunities* (n 66), Dissenting Opinion of Judge Cançado Trindade [294]; ibid, Separate Opinion of Judge Bennouna [9]; Bianchi (n 131) 462.

[168] Wolitz (n 11) 535.

decision-maker, who is normally both personally and legally accountable, decides what to do.

Unable to take advantage of legal distancing devices a legal dilemma is bound to instil in sovereigns an 'inner anxiety'[169] that triggers a most intense, conscious,[170] and reflective decision-making process.[171] It is, at least in part, this anxiety and the sovereign's corresponding, honest struggle to determine how a dilemma should be decided that ensures that a dilemma is decided in the best, though still sub-optimal, manner. The accountability of sovereign decision-makers locates them directly in the disputed borderlands between conflicting norms. Depending on the circumstances, this might not be a comfortable position to be in. While sovereigns might be eager to claim the right to choose between some conflicting treaty obligations where they stand to benefit significantly by choosing to comply with one obligation rather than another,[172] they might be much less willing to accept responsibility for choosing between more unpleasant options, in nuclear self-defence or dilemmatic water scenarios, for example.[173] The mere unwillingness of sovereign decision-makers, however, is no reason to relieve them of their burden.[174] This is so especially if one recalls that the sovereigns are on balance still more accountable and more competent to decide dilemmas than judicial actors.[175]

Ideally, there is a link between the extent to which a decision-maker relies on subjective reasons in support of a decision and the extent to which a decision-maker is accountable for the decision taken (see Figure III.1). If judicial actors decided legal dilemmas, there would be a marked mismatch between their lack of accountability and their extraordinary reliance on subjective factors. The particular competence and accountability of sovereign actors means that they are better placed to decide dilemmas than judicial actors.

It should be stressed, however, that this section does not seek to question the legitimacy of international judicial decision-making processes per se. In contrast, the proposed procedure for dealing with legal dilemmas explicitly envisions that judicial actors and sovereigns play a complementary role in dilemmatic circumstances.[176] Judicial actors should utilize all applicable conflict resolution devices in

[169] Martti Koskenniemi, 'The Lady Doth Protest Too Much—Kosovo, and the Turn to Ethics in International Law' (2002) 65 MLR 159, 175.

[170] Jaspers (n 41) 231; Mason (n 49) 233.

[171] This also means that dilemmas should not be decided by arbitrary or automated means such as lotteries or mechanical decision-making support systems. Another reason is the absence of an agent who could bear the responsibility in such situations; lotteries and automatons are not susceptible to the impression of sanctions. See Neil Duxbury, *Random Justice: On Lotteries and Legal Decision-Making* (OUP 1999) 13.

[172] See in this regard text to note 34 in the Introduction.

[173] See Part II.A.1.

[174] See also Part III.C.3 which discusses the potentially perceived unfairness of legal dilemmas.

[175] Even if they were not more competent, sovereigns, being the actors confronting the dilemma, have a direct and immediate stake in how the dilemma is being decided. Since the law is unable to express an unequivocal preference in dilemmatic circumstances, those who actually have a stake in the matter should, on balance, have a more justified entitlement to decide the question in dispute compared to actors, who have no, or a more remote stake in the matter, such as judicial actors.

[176] See in this regard especially the distinction between the proposal introduced here and the concept of a state of exception discussed below in Part III.C.2.

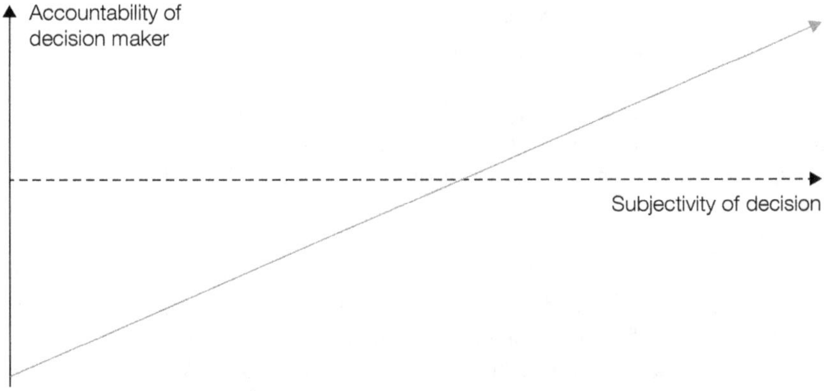

Figure III.1: This graph provides a rough illustration of the argument that the extent to which a decision-maker relies on subjective reasons in support of a decision should correspond to the extent to which a decision-maker is accountable for the decision. Legal dilemmas require very subjective decisions and should thus have a high value on the accountability axis.

order to resolve norm conflicts on clearly articulated grounds.[177] If such efforts fail, it is still judicial actors who are responsible for establishing the existence of a legal dilemma and, subsequently, for holding sovereign decision-makers to account.[178] Accordingly, the argument advanced here in favour of sovereign decision-making applies only to dilemmatic situations when legal reasoning has run its course, when 'further distinctions and exceptions are no longer possible, and legal statements seem simply to oscillate between contradictions that cannot be accounted for through further refinement'.[179] Only in such situations does the current proposal allow for a controlled politicization of the decision-making process, which aims to guarantee that dilemmas are decided by competent and accountable decision-makers, thereby increasing the chance for otherwise disenfranchised stakeholders to make their voices heard.[180] The legitimate decision of dilemmas matters not only for academic reasons. It also ensures that States and other stakeholders accept dilemmatic decisions, since illegitimate dilemmatic decisions may lead to an exacerbation of international disputes.[181]

177 *Nuclear Weapons Advisory Opinion* (n 15), Dissenting Opinion of Judge Higgins [40].

178 See Part III.A.3. 179 Nobles and Schiff (n 8) 508.

180 Concerning the benefits of the 'political decision principle', Klabbers observes, eg, that the principle's indeterminacy 'allows others to pressure the state or the tribunal concerned into making the right choice: human rights advocates, eg, may use the principle of political decision in advocating that in a conflict between a human rights convention and another treaty, the state concerned ought to give preference to the human rights treaty; environmentalists may invoke it to advocate the priority, in any given case, of an environmental treaty over a conflicting treaty'. See Klabbers (n 30) 90.

181 Stone (n 110) 150. Elsewhere, Stone argues that it is indeed questionable whether 'rules created by judges who themselves recognize that they still lack the relevant knowledge, understanding, insights and wisdom for adequate solutions will nevertheless be just'. See Julius Stone, 'Non Liquet and the International Judicial Function' in Chaim Perelman (ed), *Le problème des lacunes en droit* (Bruylant

Irrespective of the reasons offered here in favour the decision of legal dilemmas by the actor facing it, some may remain concerned that the proposal is susceptible to abuse, that it creates a legal black hole whose destabilizing forces may be felt beyond the narrow confines of a given legal dilemma. These concerns will in part be addressed by the next sub-section that focuses on a sovereign's responsibility for the sovereign's act and, in any event, the second and third sections of this part.

3. Responsibility

Once a sovereign has decided a legal dilemma, having necessarily unduly impaired at least one norm in the process, a State's international legal responsibility is engaged to the extent that a prescriptive norm was unduly impaired. Above, it was argued that the 'law must be applied even if the heavens fell'.[182] In a sense, the argument now advanced provides that the 'law must be applied even once the heavens have fallen'. However, (a group of) injured States should consider whether, given the dilemmatic circumstances, it would be apposite to temper law with mercy by suspending otherwise applicable sanctions partially or completely. Both elements, State responsibility and mercy, will be considered in turn.

a) State responsibility

A sovereign's undue impairment of a prescriptive norm by deciding a given legal dilemma should give rise to international legal State responsibility.[183] Dilemmatic circumstances should not be accepted as an excuse or a justification for the impairment of a given norm. This is so for at least three reasons.

First, the refusal to accept dilemmatic circumstances as a justification or an excuse for violating any norm unduly, corresponds to positive contemporary international law. As argued previously,[184] the legal impossibility of simultaneous compliance with two or more norms does not justify or excuse the undue impairment of any norm. Contrary to what some have argued,[185] there is no 'general rule'[186] that prohibits the enforcement of 'mutually exclusive rules of conduct'.[187] Absent any norms to the contrary, or an authorization to decide a case *ex aequo et bono* and to dispense with the enforcement of a norm on that basis, judicial actors must

1968) 310–11. Luhmann, in contrast, observes that 'courts have to decide every case submitted to them. The corresponding norm is called … the prohibition of the denial of justice.' See Luhmann, *Law as a Social System* (n 19) 284.

182 See text to note 23 in Part III.A.1.

183 The corresponding sanctions may differ from norm to norm (except when twin norms conflict).

184 Part II.B.2.

185 Hersch Lauterpacht, 'The Covenant as the "Higher Law"' (1936) 17 BYIL 54, 63.

186 Lauterpacht (n 185) 63.

187 Lauterpacht (n 185) 63. One may still argue, of course, that it would be desirable if such a rule existed. This book, however, argues that, on balance, the merits of the argument in favour of the possibility of legal dilemmas outweigh the merits associated with the argument that it should be impossible to enforce mutually exclusive norms.

hold sovereigns accountable for unduly impairing the norm they chose not to comply with.

Moreover, the ultimate enforcement of the unduly impaired norm is a necessary consequence of the view that, although sovereign decision-makers can decide dilemmas, they cannot thereby alter the relationship between the norms that constitute the dilemma. As explained previously,[188] a sovereign's decision of a dilemmatic conflict does not affect the irreconcilability of the conflicting norms, to the extent that the sovereign's decision in favour of one norm does not displace the unduly impaired norm's 'justificatory force'.[189] Thus, the impairment of a norm, which was unjustified/inexcusable[190] before the sovereign's decision, must remain unjustifiable/inexcusable after the sovereign's decision. Consequently, the undue impairment of at least one norm must engage the responsibility of States and courts should accordingly be prepared to hold States accountable.[191] This way, the proposal ensures that both conflicting norms are given effect: one as a result of the sovereign actor's decision, the other by means of *ex post facto* judicial enforcement of countermeasures.

The situation differs slightly when a dilemma arises between a prescriptive and a permissive norm and where the sovereign chooses to forgo the exercise of the permissive norm in favour of complying with the prescriptive norm.[192] For example, if a sovereign decides not to exercise the right to self-defence in the context of a *Nuclear Weapons* scenario, in favour of complying with international humanitarian law's 'intransgressible' norms, the sovereign's State responsibility is not engaged. While the impossibility of exercising the right to self-defence without unduly impairing another norm means that the right to self-defence is unduly impaired, holding the State responsible for the undue impairment of that State's right would result in the State's being penalized twice: once by losing the entitlement to exercise the permissive norm entailing the deprivation of the benefit that would have accrued from the permissive norm, and a second time by being held legally responsible for the undue impairment of the permissive norm. For that reason, it would make little sense to enforce unduly impaired permissive norms vis-à-vis the sovereign who confronted the dilemma.[193] However, in no case can sovereigns escape from a dilemma unscathed. In conflicts involving prescriptive norms, at least one prescriptive norm will be unduly impaired, engaging State responsibility. Similarly, in conflicts involving a permissive norm, a State may either be deprived of the benefit

[188] See Part III.A.2.

[189] Christopher L Kutz, 'Just Disagreement: Indeterminacy and Rationality in the Rule of Law' (1994) 103 Yale Law Journal 997, 1027–8.

[190] If the impairment of a norm were excusable/justifiable before the decision of the norm conflict, no dilemma would have existed in the first place. See Part I.A.2.e.

[191] For a discussion addressing the potential unfairness of this part of the proposal, see Part III.C.3.

[192] For a discussion of the significance of the distinction between permissive and prescriptive norms, see Part I.A.2.d.

[193] However, the fact that the State facing the dilemma may not be held accountable for the undue impairment of that State's right to self-defence, eg, does not, in principle, and depending on the facts of a particular situation, preclude the possibility of holding another State, the attacking State, eg, accountable for depriving the attacked State of the attacked State's right to self-defence.

of that permissive norm or, again, will incur State responsibility for choosing to exercise the permissive norm rather than complying with the prescriptive norm.

The second reason supporting the enforcement of an unduly impaired norm following the decision of a dilemma is that it safeguards the survival of the impaired norm's normative, 'justificatory force' beyond the moment of a legal dilemma's decision. It ensures that the unduly impaired norm does not 'drop out of the picture'. It acknowledges that the sovereign's conduct occurred 'against the background of the possibility of an alternative decision'[194] in favour of another norm and recognizes the continued validity and applicability of the norm the sovereign chose to impair. This matters not only because it allows courts to enforce such norms, but also because it provides other relevant parties with a means for seeking redress for the impairment of any of their interests that the decision of a legal dilemma detrimentally affected. The benefit of this approach is particularly apparent with respect to legal dilemmas triggered in response to two or more treaty norms. In the *Military Alliances* scenario, for example, the proposed procedure for dealing with legal dilemmas would ensure that any treaty party whose interests Egypt chose to violate (by honouring Egypt's commitment to the respective other treaty party) could seek legal redress for Egypt's violation of the respective treaty. Similarly, in the *Canal Treaties* scenario the proposal espoused here would entitle either the US or Costa Rica to seek compensation from Nicaragua for violating Nicaragua's commitment to either of the two parties. In this regard, the proposal should be uncontroversial, at least to the extent that it reflects[195] treaty law's 'political decision principle'[196] that provides that a sovereign is entitled to decide between two irreconcilably conflicting treaty norms subject to compensating any detrimentally affected treaty party.[197] However, even beyond the treaty context, in a *Nuclear Weapons* scenario, for example, the proposal espoused here would allow wronged international legal actors to resort to any applicable countermeasures.[198]

Finally, holding a sovereign accountable for unduly impairing at least one norm in the course of deciding a dilemma is desirable since it creates an incentive for sovereigns to revisit the causes of particular dilemmas with a view to prevent the dilemma's future reoccurrence.[199] To recall, a sovereign's decision of a dilemma will

[194] Freely translated from Christoph Möllers, *Möglichkeit der Normen: Über eine Praxis jenseits von Moralität und Kausalität* (Suhrkamp 2015) 272.

[195] At the same time, however, the proposal goes beyond the 'political decision principle' by considering norms beyond the treaty context, by allowing for the possibility of conflicts between permissive and prescriptive norms, and by avoiding a trivialization of the sovereign's decision of a dilemma.

[196] Zuleeg (n 35) 267.

[197] Zuleeg (n 35) 267. See also Klabbers (n 30) 18–19, 88, 99; Antonios Tzanakopoulos, 'Collective Security and Human Rights' in Erika de Wet and Jure Vidmar (eds), *Hierarchy in International Law: The Place of Human Rights* (OUP 2012) 45.

[198] The availability of and resort to countermeasures depends on the factual circumstances of a particular dilemma and is subject to the satisfaction of the applicable provisions of the ARSIWA. See in particular ILC, 'Articles on the Responsibility of States for Internationally Wrongful Acts' annexed to UNGA Res 56/83 (12 December 2001) UN Doc A/Res/56/83 ('ARSIWA') Arts 49–54.

[199] Compared to the suggestion to issue *non liquet* declarations in response to serious norm conflicts (see, eg, von Bernstorff (n 122) 49–50; Joost Pauwelyn, *Conflict of Norms in Public International Law* (CUP 2003) 152, 419), a 'dilemmatic declaration' that insists on the continued applicability of sanctions provides States with a much stronger incentive to consider reforming a particular dilemmatic

not prevent that dilemma from reoccurring in the future, due to the sovereign decision's lack of precedential value, and dilemmatic circumstances cannot furnish an excuse or justification for violating norms. Thus, affected States have good reasons to strive towards reforming international law by engaging in serious debate with other members of the international community concerning the desirability or curability of a given dilemma. Such debates may conclude quickly if it becomes clear that the dilemma was caused by a legally suboptimal regulation of a given issue.[200] For example, having learned of the tension between the articles of the 1922 Submarine Treaty in the *Submarine Warfare* scenario,[201] States may reconvene and attempt to rectify the inconsistency by modifying the treaty. Similarly, following the *Kadi Cases*,[202] EU member States may contemplate whether there are ways to avoid irreconcilably conflicting obligations in the future.

It is of course also possible that States realize that their opinions are divided to such an extent that a legal norm conflict cannot be rectified before relevant normative questions have been settled.[203] Concerning the *Nuclear Weapons* scenario, for example, it could be argued that a comprehensive and absolute prohibition of nuclear weapons requires a considered engagement with the fundamental question whether it is ultimately the sovereignty of States or the interests of individuals that should prevail in scenarios of extreme self-defence. Sovereigns need to ask themselves whether it is desirable to live in a world where a very small number of States should possess the right to self-defence even at the expense of causing horrendous harm to civilians, or of rendering large portions of the planet uninhabitable. Conversely, States need to consider whether sovereign States as subjects of the international legal order could be deprived of their right to self-defence even at the expense of losing at least their legal personality: in other words, whether the legal order is, under certain circumstances, prepared to expect States to submit to an attack rather than to defend themselves. A similar set of issues presents itself in the context of the relationship of a people's right to self-determination and the principle of respect for the territorial integrity of States,[204] in situations where the circumstances are such that both norms cannot be realized simultaneously. These are difficult questions and contemporary international legal documents—themselves a product of the legal order that generated the dilemma in the first place—are not going to provide any definitive answers in this regard. Nonetheless, dilemmatic

conflict. Similarly, in the context of moral dilemmas, it has been argued that 'ascriptions of guilt' strengthen the 'impulse' to 'strive ... to prevent ... future conflicts from arising'. See Ruth Barcan Marcus, 'Moral Dilemmas and Consistency' (1980) 77 The Journal of Philosophy 121, 131, 133. Pauwelyn holds a different view. He argues that *non liquet* declarations 'may provide [an incentive] for *states* to fill the gap by normal law-making processes'. See Pauwelyn (n 199) 152 (emphasis in original). However, whether or not a State has an incentive to 'fill the gap' depends on a given State's relevant interests. If paragraph 105(2)(E) of the *Nuclear Weapons Advisory Opinion* is interpreted as a *non liquet* declaration, eg, the nuclear powers may not have any incentive to resolve the underlying irresolvable norm conflict. They could rest assured that the use of nuclear weapons is lawful in accordance with the orthodox interpretation of the 'Lotus-Principle'. See Part II.C.

200 See Part I.B.2.

201 See also section B.2 in the Introduction.

202 See the discussion of the *Kadi Cases* in Part I.B.3 (text to notes 253–61).

203 See Part I.C.

204 See generally Christófolo (n 72).

declarations combined with the subsequent enforcement of any unduly impaired norm can increase the chance of productive negotiations, leading to sustainable solutions, by pointing out that the conflicting norms are of equal rank, that no State's interests are inherently paramount,[205] and by avoiding prematurely prioritizing one party's legal claim in an ongoing dispute.[206]

Ultimately, there is admittedly no guarantee that solutions to legal dilemmas caused by fundamental normative disagreements can always be found, and that international law can be modified accordingly. However, even the conclusion that a given legal dilemma is, at least for the time being, incurable will enhance international law's ability to address such dilemmas, as all affected actors are fully aware of what they are dealing with when such dilemmas arise in the future.

b) Mercy

While judicial actors should hold States accountable for unduly impairing a prescriptive norm, the sovereign who decided the dilemma may hope for mercy. Mercy may consist of the partial or complete suspension of otherwise applicable sanctions.[207] Mercy should not be dispensed by a judicial actor, but by (a group of) affected States.[208] An act of mercy is not a special legal instrument and has no precedential value whatsoever.[209] Rather, mercy is an act *sui generis*[210] which is inherently discretionary, subjective,[211] exceptional,[212] and irregular.[213] When contemplating whether or not to be merciful, affected States may be motivated by a variety of very

[205] Robinson argues, eg, that the awareness that all available options are 'by some metric "flawed"' leads to discussions less dominated by 'ascriptions of bad faith, incompetence, hidden agendas, or moral shortcomings' than by a 'more generous, more collegial, and more open-minded' atmosphere. See Darryl Robinson, 'Inescapable Dyads: Why the International Criminal Court Cannot Win' (2015) 28 Leiden Journal of International Law 323, 345.

[206] Specifically, in the context of water disputes, Scott notes, eg, that '[o]nce a State is certain about its rights, or part of them, these rights will stand in the way of easy agreement'. See Robert D Scott, 'Kansas v. Colorado Revisited' (1958) 52 AJIL 432, 454.

[207] See also Robert A Ferguson, 'The Place of Mercy in Legal Discourse' in Austin Sarat (ed), *Merciful Judgments and Contemporary Society* (CUP 2011) 19; Ludvig af Holberg, *Einleitung in das Natur- und Völkerrecht* (Wentzel 1748) 679. In principle, mercy could also consist of any other applicable measure.

[208] Martha Minow, *Between Vengeance and Forgiveness: Facing History After Genocide and Mass Violence* (Beacon Press 1998) 17.

[209] See also Part III.A.3.a.

[210] Ferguson (n 207) 57.

[211] Austin Sarat, 'When Can or Should Legal Judgment Be Merciful? An Introduction' in Austin Sarat (ed), *Merciful Judgments and Contemporary Society* (CUP 2011) 3. Characterized in this manner, mercy is not entirely dissimilar to the concept of imperfect rights/obligations, with respect to which 'each state has to follow its own conscience in deciding what it is obliged to do' (Alfred Verdross and Heribert Franz Koeck, 'Natural Law: The Tradition of Universal Reason and Authority' in Ronald St John MacDonald and Douglas M Johnston (eds), *The Structure and Process of International Law: Essays in Legal Philosophy, Doctrine, and Theory* (Brill 1986) 37–38), employed by Vattel (Emer de Vattel, *The Law of Nations* (Luke White 1792), Preliminaries, para 17) and Pufendorf (Samuel Pufendorf, *The Political Writings of Samuel Pufendorf* (Craig L Carr ed, Michael J Seidler tr, OUP 1994) bk 1, ch 7, paras 7–8).

[212] Susan Williams, 'A Feminist View of Mercy, Judgment and the "Exception" in the Context of Transitional Justice' in Austin Sarat (ed), *Merciful Judgments and Contemporary Society* (CUP 2011) 252; Sarat (n 211) 2, 8, 13, 15.

[213] Williams (n 212) 251.

different (legal and non-legal) factors including a willingness to 'end [a] cycle of offense',[214] to '[f]orge constructive alliances',[215] to 'facilitate a new beginning'[216] of bilateral relations, or to 'foster peace and reconciliation'.[217] Additionally, States may consider, for instance, the extent to which the emergence of a dilemma was a strategic conflict, whether a given dilemma was caused by a State's prior fault,[218] whether the emergence of a dilemma was foreseeable, or whether a given irresolvable norm conflict reflects underlying metaphysical disagreement.

Sovereigns confronting treaty-related dilemmas, for example, such as those concerning the *Military Alliances, Canal Treaties*, and *Submarine Warfare* scenarios are probably less likely to be deserving of mercy since these norm conflicts were either foreseeable and/or results of the prior fault of the respective actors. Both in the *Nuclear Weapons* and in the *Distress at Sea* scenarios, however, as well as in the domestic cases concerning the *Conjoined Twins* and the *Hijacked Airplane*, it might be possible, depending strictly on the specific circumstances of a given situation, to make a better argument in favour of the dispensation of mercy.

At this stage, the proposal may still raise more questions than it answers. Thus, the next two sections of this part consider two clusters of potential objections to the proposed method of dealing with dilemmas in detail.

B. Theoretical Objections

This section addresses three theoretical objections to the proposal outlined above. The three objections respectively relate to classical logic's law of non-contradiction, to the 'ought implies can maxim', and to the effects which legal dilemmas may have on international law's regulatory monopoly of violence.

1. The law of non-contradiction

Some might argue[219] that dilemmatic declarations do not improve law's conceptual accuracy but that they are, rather, conceptually inaccurate and illogical. Specifically,

[214] Minow (n 208) 14. [215] Minow (n 208) 14.

[216] Alfred M De Zayas, 'Amnesty Clause' in Rudolf Bernhardt (ed), *Encyclopedia of Public International Law* (Max Planck Institute for Comparative Public Law and International Law 1981) 14, 18. Historic examples of clauses facilitating a 'new beginning' include the Peace Treaty between the Holy Roman Emperor and the King of France and their respective Allies (24 October 1648) 1 CTS 271 Art 2; Definitive Treaty of Peace and Amity between His Britannic Majest and His Most Christian Majesty (Great Britain–France) (30 May 1814) 63 CTS 171 Art 16.

[217] Ronald C Slye, 'The Legitimacy of Amnesties under International Law and General Principles of Anglo-American Law: Is a Legitimate Amnesty Possible' (2002) 43 Virginia Journal of International Law 173, 174.

[218] See Part I.B.1.

[219] Kelsen dismisses the logical possibility of irresolvable norm conflicts, for example. See Hans Kelsen, *General Theory of Law and State* (Harvard UP 1945) 374–5. See also Nicholas Rescher, *Paradoxes: Their Roots, Range, and Resolution* (Open Court 2001) 9; George P Fletcher, 'Paradoxes in Legal Thought' (1985) 85 Columbia Law Review 1263, 1264–5.

it could be argued that the acknowledgement of genuine irresolvable norm conflicts by means of a dilemmatic declaration violates logic's law of non-contradiction.[220] The law of non-contradiction stipulates *inter alia* that 'opposite assertions cannot be true at the same time'.[221] One of the strongest arguments in favour of the law of non-contradiction in the legal context is the explosion principle. The explosion principle provides that a true contradictory statement causes the statement's normative reference system (a legal system, for example) to degenerate into triviality where any statement is true.[222] This sub-section seeks to show that such concerns do not call into question the merits of the proposed procedure for dealing with legal dilemmas.

First, whether dilemmatic declarations violate the laws of logic depends on the logical system which is applied. Logic is not 'a neutral technique ... guiding correct thinking about any issue or problem in the world'.[223] Rather, any system of logic is 'inherently saturated with particular metaphysical assumptions that predetermine[e] the nature of its premises and therefore its conclusions'.[224] Indeed, the law of non-contradiction and the explosion principle are by no means necessary principles of any logical system.[225] Paraconsistent conceptions of logic, for example, possess the ability to contain contradictions and can prevent the degeneration of a logical system into triviality. For the longest part of history, the explosion principle—the most problematic consequence of violating the law of non-contradiction—was not generally accepted. Neither Aristotle nor the Stoics adhered to the explosion principle.[226] Similarly, in:

> the history of logic in Asia, there is a tendency (for example, in Jain and Buddhist traditions) to consider the possibility of statements being both true and false. Moreover, the logics developed by the major Buddhist logicians, Dignāga (5th century) and Dharmakīrti (7th century) do not embrace [the explosion principle].[227]

[220] The truth and/or necessity of the law of non-contradiction is not accepted beyond dispute. Priest has argued, eg, that '[i]t is a striking fact about the Law [of non-contradiction] that there has not been a sustained defence of it *since* Aristotle (at least, that I am aware of). Were his arguments so good that they settled the matter? Hardly.' See Graham Priest, 'What's So Bad About Contradictions?' in Graham Priest, JC Beall, and Bradley Armour-Garb (eds), *The Law of Non-Contradiction* (OUP 2004) 29 (emphasis in original).

[221] Paula Gottlieb, 'Aristotle on Non-Contradiction' in Edward N Zalta (ed), *The Stanford Encyclopedia of Philosophy* (Summer edn, 2015) <http://plato.stanford.edu/archives/sum2015/entries/aristotle-noncontradiction/> accessed 24 May 2017.

[222] This objection would, in any case, be limited to contradictory norm conflicts and would leave contrary norm conflicts in principle unaffected. See Part I.A.2.d.

[223] Wael B Hallaq, *The Impossible State: Islam, Politics, and Modernity's Moral Predicament* (Columbia UP 2012) 155.

[224] Hallaq (n 223) 155.

[225] Indeed, von Wright acknowledges, eg, that the view that 'of "norm-logical-necessity" normative orders are gapless and free from contradiction' cannot be based on logic, but rather rests on certain '*normative* ideas'. See Georg Henrik von Wright, 'Deontic Logic: A Personal View' (1999) 12 Ratio Juris 26, 33 (emphasis in original). Similarly, Luhmann argues that '[t]he world does not provide any guarantee for logical order and consistency of deductions', but that legal systems are consistent merely to the extent that they positively stipulate for their own consistency. See Luhmann, *Law as a Social System* (n 19) 286.

[226] Priest (n 220) 24–5.

[227] Graham Priest, Koji Tanaka, and Zach Weber, 'Paraconsistent Logic' in Edward N Zalta (ed), *The Stanford Encyclopedia of Philosophy* (Winter edn, 2016) <http://plato.stanford.edu/archives/

By contrast, the principle 'that truth and falsity in an interpretation are exclusive and exhaustive ... usually packed into textbooks of logic without comment',[228] is a rather 'modern phenomenon',[229] which appeared first in the Middle Ages.[230] This means that the observation that dilemmatic declarations violate the laws of logic is contingent upon the adoption of a particular, contemporary logical system, which in turn relies on the acceptance of a specific metaphysical theory.[231]

Moreover, the utility of logical principles also depends on numerous assumptions about international law. For example, norm conflicts are entirely unproblematic from a logical point of view, if each norm is considered to belong to a different legal order.[232] Only if both conflicting norms are considered to form part of the same legal order could a logical contradiction arise.[233] Such assumptions about international law are perfectly defensible, but they are assumptions, which need to be acknowledged, and which condition the validity of arguments seeking to establish the undesirability of dilemmas on grounds of logic. Any argument seeking to establish the undesirability of legal dilemmas with respect to the parameters of a given logical system would first need to establish the merits of that logical system. While a detailed consideration of the merits and shortcomings of particular conceptions of logic would go beyond the confines of this book, it is hoped that the totality of the arguments considered in this part shows that, at least for the purposes of the argument in favour of legal dilemmas advanced by this book, an understanding of legal systems that can contain and tolerate contradictions and dilemmatic declarations is desirable.

Second, even if dilemmatic declarations violate the laws of formal logic, this fact does not necessarily call into question their desirability. The principles of formal logic cannot be transplanted automatically and without more to the sphere of law.

fall2013/entries/logic-paraconsistent/> accessed 17 January 2017. Consider further the Dadaist movement or the concept of Kōan, both of which possess concepts of irresolvable conflicts of norms.

228 Priest (n 220) 26.

229 Priest further explains that, in 'the second half of the nineteenth-century, an account of negation—now often called "Boolean negation"—was championed by Boole, Frege, and others. Boolean negation is explosive, and was incorporated in the first contemporary formal logic. This logic, now usually called classical logic ... was so great an improvement on traditional logic that it soon became entrenched. Whether this is because it enshrined the Natural Light of Pure Reason, or because it was the first cab off the rank, I leave the reader to judge.' Priest (n 220) 25.

230 Priest (n 220) 25. The fact that knowledge, or a certain insight, arose at a particular time in a particular place does not, of course, automatically relativize its truth value. However, reference to the recency of the explosion principle in this case illustrates that it is possible for logics to exist that do not embrace the explosion principle.

231 Eleftheriadis makes a similar observation about von Wright's attitude towards normative inconsistency. Eleftheriadis observes that von Wright's view is 'linked to the purpose or rationale of any norm-giving project, not a logical point'. See Pavlos Eleftheriadis, *Legal Rights* (OUP 2008) 90. See also Georg Henrik von Wright, 'Deontic Logic' (1951) 60 Mind 1, 33.

232 This is, of course, of cold comfort to the addressee of the two respective norms who must nonetheless comply with each norm. See, eg, the discussion of the *Kadi Cases* Part I.B.3 (text to notes 253–61).

233 MacCormick observes, eg, that norm conflicts are 'not logically embarrassing' if conflicting legal statements are considered 'from the point of view of different [legal] systems'. See MacCormick (n 13) 530–1.

The validity of conclusions reached by applying principles of formal logic is limited to the sphere of formal logic. The validity or desirability of statements within a particular context such as international law cannot be established merely by reference to certain conclusions reached by applying principles belonging to a different context, as much as the English offence of murder cannot be established based on Swedish law. The laws of Sweden do not necessarily mirror the laws of England; the laws of physics do not mirror those of law; and the laws of logic do not necessarily mirror the logic of laws. This is not to say that logic may not be able to play a very meaningful role within legal contexts. As argued previously, deontic logic, in particular, can be helpful to map certain conflicting norm constellations.[234]

When certain logical principles are applied to law, these principles need to be carefully incorporated in order to ensure that the utilization of logical principles does not undermine or ignore law's distinct procedures,[235] which respond, in particular, to the 'social dynamics'[236] of a given society and rely heavily on value judgments,[237] rather than logical deductions.[238] It might make sense to insist that particular logical systems degenerate into triviality in accordance with the explosion principle when and if true contradictions are tolerated. However, a contradiction in the realm of law by no means entails the disapplication of every other legal norm beyond a particular conflict. It entails, least of all of, the collapse of the entire legal system, 'legal anarchy or nihilism'.[239] This is so not only because the interdependency of legal norms differs from that of logical norms, but also because legal contradictions can easily be contained by positing additional legal norms that can 'patch-up' inconsistencies.[240] Indeed, deontic logicians have themselves observed

[234] See Part I.A.2.d. See also Jordi Ferrer Beltrán and Giovanni Battista Ratti, 'Defeasibility and Legality: A Survey' in Jordi Ferrer Beltrán and Giovanni Battista Ratti (eds), *The Logic of Legal Requirements* (OUP 2012) 20–1.

[235] See, eg, Krimphove, who illustrates the discrepancy between the conclusions reached by purely logical as opposed to legal reasoning with reference to the German concept of '*Wahlfeststellung*' (lit. an 'elective determination', which allows for the conviction of a defendant for committing unlawful act A or for act B in a situation where it is uncertain whether or not the defendant has committed action A or action B, but it is certain that the defendant must have committed either one or the other). See Dieter Krimphove, 'Grenzen der Logik' (2013) 44 Rechtstheorie 315, 330–8.

[236] Oren Perez, 'Law in the Air: A Prologue to the World of Legal Paradoxes' in Oren Perez and Gunther Teubner (eds), *Paradoxes and Inconsistencies in the Law* (Hart 2005) 16–17.

[237] Canaris (n 111) 29.

[238] See also the ILC's Report on Fragmentation, which observed that 'any [legal] decision will involve interpretation and choice between alternative rule-formulations and meanings that cannot be pressed within the model of logical reasoning'. See ILC, *Fragmentation Report* (n 27) para 25. See also Lon L Fuller, *The Morality of Law* (rev edn, Yale UP 1969) 65–6; Hernandez (n 78) 278.

[239] Stone, rejecting von Wright's argument that 'moral anarchy' would ensue if true contradictions were tolerated (Georg Henrik von Wright, *An Essay in Modal Logic* (North-Holland 1951) 39), observes that, while, in spheres of formal logic and moral philosophy, the 'breaking down [of] all logical connections between deontic modalities would lead to "moral anarchy" or "moral nihilism"[,] ... this would support the ethical desirability of treating *moral* systems as if they were logically complete ... [but that] ... it would say nothing decisive about the actual situation of any particular *legal* order'. See Julius Stone, *Legal System and Lawyers' Reasonings* (Stanford UP 1964) 190–1 (emphasis in original).

[240] Consider, eg, contractual or statutory severability clauses that are designed specifically to contain a legal defect to an immediately affected clause, thereby preserving the validity of otherwise unaffected norms.

that, in the realm of law, the coexistence of two mutually exclusive norms 'in itself, need not lead to trouble'[241] since legislators could 'take steps to remove the conflict'.[242] Thus, the utility of principles of formal logic in the sphere of law is limited and a given legal concept's (non-)compliance with principles of formal logic cannot be an unqualified indicator of that concept's undesirability.

Just as the laws of logic operate within specific parameters informed by specific assumptions, so are particular understandings of law shaped by particular metaphysical theories. This means that the rejection of one or another theory of law or logic requires more than a mere reference to the fact that an alternative system appears to conflict with one's own understanding. Especially if one allows for the possibility that the non-compliance of a legal theory with principles of formal logic might be evidence of the inadequacy of the latter rather than the former.[243] Thus, a sustained argument is necessary to illustrate a given theory's ability to cope more or less well with a given task. It is hoped that the arguments preceding and following this section offer convincing reasons in favour of the merits of the proposed procedure for dealing with legal dilemmas.

2. The 'ought implies can' maxim

A related argument could be that the proposed introduction of dilemmatic declarations, and the corresponding enforcement of sanctions, ought to be rejected since they violate the 'ought implies can' maxim. Conventionally, the 'ought implies can' maxim is understood to stipulate that '[t]he action to which the "*ought*" applies must ... be possible under natural conditions'.[244] In moral philosophy, the 'ought implies can' maxim is at the heart of a dispute concerning the possibility of the existence of moral dilemmas.[245] If this maxim is accepted, severe problems could

[241] Georg Henrik von Wright, 'Norms, Truth and Logic' in AA Martino (ed), *Deontic Logic, Computational Linguistics, and Legal Information Systems* (North-Holland 1982) 157–8.

[242] von Wright (n 241), 157–8.

[243] In this regard, Geyer notes that doubts about the limited competence of logic to deal with the paradoxical 'are as old as logic itself' and that the identification of the apparent illogicality of the Christian doctrine of the Trinity in the wake of the 'triumph of Aristotelian logic' in the late Middle Ages led in the first instance to doubts concerning the utility and adequacy of latter, not the former. See Paul Geyer, 'Historisch-systematische Grundlegung' in Roland Hagenbüchle and Paul Geyer (eds), *Das Paradox: eine Herausforderung des abendländischen Denkens* (2nd edn, Königshausen & Neumann 2002) 11, 18.

[244] Immanuel Kant, *Kritik der reinen Vernunft* (Gesammelte Schriften, Preußische Akademie der Wissenschaften 1900) ('*Kritik der reinen Vernunft*') A548/B576 (tr Robert Stern, 'Does 'Ought' Imply 'Can'? And did Kant Think it Does?' (2004) 16 Utilitas 42, 55). For a consideration of different meanings and interpretations of the meaning of 'ought implies can', see Stern (n 244); Jens Timmermann, 'Sollen und Können. "Du kannst, denn du Sollst" und "Sollen impliziert Können" im Vergleich' (2003) 6 Logical Analysis and History of Philosophy 113, 118. To von Wright, the maxim reflects the principle of consistency, which is satisfied 'if, and only if, it is logically possible, under any given condition of application, to obey all the commands collectively and avail oneself of each one of the permissions individually which apply on that occasion.' See Georg Henrik von Wright, *Norm and Action: A Logical Enquiry* (Routledge & Kegan Paul 1963) 144.

[245] Walter Sinnott-Armstrong, '"Ought" Conversationally Implies "Can"' (1984) XCIII The Philosophical Review 249, 249; Ruth Barcan Marcus, 'More about Moral Dilemmas' in HE Mason (ed), *Moral Dilemmas and Moral Theory* (OUP 1996) 28; Dougherty (n 20) 35.

arise with respect to irresolvable norm conflicts. This is so because irresolvable norm conflicts confront actors with mutually exclusive norms that apparently impose two simultaneous 'oughts' despite an actor's inability to comply with at least one of them. Similarly, once a dilemma has been decided, actors appear to be sanctioned for conduct they had no choice but to commit.

This section argues, however, that the 'ought implies can' maxim cannot be invoked to establish the undesirability of dilemmatic declarations, and by extension, of legal dilemmas, for at least three reasons. First, the conventional understanding of the maxim arguably misconstrues the maxim's original meaning. Second, even if the maxim's conventional understanding is preferred, legal dilemmas do not engage the maxim. Third, even if legal dilemmas engage the maxim, the maxim's applicability to law is limited for law has always tolerated exceptions to the 'ought implies can' maxim.

With respect to the first argument, the 'ought implies can' maxim is conventionally interpreted to mean that the existence of an 'ought' presupposes the existence of a 'can'. This means that a moral actor's ability (the 'can') determines the range of possible obligations (the 'ought'). However, it has been argued that the maxim is most properly understood to stipulate that it is the 'ought' that determines a moral actor's ability (the 'can') to comply with a given set of obligations. Indeed, it has been observed, that while one of the maxim's most renown proponents stipulates, 'duty commands nothing but what he can do':[246]

> [Kant] does so because his conception of our agency is such that he holds us to be essentially capable of acting as right requires, not because our capacities as human agents naturalistically conceived put limits on what the moral law can comprise.[247]

Indeed, Kant himself made it clear that:

> [e]thical duties must not be determined in accordance with the capacity to fulfil the law that is ascribed to human beings; on the contrary, their moral capacity must be estimated by the law, which commands categorically, and so in accordance with our rational knowledge of what they ought to be in keeping with the idea of humanity, not in accordance with the empirical knowledge we have of them as they are.[248]

Accordingly, and with reference to additional passages of Kant's *Critique of Pure Reason*[249] and *Critique of Practical Reason*,[250] it has been argued that:

> the Kantian principle in these cases is best rendered not as 'ought implies can', but as 'you can because you ought' in so far as here the 'ought' is presupposed rather than being used to determine whether a duty can properly be demanded of an agent.[251]

[246] Immanuel Kant, *Die Religion innerhalb der Grenzen der bloßen Vernunft* (Gesammelte Schriften, Preußische Akademie der Wissenschaften 1900) 6:47 (tr by Stern (n 244) 54).

[247] Stern (n 244) 57.

[248] Immanuel Kant, *Grundlegung zur Metaphysik der Sitten* (Gesammelte Schriften, Preußische Akademie der Wissenschaften 1900) 6:404–405 (tr by Stern (n 244) 57).

[249] Kant, *Kritik der reinen Vernunft* (n 244) A548/B576.

[250] Immanuel Kant, *Kritik der praktischen Vernunft* (Gesammelte Schriften, Preußische Akademie der Wissenschaften 1900) 5:30.

[251] Stern (n 244) 61.

In the context of international law, some also appear to deduce a 'can' from an 'ought'. For example, it has been argued that in accordance with the '[o]ught implies can'[252] principle, national courts 'may infer [the ability] to exercise jurisdiction'[253] to 'prevent their states acting in contravention of international obligations'[254] from the fact that they ought, or 'should ... do so'.[255]

Construed in this manner, the maxim ceases to pose any difficulties for dilemmatic declarations. Instead, 'ought implies can' would encourage actors facing a dilemma to engage in an intensified contemplative process in search of the best reason to decide a dilemma one way or another.[256] Actors would be in a position similar to human judges who, fully aware that they will never be as omnipotent as Dworkin's Hercules, are nonetheless striving to resemble the Greek god's inimitable perfection,[257] in line with the proverbial necessity to reach for the unachievable to realize the possible.[258] Compared to the conventional version of the 'ought implies can' maxim, this latter understanding of the maxim does not lead to a trimming of the ideal in response to an actor's limited abilities. Instead, it would trigger renewed efforts to identify the best means to overcome a legal dilemma.[259]

Second, even if the conventional understanding of the 'ought implies can' maxim were favoured, legal dilemmas do not actually engage the 'ought implies can' maxim, despite an understandable and initial appearance to the contrary. The conflicting norms in a legal dilemma are distinct norms, each of which an actor can separately (though not concurrently and not necessarily successively) comply with.[260] Legal dilemmas are not situations where legal actors are 'required to abide by some [ungraspable and unrecognizable] standard that hovers esoterically beyond [their] comprehension'.[261] In dilemmatic situations, decision-makers have

[252] André Nollkaemper, *National Courts and the International Rule of Law* (OUP 2012) 42.

[253] Nollkaemper (n 252) 43.

[254] Nollkaemper (n 252) 43.

[255] Nollkaemper (n 252) 43.

[256] This situation resembles the view of Dworkin, who recommended that legal actors faced with apparent dilemmas should resolve them by thinking 'long and hard' about what to do. See Dworkin (n 66) 343–4. See also Gerald Fitzmaurice, 'The Problem of Non-Liquet: Prolegomena To a Restatement' *Mélanges offerts à Charles Rousseau: la communauté internationale* (A Pedone 1974) 97–8. Aquinas, too, held the view that dilemmas could be resolved by rightful thinking and a rigorous analysis of the available options. See Dougherty (n 20) 132.

[257] Dworkin (n 66) 129–30.

[258] Weber observes that 'the possible was very often achieved only by reaching for that which lay beyond the impossible'. See Max Weber, 'Der Sinn der "Wertfreiheit" der soziologischen und ökonomischen Wissenschaften' *Gesammelte Aufsätze zur Wissenschaftslehre* (Mohr Siebeck 1922) 476 (tr by author).

[259] One might argue that such efforts might be futile if an actor faces a dilemma arising in response to entrenched metaphysical undecidability (see Part I.4). However, even dilemmas that are presently incurable owing to fundamental normative disagreements (possibly the regulation of the use of nuclear weapons, eg) do not by necessity need to remain incurable. Actors facing norm conflicts triggered by normative undecidability may still attempt to identify the normative parameters that caused the dilemma and they may still try to re-negotiate or modify such parameters even if only with a view to finding an interim solution. See also Part III.A.3.a.

[260] Marcus (n 199) 134.

[261] Matthew H Kramer, 'When Is There Not One Right Answer?' (2008) 53 American Journal of Jurisprudence 49, 55.

an actual choice between two possible options. That choice is not made impossible just because each alternative engages the legal responsibility of a State. For example, if there is a conflict between the obligations to comply with a command to save *A* and a command to save *B* and, due to external circumstances (for example, there is only one seat left in a lifeboat in the *Distress at Sea Scenario*),[262] the actor can save only one, then the first and the second command could individually be complied with.[263] Even once the dilemma has been decided, and either *B* or *A* has not been saved, there is something that the actor 'ought to have done and could have done and which he did not do'.[264] Thus, dilemmatic situations differ from the scenario in the *Lighthouses Case*, for instance, where Greece's outright inability to restore and return the bombarded Lighthouse was held to defeat Greece's obligation to do so.[265] As such the 'ought implies can' maxim does not necessarily apply to legal dilemmas.

The 'ought implies can' maxim comes into play only if one accepts the agglomeration principle[266] of deontic logic. The principle provides that '*X* ought to do *a*' and '*X* ought to do *b*' cannot be kept distinct, but that the two obligations result in '*X* ought to do *a* and *b*'. The unconsidered application of deontic logic's agglomeration principle to dilemmatic situations can, however, have unintended side effects. For example, in the *Conjoined Twins* scenario, it would be inappropriate to apply the agglomeration principle as it would transform a conflict between two norms ('save twin 1', 'do not kill twin 2') into a unilateral normative statement ('do (save twin 1 and not kill twin 2)'), with unintelligible content.[267] It would be similar to a command: 'close open the window', which makes sense, if any, only if it is left in its un-agglomerated form: 'open the window'; 'close the window'. Here the actor is caught between two 'oughts', with each of which the actor could comply, for different, considered reasons.[268]

262 See section B.5 of the Introduction.

263 This example could be contrasted with a norm that requires an actor to fly to the moon in ten minutes, which at least at present, would be a norm impossible to comply with.

264 Marcus (n 199) 134. See also Sinnott-Armstrong (n 245) 251.

265 *Ottoman Empire Lighthouses Concession (Greece/France)* (1956) 12 RIAA 155; James Crawford, *State Responsibility: The General Part* (CUP 2013) 296.

266 Cf Bernard Williams, *Problems of the Self: Philosophical Papers 1956-1972* (CUP 1976) 180–4; Terrance McConnell, 'Moral Dilemmas' in Edward N Zalta (ed), *The Stanford Encyclopedia of Philosophy* (Fall edn, 2014) <http://plato.stanford.edu/archives/fall2014/entries/moral-dilemmas/> accessed 27 January 2017.

267 Kramer observes that 'the structure of a conflict between moral duties does not consist in one's being obligated to do *X* and to abstain from doing *X*. Rather, it consists in one's being obligated to do *X* and one's being obligated to abstain from doing *X*.' See Matthew H Kramer, 'Moral Rights and the Limits of the Ought-Implies-Can Principle: Why Impeccable Precautions Are No Excuse' (2005) 48 Inquiry 307, 351 (fn 3).

268 Strictly speaking, dilemmatic decisions are supported by reasons rather than justifications, as the grounds on which a decision-maker's decision rests, do not 'just-ify' a particular decision, to the extent that the term 'just-ify' implies a transformation of the justness status of a given course of conduct. The German equivalent—'*Rechtfertigung*' (lit. *Recht*—law; *Fertigung*—manufacture)—makes this distinction clearer: the reasons supporting a dilemmatic decision do not *manufacture law* where none previously existed since the proposal explicitly stipulates that dilemmatic decisions have no precedential value. See Part III.A.2.

However, the application of the agglomeration principle leads to the conflation of two norms into one, which cannot be complied with. As a result, in this case, the application of the agglomeration principle in conjunction with the 'ought implies can' maxim to irresolvable norm conflicts eliminates the normative content of each norm and removes the ability to consider any reasons for complying with one or the other norm. In the *Conjoined Twins* scenario, this would mean that the obligation to 'save *A*' and the obligation to 'not kill *B*' equates to 'save *A;* do not kill *B*' and if this agglomerated 'ought' were impossible to realize, then one would have to conclude that one ought not, or at least that one was not obliged, to 'save *A*; do not kill *B*'. Consequently, the agglomeration principle transforms a conflict between two otherwise intelligible norms into a '*dispositio perplexa*'[269] and distorts the original norm conflict.

A second reason questioning the utility of linking the agglomeration principle with the 'ought implies can' maxim, concerns the resulting impossibility of enforcing norms successively. Considering again the two commands to open and to close the window, it is evident that, in its agglomerated form, the command to 'close open the window' cannot be complied with. However, keeping the commands distinct allows for the possibility to comply with the second norm, once the first one has been realized. The following is an example where keeping two norms agglomerated allowed for the successive enforcement of each norm:

> At one time in canonical law there was a principle according to which any promise made under oath was binding and another principle according to which certain kinds of promises, such as those extorted or usurious, imposed no obligation. What should the courts do then in the case of a usurious promise under oath? The solution was to order the promisor to render performance to the promisee and then immediately to compel the promisee to return what he had just received.[270]

In this case, the maintenance of a distinction between the two norms, rather than their agglomeration into the form of 'enforce-not-enforce' the contract, allows for the successive enforcement of the norms. In a not too dissimilar manner, the proposed procedure for dealing with legal dilemmas insists on the subsequent enforcement of any unduly impaired norm after a dilemma has been decided. This would not be possible if a dilemmatic conflict would be treated as an unintelligible set of norms *ab initio*. Overall, therefore, the 'ought implies can' maxim should not be invoked to question the desirability of the proposal outlined here unless the agglomeration principle with its questionable implications is accepted as well.

Finally, even if the 'ought implies can' maxim were understood conventionally and even if it were applicable to legal dilemmas, the maxim applies in the legal sphere only to a limited extent.[271] It has been argued, for example, that generally,

[269] Leibniz (n 20) 137.

[270] Fuller (n 238) 66. Fuller borrowed the example from Rudolf von Jhering, *Geist des römischen Rechts auf den verschiedenen Stufen seiner Entwicklung* (Breitkopf & Härtel 1858) vol 2, §45, 517–18.

[271] HLA Hart, 'Kelsen's Doctrine of the Unity of Law' in Howard E Kiefer and Milton K Munitz (eds), *Ethics and Social Justice* (State University of New York Press 1968) 188; Kramer (n 261) 55.

but specifically with respect to the application of 'objective standards',[272] '[a]ll legal systems temper their respect for the principle that persons should not be punished if they could not have done otherwise, i.e. had neither the capacity nor a fair opportunity to act otherwise'.[273] Similarly, it has been observed that 'there is some sense in saying that our duties persist even when we are unable to perform them'.[274] Some go even further and hold that not only does the 'ought implies can' maxim not necessarily apply to legal obligations, but also that the maxim's applicability in moral contexts ought to be questioned.[275]

There is no question that legal norms are generally enacted with a view to ensure that the intended norm addressees are able to comply with the 'ought implies can' maxim. Most conduct norms could be positioned near the centre of a spectrum that features norms detached from an actor's capabilities under 'natural conditions'[276] (for example, strict liability crimes) on one end, and norms that are completely dependent on an actor's capabilities on the other (see Figure III.2).

International norms that occupy the left extreme of the spectrum are, for example, *ius cogens* norms, from which 'no derogation is permitted'.[277] As established previously,[278] neither consent or *force majeure*, nor distress or necessity can justify violating a peremptory norm—when, for example, taking countermeasures.[279] The ILC Commentary makes it expressly clear that:

> the circumstances precluding wrongfulness … do not authorize or excuse any derogation from a peremptory norm of general international law. For example, a State taking countermeasures may not derogate from such a norm: … a genocide cannot justify a counter-genocide. The plea of necessity likewise cannot excuse the breach of a peremptory norm.[280]

The obligation to comply with *ius cogens* norms persists, even when the legal actor to which they are addressed is in distress; when 'natural conditions'[281] are not

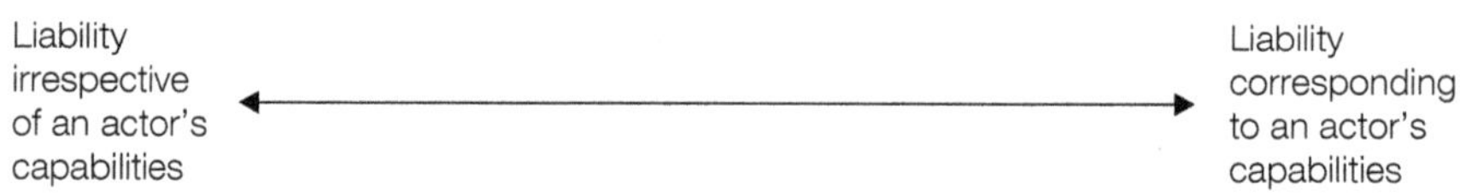

Figure III.2: Legal conduct norms may be depicted on a spectrum featuring norms that exist irrespective of an actor's capability to comply with them on one end, and norms that are completely dependent on an actor's capabilities on the other.

[272] HLA Hart, *Punishment and Responsibility* (2nd edn, OUP 2008) 153. See also Hart (n 271) 188.
[273] Hart (n 272) 153. Cf HLA Hart, *The Concept of Law* (2nd edn, Clarendon Press 1994) 178–9.
[274] Victor Tadros, *The Ends of Harm: The Moral Foundations of Criminal Law* (OUP 2011) 255.
[275] Kramer (n 267) 307–8, 311–12; Kramer (n 261) 55.
[276] Kant, *Kritik der reinen Vernunft* (n 244) A548/B576.
[277] VCLT (n 86) Art 53. See also Part I.B.3.
[278] See Part II.B.1–3.
[279] ILC, *ARSIWA* (n 198) Arts 26, 50(1)(d).
[280] ILC, Commentary to the ILC Articles on Responsibility of States for Internationally Wrongful Acts, ILC Ybk 2001/II(2) 31 ('*ARSIWA Commentary*') Art 26 [4]. See also *Application of the Convention on the Prevention and Punishment of the Crime of Genocide (Bosnia and Herzegovina v Yugoslavia)* (Counter-Claims: Order) [1997] ICJ Rep 243 [35].
[281] Kant, *Kritik der reinen Vernunft* (n 244) A548/B576.

in place; when the legal actor may have no choice but to violate its obligations. This example alone suffices to show that the 'ought implies can' maxim is no inevitable axiom underpinning liability and the existence of obligations in international law.

However, one need not even limit this observation to *ius cogens* norms. The important dogma of international law, according to which domestic laws cannot excuse the violation of international law,[282] can also give rise to situations where international legal actors have obligations that conflict with domestic provisions. Indeed, had the ICJ's Order of Provisional Measures[283] in the *LaGrand Case*[284] obliged the US to stay the execution of Walter LaGrand,[285] the US would have been obliged to do so despite the known fact that the US Federal Government lacked the required domestic constitutional competence in this regard.[286]

A domestic example of a norm on the left end of the spectrum is provided by the King's Bench's decision in *Paradine* v *Jane*,[287] where the Court held that: 'if the lessee covenant to repair a house, though it be burnt by lightning, or thrown down by enemies, yet he ought to repair it'.[288] Here, the lessee was held to his covenant despite the change of the 'natural conditions'[289] and the obligation to repair the now no-longer existing house continued to exist.[290]

Conversely, international law also countenances obligations of degree that take an actor's abilities into account and that may occupy the right end of the spectrum.

[282] See, eg, VCLT (n 86) Art 27; ILC, *ARSIWA* (n 198) Art 3. The ICJ has confirmed this principle as a norm of customary international law on numerous occasions. See, eg, *Fisheries (United Kingdom v Norway)* (Merits) [1951] ICJ Rep 116, 132; *Nottebohm (Liechtenstein v Guatemala)* (Preliminary Objection) [1953] ICJ Rep 111, 123; *LaGrand (Germany v United States of America)* (Judgment) [2001] ICJ Rep 466 ('*LaGrand (Judgment)*') [91].

[283] *LaGrand (Germany v United States of America)* (Request for the Indication of Provisional Measures: Order) [1999] ICJ Rep 9 ('*LaGrand (Provisional Measures)*').

[284] *LaGrand (Judgment)* (n 282).

[285] In its Order of Provisional Measures, the ICJ did not go as far but merely imposed upon the US the binding obligation to 'take all measures at its disposal to ensure that Walter LaGrand is not executed pending the final decision' of the ICJ. See *LaGrand (Provisional Measures)* (n 283) [29(1)(a)].

[286] During the proceedings, the US argued *inter alia* that the 'character of the United States of America as a federal republic of divided powers' was a factor 'constraining the United States ability' to implement the ICJ's Order of Provisional Measures. See *LaGrand (Judgment)* (n 282) [95].

[287] *Paradine v Jane* 82 Eng Rep 897 (KB 1647) ('*Paradine v Jane*') (King's Bench, England and Wales).

[288] *Paradine v Jane* (n 287) [3]. The decision's rationale was confined to obligations undertaken voluntarily (such as the contractual obligation to repair a house). With respect to involuntary obligations imposed by law, the Court held that legal subjects are excused from complying with such obligations where the subject 'is disabled to perform [the obligation] without any default in him', ibid [3].

[289] The lessee had argued that a 'certain German prince, by the name Prince Rupert, alien born [and] enemy to the King and kingdom', had invaded the realm 'with a hostile army of men', and had expelled and deprived the lessee of the possession of the lessee's house. See *Paradine v Jane* (n 287).

[290] A very fitting contemporary example of domestic absolute liability is also provided by the *Oleum Gas Leek Case* (India), in which the Indian Supreme Court held that enterprises engaged in 'hazardous or inherently dangerous' activities are 'strictly and absolutely liable to compensate all those who are affected by the accident and such liability is not subject to any … exceptions'. See *MC Mehta v Union of India (UOI) and Ors* 1987 SCR (1) 819 [32] (Supreme Court of India).

Article 2(3) of the 1966 International Covenant on Economic, Social and Cultural Rights, for example, provides that:

> [d]eveloping countries, with due regard to human rights and their national economy, may determine to what extent they would guarantee the economic rights in the present Covenant to non-nationals.[291]

This provision indicates that States may not be under an obligation to guarantee certain rights to non-nationals, where the capability of a State to do so is limited by the condition of the State's national economy. In this regard, the provision reflects the conventional understanding of the 'ought implies can' maxim. One might also argue that the very existence of the ARSIWA's 'circumstances precluding wrongfulness'[292] or the ICCPR's 'public emergency' provision[293] show, to some extent, that in certain cases a 'cannot' may lead to a preclusion of liability.[294] A domestic example of a norm at the right end is the rescue-duty in German law, which imposes an obligation to rescue another human in danger only if it can be 'expected [of the rescuer] under the circumstances, particularly if it is possible without substantial danger to [the rescuer] himself'.[295] Here the very possibility of being able to assist without being exposed to 'substantial danger' forms part of the offence. Thus, a plea of impossibility is no defence, but rather an outright denial that an obligation existed at all. Consequently, a 'cannot' leads to an 'ought not'.[296]

It would go too far to argue that the 'ought implies can' maxim has not informed international law at all or is alien to legal systems in general. Nonetheless, there are clearly situations where law derogates from the maxim and where an actor faces an 'ought' irrespective of the actor's ability to comply with it. Consequently, the maxim does not constitute a non-derogable, absolute legal principle that can be invoked to establish the undesirability of legal dilemmas in principle. Rather, the maxim is no more than a general principle that can be applied in accordance with the requirements of particular situations.

Overall, it should now be apparent that the 'ought implies can' maxim cannot be invoked to categorically rule out the desirability of dilemmatic declarations, and,

[291] International Covenant on Economic, Social and Cultural Rights (adopted 16 December 1966, entered into force 3 January 1976) 993 UNTS 3 Art 2(3).

[292] ILC, *ARSIWA* (n 198) Arts 20–27.

[293] International Covenant on Civil and Political Rights (adopted 16 December 1966, entered into force 23 March 1976) 999 UNTS 171 Art 4.

[294] This observation is limited to the extent to which those provisions constitute justifications as 'ought implies can' is not the same as 'liability implies can'. The former, like justifications, defeats the very existence of the 'ought'; the latter, like excuses, preserves the 'ought' but precludes the liability for its violation.

[295] German Criminal Code 1871 (Germany) s 323(c). For similar provisions in other domestic legal systems, see Ferdinand Joseph Maria Feldbrugge, 'Good and Bad Samaritans: A Comparative Survey of Criminal Law Provisions Concerning Failure to Rescue' (1965) 14 American Journal of Comparative Law 630, 635.

[296] Consider also the Roman law principle that '[t]here is no obligation to the impossible'. See Justinian, *Digesta* (Theodor Mommsen and Paul Krüger eds, Weidmann 1954) 50.17.185 (Celsus). For additional examples of impossible obligations in domestic law, see Fuller (n 238) 70–8.

by extensions, that of legal dilemmas. The maxim is inapplicable to legal dilemmas that do not impose agglomerated or meaningless obligations but which, instead, consist of two or more distinct norms. An alternative construction of the maxim shows, that rather than calling the normativity of mutually exclusive norms into question, the maxim may militate in favour of an intensified search for the one right answer. Finally, although the maxim possesses considerable 'normative power',[297] the maxim's legal authority is limited and law frequently imposes obligations in violation of the maxim.

3. International law's monopoly of violence

A third theoretical objection to the proposed method of dealing with dilemmas relates to the proposal's effect on international law's regulatory monopoly of violence. Since the open acknowledgement of a legal dilemma does not provide parties with an unequivocal answer, some might argue that international law's ability to settle disputes is undermined, that dilemmatic declarations are contradictory statements and that they are, as such, absurd, 'deficient',[298] 'pointless',[299] 'senseless',[300] or 'singularly useless in communicating any ideas, expectations or procedures'.[301] As a result, law's 'primordial duty ... is abandoned and the reign of force is sanctioned'[302] if law fails to provide an unequivocal answer.[303] If States accept international law's regulatory monopoly of violence in return for international law's provision of mechanisms for the peaceful decision of disputes[304] and if dilemmatic declarations and decisions do not constitute such a mechanism,[305] respect for international law is bound to suffer. Ultimately, dilemmatic

[297] Nollkaemper (n 252) 44. [298] Marcus (n 245) 27.

[299] James Griffin, 'The Human Good and the Ambitions of Consequentialism' (1992) 9 Social Philosophy and Policy 118, 123.

[300] Christian Bumke, *Relative Rechtswidrigkeit: Systembildung und Binnendifferenzierungen im Öffentlichen Recht* (Mohr Siebeck 2004) 40.

[301] Martti Koskenniemi, *From Apology to Utopia: The Structure of International Legal Argument* (CUP 2005) 27. Luhmann argues that departing from law's inherent binary code of legal or illegal events would lead to a 'break-down' of legal communications. See Richard Nobles and David Schiff, 'Introduction' in Fatima Kastner and others (eds), Klaus A Ziegert (tr), *Law as a Social System* (Oxford Socio-Legal Studies 2004) 12.

[302] Hersch Lauterpacht, *The Function of Law in the International Community* (Clarendon Press 1933) 72. See also Luhmann, who argues that a court's refusal to answer a legal question definitively amounts to a 'denial of justice'. See Luhmann, *Law as a Social System* (n 19) 284.

[303] Prosper Weil, '"The Court Cannot Conclude Definitively ..." *Non Liquet* Revisited' (1998) 36 Columbia Journal of Transnational Law 109, 114; Lauterpacht (n 20) 235; Juliane Kokott, *The Burden of Proof in Comparative and International Human Rights Law: Civil and Common Law Approaches with Special Reference to the American and German Legal Systems* (Martinus Nijhoff 1998) 157.

[304] Posner (n 127) 35.

[305] Marcelo G Kohen, 'The Notion of "State Survival" in International Law' in Laurence Boisson de Chazournes and Philippe Sands (eds), *International Law, the International Court of Justice and Nuclear Weapons* (CUP 1999) 299–300; CF Amerasinghe, 'The Legality of the Use of or Threat to Use Nuclear Weapons' (1999) X Finnish Yearbook of International Law 5, 45; Wolitz (n 11) 572; Koskenniemi, *From Apology to Utopia* (n 301) 26–7.

declarations and decisions could thus undermine international law's regulatory monopoly[306] on violence.[307]

Such views might be informed by the fear that a departure from law's binary code, which dilemmatic declarations entail, could lead to a 'break down'[308] of legal communications and stability.[309] In principle, these concerns are understandable. They presuppose, however, that '[a]ll [legal] communications make, or are linked to … this [binary] distinction'[310] between legal and illegal states of affairs. But there is no necessary link between legal communications and the binary distinction between the legal and the illegal. Rather, it is a choice that needs to be justified.[311] It may be that binary legal classifications are in general preferable and that they tend to further the interests of stability, coherence, and clarity. But in some instances, the binary distinction can be problematic. It can impair law's ability to contribute to the peaceful settlement of disputes and it can call into question international law's regulatory monopoly of violence. Binary distinctions can obscure normative relationships by enforcing a binary structure on states of affairs that are not susceptible to binary representations. A binary approach to the irresolvable norm conflict in the *Nuclear Weapons* scenario, for instance, forces judicial actors to establish a legal priority between two norms where none exists. In such a case, the benefit of communicating legal conditions by means of binary codes is all but evident. To the contrary, the insistence on the binary distinction confronts judicial actors with a choice between two undesirable extremes—law's speechlessness, and thus the collapse of legal communication (manifesting itself by issuing a *non liquet* declaration, for example) on the one hand, and judicial lawmaking with reference to non-legal considerations, and thus less accountable and less competent reconfiguration of

[306] The reference is strictly only to international law's monopoly on the regulation on violence. Lacking general enforcement agencies, international law does not possess, administer, or enforce a monopoly of violence per se. See also Möllers who refers to the 'monopolisation of the regulation on violence' (Möllers (n 194) 329 (tr by author)) and Weber who speaks of the 'monopoly on legitimate force' (Max Weber, *Wirtschaft und Gesellschaft. Grundriß einer verstehenden Soziologie* (Mohr 1980) 29 (tr by author)).

[307] Engisch observes in the domestic context that a court that refuses to decide a case would fail in its task of 'concrete pacification of the circumstances'. See Karl Engisch, *Einführung in das juristische Denken* (9th edn, Kohlhammer 1997) 70 (tr by author). Engisch argues that courts must definitively dispose of disputes even if they cannot dispose of the doubts surrounding a given judicial answer. However, it seems questionable whether definitive dispositions of disputes shrouded in doubt could further 'the pacification' of a given situation in a sustainable manner. Engisch (n 307) 69–70. See also Weil (n 303) 114.

[308] Nobles and Schiff (n 301) 12.

[309] Nobles and Schiff (n 301) 17.

[310] Nobles and Schiff (n 301) 9.

[311] Luhmann accepts that 'the two sides of the code [(legality and illegality)] are always applied simultaneously to the same situation' in the sense that in a bilateral norm conflict scenario 'one party wins the dispute (acted legally) and another party loses (acted illegally)' but Luhmann would deny that the 'two sides of the code' could simultaneously apply in the same situation *to the same subject.* See Nobles and Schiff (n 301)18; Luhmann, *Law as a Social System* (n 19) 175. Even in the context of information technology, the utility of binary codes is increasingly questioned. See, eg, Paul Marks, 'Ditching Binary Will Make Quantum Computers More Powerful' *NewScientist* (10 August 2009). See also Franco Nori, 'Quantum Football' (2009) 325 Science 689; Jonathan P Home and others, 'Complete Methods Set for Scalable Ion Trap Quantum Information Processing' (2009) 325 Science 1227.

legal norms, on the other.[312] Unsurprisingly, it was thus observed in the *Nuclear Weapons Advisory Opinion*, with direct reference to law's supposedly necessary reliance on binary codes, that 'the statement of the law' could in that case 'not be limited to the alternatives of permitted/prohibited'.[313] The fears associated with a punctual departure from law's otherwise existing binary structure and potential knock-on effects regarding respect for international law's regulatory monopoly of violence should thus not be overstated.

After all, the proposed method of dealing with dilemmas does explicitly not entail a judicial refusal to give an answer. It simply argues that judges should acknowledge the existence of dilemmatic norm conflicts when and if they exist. Acknowledging such legal superposition states by means of dilemmatic declarations may be unorthodox. But in some circumstances dilemmatic declarations are more likely to further the pursuit of the peaceful settlement of disputes and respect for international law than unswerving insistence on law's binary code.

If one assumes, for example, that it is, once more in the context of a *Nuclear Weapons* scenario, 'pragmatically unthinkable that a statesman might be deterred [by a legal prohibition] from using'[314] a nuclear weapon in a circumstance of extreme self-defence, and if one assumes, likewise, that the conflicting norm—the inherent right to self-defence—is of equal status to the weapon's prohibition, then one might conclude that 'an absolute prohibition would ... condem[n] the law to irrelevance'.[315] In such circumstances, it would seem as if the law makes an unjustified, and perhaps even unrealistic, choice in favour of the attacked State's compliance with the prohibition of nuclear weapons at the expense of the attacked State's destruction. Indeed, in the course of the proceedings concerning the *Nuclear Weapons Advisory Opinion* one State suggested that a system where an attacked State loses the right to self-defence in response to an attack that is so overwhelming that only otherwise unlawful measures could be taken in the attacked State's defence, would not be 'rule[d] by law' but by an 'aggressor's charter'.[316] Statements of this kind indicate that respect for international law's regulatory monopoly of violence may become extremely difficult to justify if an absolute prohibition is insisted upon. Conversely, however, if the law unqualifiedly favoured the inherent right to self-defence under such circumstances, States would possess a 'right to embark on a course of conduct which could result in the

[312] Nonetheless, this is the option favoured by Luhmann, who argues that 'Courts must also decide in cases where they cannot decide; or at least, not within tenable standards of rationality. If the law cannot be found, it must simply be invented.' See Niklas Luhmann, *Das Recht der Gesellschaft* (Suhrkamp 1995) 317 (tr by von Bernstorff (n 122) 41 (fn 31)).

[313] *Nuclear Weapons Advisory Opinion* (n 15), Separate Opinion of Judge Ranjeva, 300.

[314] Koskenniemi (n 167) 142.

[315] Koskenniemi (n 167) 142, 145–7. For a classic critique of international law's favour for apparently utopian standards, see Carr, who observes, *inter alia*, that '[i]n theories of international law, utopia tends to predominate over reality to an extent unparalleled in other branches of jurisprudence.' See Edward Hallett Carr, *The Twenty Years' Crisis 1919-1939: An Introduction to the Study of International Relations* (2nd edn, Macmillan 1946) 174.

[316] Oral statement by the Attorney-General of the United Kingdom, Nicholas Lyell, cited by Judge Schwebel in *Nuclear Weapons Advisory Opinion* (n 15), Dissenting Opinion of Judge Schwebel, 321.

extinction of civilization, and ... the dissolution of all forms of life on the planet, both flora and fauna'.[317] In particular, those at the receiving end of a nuclear launch might well question both the relevance and the legitimacy of international law with respect to its ability to protect their interests (which, for the purposes of this argument, are assumed to be of the same status as the interests protected by the inherent right to self-defence). By analogy, this rationale could be extended to various other kinds of dilemmatic states.

In dilemmatic situations of this kind, the concept of a legal dilemma can help ensure the continued relevance of and respect for international law by granting both legal norms equal rank and by imposing the responsibility to choose between the two options on the decision-maker. With respect to courts, legal dilemmas save judicial actors from having to pronounce that a State is legally expected to forfeit the core of its sovereign rights in the interest of international law. At the same time, dilemmas save courts from having to engage in brute 'calculations of utility'[318] that could sanction the violation of some of international humanitarian law's most fundamental norms, subject to the satisfaction of particular, and easily abused, legal tests.[319] With respect to States, dilemmatic declarations strengthen, rather than weaken, international law's ability to guide its subjects' conduct as a 'wise ... counsellor',[320] by helping legal actors to deal with legal dilemmas and by clarifying the legal relations of parties to a given legal dispute. In response to a dilemmatic declaration, a decision-maker may, for example, choose to revisit the causes of a dilemma, after or before the dilemma has been decided.[321] The State facing the dilemma may also, consulting with other States whose interests the dilemma affects, seek to identify whether it is possible to re-negotiate or modify the conflicting norms.[322] If that is not possible, a sovereign decision-maker will need to make a decision.

Overall, therefore, there is little cause for concern that the acknowledgement of the possibility of legal dilemmas and corresponding dilemmatic declarations could disrupt international law's ability to settle disputes or call into question international law's regulatory monopoly of violence. To the contrary, in dilemmatic circumstances, dilemmatic declarations enhance international law's potential to contribute towards a conscientious approach to conflicts and, where possible, to their peaceful resolution. Irrespective of the attempts to defend the proposed method for dealing with legal dilemmas against these three theoretical objections, the proposal attracts at least three additional and more practical concerns. These will be addressed in the next section.

[317] *Nuclear Weapons Advisory Opinion* (n 15), Dissenting Opinion of Judge Shahabuddeen, 391.

[318] Thomas Nagel, *Mortal Questions* (CUP 1979) 59.

[319] Koskenniemi, 'Case Analysis' (n 167) 152–3. Chamberlain opposed the codification of the crime of aggression for similar reasons. See Austen Chamberlain, 'Contribution to a Parliamentary Debate on International Peace and Disarmament' HC Deb 24 November 1927, vol 210, col 2105; Ian Brownlie, 'Some Legal Aspects of the Use of Nuclear Weapons' (1965) 14 ICLQ 437, 438.

[320] Stone (n 110) 153.

[321] See Part III.A.3.a.

[322] An attempt to modify the conflicting norms differs from an attempt to avoid a dilemma, eg, by means of interpretation. See Part I.A.2.c.

C. Practical Objections

This section addresses three practical objections to the proposal outlined above. The three objections respectively relate to the jurisdiction of courts to issue dilemmatic declarations, to the abuse of dilemmatic conditions by sovereigns, and to the potential unfairness of dilemmatic states of affairs.

1. Jurisdictional concerns

Some might respond to the suggestion that courts should issue dilemmatic declarations by questioning that courts possess the jurisdiction to do so. The fact that, to date, no court has, at least not explicitly, issued a dilemmatic declaration may be taken as an indicator that the issuance of dilemmatic declarations is beyond a court's jurisdiction. This section seeks to show, with reference to the ICJ, that the competence to issue dilemmatic declarations could be accommodated within the existing provisions of the ICJ Statute. While there are various international legal jurisdictions, the focus on the ICJ is justified not just on grounds of expediency but also because the ICJ's Statute has shaped the jurisprudence of, and is being frequently utilized by, other courts and tribunals.[323]

For the purposes of the present argument, Article 38(1) of the ICJ Statute constitutes the starting point for an analysis of the ICJ's jurisdiction. The article provides that it is the ICJ's function 'to decide in accordance with international law such disputes as are submitted to it'.[324] The key question is whether the term 'decide'[325] can accommodate the issuance of a dilemmatic declaration or, in other words, whether a dispute can be decided by means of a dilemmatic declaration.

There is no evidence to suggest that the term 'decide' was used in Article 38(1) as a legal term of art. In accordance with the VCLT, one may thus refer to the term's 'ordinary meaning' and the ICJ Statute's 'object and purpose' in order to ascertain the meaning of 'decide'. One ordinary meaning[326] of the term is 'to arrive at an opinion or conclusion about ... a matter under consideration';[327] another is 'to bring to an end ... a controversy ... by finding in favour of one party'.[328] A dilemmatic declaration would certainly be compatible with the first interpretation, since it constitutes a 'conclusion', albeit an unequivocal one, about 'a matter under consideration'.[329] However, considering the object and purpose of the ICJ Statute,

[323] Pellet (n 79) 691–2. [324] ICJ Statue (n 79) Art 38(1).

[325] The League of Nations Covenant used the slightly softer term 'determine' with reference to the PCIJ: 'The Court shall be competent to hear and determine any dispute of an international character which the parties thereto submit', Covenant of the League of Nations (adopted 29 April 1919, entered into force 10 January 1920) 225 CTS 195 art 14.

[326] VCLT (n 86) Art 31(1).

[327] 'decide, v.1' (*OED Online*, OUP December 2016) <http://www.oed.com/view/Entry/48173> accessed 27 January 2017.

[328] *OED Online* (n 327).

[329] In the domestic context, Dworkin observes, eg, that a 'tie judgment is a judgment of the same character as the judgment that one of the other of these contrary propositions is true and the other

a legal instrument specifically designed to settle inter-State disputes, the second interpretation of 'decide', referring to the settlement of a dispute 'by finding in favour of one party',[330] might be preferable. Indeed, it has been observed that even in situations when a court's decision 'might well have gone the other way … [a] decision, final and authoritative, there must be …'.[331] If that is the case, dilemmatic declarations that find both in favour and against one or more parties are, at least at first sight, difficult to accommodate within Article 38(1) of the ICJ Statute. In the same vein, one might argue that international law's adversarial nature requires that Article 38(1) must be interpreted to mean that the ICJ must reach an unequivocal decision in every case.[332]

It has been noted, however, that the restriction of the ICJ's competence to the 'decision' of disputes in accordance with Article 38(1) is unnecessarily narrow and disregards various other competences of the Court including the ICJ's 'duty … to ascertain and apply the … law'.[333] Indeed, apart from the 'definitive and authoritative resolution of a dispute',[334] pronouncements of the ICJ serve numerous additional functions. They include, most importantly, assistance with and facilitation of negotiations,[335] legal classification of particular activities,[336] and clarification of legal relations between parties.[337] The ICJ's own jurisprudence echoes such observations. In the *Haya De La Torre Case*, the ICJ was content, for example, to observe that although:

> [the Court] is unable to give any practical advice … the Parties, now that their mutual legal relations have been made clear, will be able to find a practical and satisfactory solution.[338]

Similarly, in *Frontier Between Turkey and Iraq*, the PCIJ acknowledged that it would not and could not settle the actual dispute between the UK and Turkey.[339] Instead, the PCIJ shed some light on the framework within which the actual dispute could be resolved. Further, in the *Minquiers and Ecrehos Case*,[340] which

false. But the tie judgment is a positive judgment of the same character … as the judgment that one of the other of these contrary propositions is true and the other false … and makes exactly the same epistemological or ontological presuppositions (whatever these might be).' See Dworkin (n 66) 342.

330 *OED Online* (n 327).

331 Lauterpacht, *Some Observations* (n 20) 235.

332 Stone (n 110) 134; Daniel Bodansky, 'Non Liquet and the Incompleteness of International Law' in Laurence Boisson de Chazournes and Philippe Sands (eds), *International Law, the International Court of Justice and Nuclear Weapons* (CUP 1999) 160–1.

333 *Fisheries Jurisdiction (United Kingdom v Iceland)* (n 83) [17]–[18]. See also Pellet (n 79) 693.

334 Ian Brownlie, 'Why Do States Takes Disputes to the International Court?' in Nisuke Ando, Edward McWhinney, and Rüdiger Wolfrum (eds), *Liber Amicorum—Judge Shigeru Oda* (Kluwer Law International 2002) vol 2, 829–34.

335 C Wilfred Jenks, 'The Conflict of Law-Making Treaties' (1953) 30 BYIL 401, 434. Going further, Ian Hurd has suggested that international law should become a 'resource' rather than a definitive standard by reference to which State conduct can be measured. See Ian Hurd, 'Is Humanitarian Intervention Legal? The Rule of Law in an Incoherent World' (2011) 25 Ethics & International Affairs 293, 293–4.

336 See, eg, *Nuclear Weapons Advisory Opinion* (n 15) [18].

337 Brownlie (n 334) 834.

338 *Haya De La Torre (Colombia/Peru)* (Judgment) [1951] ICJ Rep 71 ('*Haya De La Torre*') 83.

339 *Interpretation of Article 3, Paragraph 2 of the Treaty of Lausanne (Advisory Opinion)* [1925] PCIJ Series B No 12, 18.

340 *Minquiers and Ecrehos (France/United Kingdom)* (Judgment) [1953] ICJ Rep 47 ('*Minquiers and Ecrehos*')

concerned a dispute between France and the UK over 'islets and rocks of the Minquiers and Ecrehos groups',[341] the ICJ:

> might ... have found—and this would have been quite a likely possibility if the *compromis* had not been interpreted as excluding it—that *each* party had a claim which, *were it not for the claim of the other*, would have been strong enough to *outweigh* the other. In that event, the Court must either have found that the sovereignty belonged jointly to the parties, or that it belonged to neither exclusively, while at the same time belonging to no one else, either actually or even potentially,—for clearly the islets and rocks could not, on this basis, have been adjudged open to acquisition by any third party.[342]

The comment supports the view that it is not unthinkable that the ICJ could even in contentious cases conclude—forgoing a *non liquet* declaration—that an irresolvable norm conflict exists. Similar situations could arise in border disputes, where the ICJ itself is asked to draw a boundary rather than to determine the ownership of a given territory (for example, an island) *in toto*.[343] Likewise, dilemmatic declarations could facilitate the decision of disputes despite their defiance of the conventional practice of passing judgments in favour of one party.

This is so, in particular, with respect to the ICJ's advisory jurisdiction.[344] Advisory opinions are, by their very nature, not designed to provide a 'definitive and authoritative resolution'[345] of a dispute.[346] Instead, they may guide the behaviour of the requesting organs[347] or they may prevent 'the development of an

[341] *Minquiers and Ecrehos* (n 340) 50. [342] Fitzmaurice (n 256) 107 (emphasis in original).

[343] In the recent *Frontier Dispute Case* between Burkina Faso and Niger, such a question could have arisen regarding the status of a 'triangle' of territory that was claimed by neither party. See *Frontier Dispute (Burkina Faso/Niger)* (Judgment) [2013] ICJ Rep 44 [74]. See also *North Sea Continental Shelf Cases (Federal Republic of Germany/Denmark; Federal Republic of Germany/Netherlands)* (Judgment) [1969] ICJ Rep 3; Fitzmaurice (n 256) 107.

[344] ICJ Statute (n 79) Arts 65–68; Charter of the United Nations (adopted 26 June 1945, entered into force 25 October 1945) 1 UNTS XVI Art 96. With respect to the advisory jurisdiction of the ICJ, see also, eg, the *Nuclear Weapons Advisory Opinion* (n 15). As of January 2017, the ICJ had been asked to provide an advisory opinion on twenty-six occasions. However, the concept of an advisory jurisdiction is not unique to the ICJ. The European Court of Human Rights, eg, which oversees the implementation of the ECHR, very recently acquired an advisory jurisdiction. See Protocol No 16 to the Convention for the Protection of Human Rights and Fundamental Freedoms (2013) CETS No 214. Generally, see also Kenneth J Keith, 'The Advisory Jurisdiction of the International Court of Justice: Some Comparative Reflections' (1996) 16 Australian Yearbook of International Law 39, 40; Kenneth J Keith, *The Extent of the Advisory Jurisdiction of the International Court of Justice* (Sijthoff 1971) 16.

[345] Brownlie (n 334) 829–34; Hernandez (n 78) 256–7.

[346] Franklin Berman, 'The Uses and Abuses of Advisory Opinions' in Nisuke Ando, Edward McWhinney, and Rüdiger Wolfrum (eds), *Liber Amicorum—Judge Shigeru Oda* (Kluwer Law International 2002) vol 2, 824–5. Even Lauterpacht accepts that, in advisory opinions, the 'apparent indecision [of the International Court of Justice], which leaves room for discretion on the part of the organ which requested the Opinion, may—both as a matter of development of the law and as a guide to action—be preferable to a deceptive clarity which fails to give an indication of the inherent complexities of the issue'. See Lauterpacht (n 18) 152.

[347] Mohamed Sameh M Amr, *The Role of the International Court of Justice as the Principal Judicial Organ of the United Nations* (Martinus Nijhoff 2003) 48; Rosenne (n 78) 174.

adversarial relationship'[348] between particular parties, by 'stat[ing] the law as it finds it at the present stage of its development'[349] in order to offer 'persuasive guidelines for peaceful settlement of [a] dispute'.[350] Despite their inability to decide the issue in favour of one or the other norms in conflict, the judges in the *Nuclear Weapons Advisory Opinion*, for example, were nonetheless convinced that their decision:

> would have relevance for the continuing debate on the matter in the General Assembly and would present an additional element in the negotiations on the matter.[351]

In this way, advisory opinions can be of normative importance[352] despite the fact that they are non-binding. Some have even gone so far as to argue that advisory opinions can be 'more influential and authoritative than a judgment in a contentious case, [since they] affect[t] the general interpretation of international law for all States'.[353] They 'offer the Court a much greater potential to further develop the law than judgments in contentious proceedings'.[354] Overall, therefore, the competence conferred upon judges by the ICJ Statute is not limited to the mere settlement of disputes in favour of one party. It extends to the issuance of advisory opinions and judgments that clarify and ascertain international law. Dilemmatic declarations serve exactly this purpose and should fall, as such, within the ordinary competence conferred upon judicial actors by the ICJ Statute.

Compared to the jurisdictional concerns related to dilemmatic declarations, the suggestion that courts should enforce any norm that a sovereign chose to impair in the course of deciding a dilemma should, at least from a jurisdictional perspective, be less controversial. At the enforcement stage, a court scrutinizes the legality of a sovereign's actions in the conventional manner. If the court concludes that a given violation of a particular norm was, for example with reference to the ARSIWA or any other applicable legal instrument, neither justified nor excused, a State's responsibility will be engaged. One could still argue, of course, that a court should consider treating dilemmatic circumstances, where a legal subject cannot but impair at least one norm, as a circumstance precluding, excusing, or justifying the wrongfulness of impairing the impaired norm. That argument, however, does not relate to the court's jurisdiction and is thus addressed both above[355] and below.[356]

[348] Manfred Lachs, 'Some Reflections on the Contribution of the International Court of Justice to the Development of International Law' (1983) 10 Syracuse Journal of International Law and Commerce 239, 250.

[349] *Nuclear Weapons Advisory Opinion* (n 15), Declaration of Judge Vereshchetin, 279.

[350] Lachs (n 348) 250; Keith, 'The Advisory Jurisdiction of the International Court of Justice' (n 344) 53–8.

[351] *Nuclear Weapons Advisory Opinion* (n 15) [17].

[352] Mahasen Mohammad Aljaghoub, *The Advisory Function of the International Court of Justice 1946–2005* (Springer 2007) 12; *Nuclear Weapons Advisory Opinion* (n 15), Dissenting Opinion of Judge Koroma, 573.

[353] Jo M Pasqualucci, *The Practice and Procedure of the Inter-American Court of Human Rights* (CUP 2012) 37. This observation concerned the advisory jurisdiction of the IACtHR but it could be applied to the advisory jurisdiction of other courts.

[354] Lachs (n 348) 294.

[355] Part III.A.3.a.

[356] Part III.C.3.

2. Sovereign decisionism

Further practical objections could be based on the argument that deference to sovereign decision-makers in dilemmatic circumstances could lead to unfettered, sovereign decisionism, since law apparently surrenders in light of an irresolvable norm conflict. One might fear that dilemmatic declarations could 'become all things to all States' [357] and that legal dilemmas could in practice cause States to take the law into their own hands.[358] In light of the fact, however, that legal dilemmas are still identified by law, that the competence of actors facing a legal dilemma is strictly limited to deciding between the conflicting norms, and that they are legally accountable for any decision they make, these concerns are not as strong as they may appear to be.

First, compared to the classical conceptualization of the state of exception, legal dilemmas are not identified by sovereigns with reference to particular existing facts. The classical state of exception[359] is triggered by 'extreme peril, a danger to the existence of the state, or the like'.[360] Exceptions are brought about by events, which 'cannot be circumscribed factually and made to conform to a preformed law'.[361] As such, it is the sovereign, and only the sovereign,[362] who determines 'when [the normal state of affairs is] disturbed'.[363] Similarly, the related concept of *Staatsnotwendigkeit* [364] responds to a clash between law and the 'naked necessities of life',[365] which are situations impossible to be 'grasped by law'.[366] In these cases, the existence of the state of exception is an inherently subjective question in as much as the identification of whether or not a state of exception exists depends on the actor tasked with making that determination.

The conditions giving rise to legal dilemmas are different. There is no doubt that some legal dilemmas may concern situations where there is a 'danger to the existence of the state'. This could be the case in circumstances of extreme self-defence in

[357] Akande (n 21) 216; Amerasinghe (n 305) 44.

[358] Amerasinghe (n 305) 44; Lauterpacht (n 302) 7.

[359] Although Schmitt's '*Ausnahmezustand*' is usually discussed with reference to crises of various kinds, it should be noted that Schmitt intended the concept to have a more general meaning: 'the exception is to be understood to refer to a general concept in the theory of the state, and not merely to a construct applied to any emergency decree or state of siege'. See Carl Schmitt, *Political Theology: Four Chapters on the Concept of Sovereignty* (George Schwab tr, University of Chicago Press 1985) 5.

[360] Schmitt, *Political Theology* (n 359) 6.

[361] Schmitt, *Political Theology* (n 359) 6.

[362] In *Die Diktatur*, which preceded *Political Theology*, Schmitt observed that, at least historically, the task of identifying the existence of a state of exception was kept distinct from the task of deciding what to do in a state of exception. See John P McCormick, 'The Dilemmas of Dictatorship: Carl Schmitt and Constitutional Emergency Powers' in David Dyzenhaus (ed), *Law as Politics* (Duke UP 1998) 240.

[363] Schmitt, *Political Theology* (n 359) 9.

[364] Bonhoeffer (n 34) 185. It appears as if the link between Bonhoeffer's *Staatsnotwendigkeit* and Schmitt's *Ausnahmezustand* has not previously been noted (for one exception, see Petra Brown, 'Bonhoeffer, Schmitt, and the State of Exception' (2013) 26 Pacifica: Australasian Theological Studies 246). This relationship deserves further study, especially since both authors were German Christians writing at the same time and given that they were positioned at opposite ends of the political spectrum in Nazi Germany.

[365] Bonhoeffer (n 34) 185 (tr by author).

[366] Bonhoeffer (n 34) 185 (tr by author).

the context of the *Nuclear Weapons* scenario or in variations of the *Military Alliances* situation. In principle, however, legal dilemmas are not linked to a particular set of circumstances that undermine the ordinary framework of facts with respect to which the ordinary legal order is defined. As established previously,[367] certain legal dilemmas can exist entirely independent of any empirical state of affairs (intrinsic dilemmas), and those legal dilemmas that are fact-dependent (contingent dilemmas) do not necessitate that those facts possess the ability to upset the normally existing framework of law.[368] The *Canal Treaties* scenario, for instance, concerns a conflict that does not call into question the existence of a State. Neither does the norm conflict in the *Canal Treaties* scenario threaten to undermine the ordinary framework of facts with respect to which the legal order is normally defined.

Further, compared to a state of exception, the identification of a legal dilemma occurs in accordance with a pre-determined, precise definition,[369] and based on a particular legal test. The identification of a legal dilemma presupposes the application of all the legal mechanisms, principles, and devices discussed in Part II. Only once they proved unable to establish a hierarchy or compromise between the conflicting norms can a legal dilemma be established. The question of the existence of legal dilemmas is thus an objective question in so far as the identification of whether or not a legal dilemma exists does not inherently depend on the actor tasked with making that determination.

Second, while it is true that legal dilemmas, just like states of exceptions,[370] which are not susceptible to codification,[371] can ultimately only be decided by means of a sovereign decision, decision-makers facing a dilemma can choose only to comply with one of the two conflicting norms. In the *Nuclear Weapons* scenario, a sovereign could either launch a nuclear weapon or decide not to exercise its right to self-defence; in the *Submarine Warfare* scenario the choice exists merely between destroying and not destroying a merchant vessel; in the *Hijacked Airplane* scenario a sovereign's choice is between shooting down the airplane or not. In other words, an actor facing dilemmatic circumstances can choose from precisely two options. A dilemmatic declaration's suggestion that any one of the available options 'is not legally reprehensible'[372] is always accompanied by a statement that any one of the available options 'is legally reprehensible'.[373] By contrast, sovereign decision-makers within a state of exception possess 'principally unlimited authority'[374] and

[367] For the distinction between contingent and intrinsic conflicts see Part I.A.2.d.

[368] See Part I.A.2.d.

[369] See Part I.A.2.

[370] Schmitt, *Political Theology* (n 359) 5; Tracy B Strong, 'Foreword' in Schmitt, *Political Theology: Four Chapters on the Concept of Sovereignty* (George Schwab tr, University of Chicago Press 2005) xii.

[371] Schmitt, *Political Theology* (n 359) 13; Lars Vinx, 'Carl Schmitt' in Edward N Zalta (ed), *The Stanford Encyclopedia of Philosophy* (Spring edn, 2016) <https://plato.stanford.edu/archives/spr2016/entries/schmitt/> accessed 26 January 2017.

[372] *Nuclear Weapons Advisory Opinion* (n 15), Dissenting Opinion of Judge Koroma, 559

[373] Thus, the potential concerns of Judge Koroma (*Nuclear Weapons Advisory Opinion* (n 15), Dissenting Opinion of Judge Koroma, 559) regarding the *Nuclear Weapons Advisory Opinion* would not apply to a dilemmatic reading of the ICJ's decision in that case.

[374] Schmitt, *Political Theology* (n 359) 12, 6–7. See also Oren Gross and Fionnuala Ní Aoláin, *Law in Times of Crisis: Emergency Powers in Theory and Practice* (CUP 2006) 165.

decide what to do in a 'moment of indifference'[375] from a potentially 'infinite number of options'.[376] Decision-makers facing 'extraordinary situations of ultimate necessity'[377] must decide 'unshackled from law'.[378]

Compared to the 'unlimited authority' of a sovereign faced with a state of exception, the scope of the decision-making power of an actor faced with a legal dilemma is expressly limited to those conduct norms that form part of a particular dilemma. Dilemmas may certainly entail an 'element of indifference'[379] regarding the comparative value of two or more conduct norms, and, in light of the limited assistance that legal reason can provide in dilemmatic cases, it might also be adequate to state that an actor's decision 'emanates from nothingness' [380] (at least from law's point of view).[381] Nonetheless, legal dilemmas concern a choice between two or more previously identified conduct norms, and they do not contain a notion of unlimited power. Therefore, the risk of abuse is much more limited compared to classical states of exception.

Finally, compared to states of exception, actors facing dilemmas are legally accountable for their actions. It follows from classical conceptualization of the state of exception as a space, if not devoid of order,[382] then at least devoid of law, that a sovereign's conduct within a state of exception is not susceptible to legal sanction. As the entire legal order is suspended,[383] the sovereign's conduct does not engage a legal order's ordinary and regulatory functions. Indeed, while the sovereign is part of the legal system by deciding the state of exception, the sovereign simultaneously 'stands outside'[384] of the legal order. To say that anything a sovereign does in a state of exception is 'legal and constitutional',[385] would probably go too far, as the legal order that serves as the required frame of reference for such a qualification is suspended.[386] However, there is no doubt that a sovereign's conduct in a classical

[375] Schmitt, *Political Theology* (n 359) 30, 32; Hasso Hofmann, *Legitimität gegen Legalität: Der Weg der politischen Philosophie Carl Schmitts* (Duncker & Humblot 2010) 52. See also William E Scheuerman, *Carl Schmitt: The End of Law* (Rowman & Littlefield 1999) 32–4.

[376] Thalin Zarmanian, 'Carl Schmitt and the Problem of Legal Order: From Domestic to International' (2006) 19 Leiden Journal of International Law 41, 49. Note, however, that sovereigns may be subject to certain teleological restrictions, depending on whether they are sovereign or commissarial dictators. See Carl Schmitt-Dorotić, *Die Diktatur: von den Anfängen des modernen Souveränitätsgedankens bis zum proletarischen Klassenkampf* (Duncker & Humblot 1921) 139–40, 145–6; Joseph J Bendersky, *Carl Schmitt: Theorist for the Reich* (Princeton UP 2014) 33.

[377] Bonhoeffer (n 34) 185 (tr by author).

[378] Bonhoeffer (n 34) 185 (tr by author).

[379] Schmitt, *Political Theology* (n 359) 30, 32; Hofmann (n 375) 52. See also Scheuerman (n 375) 32–4.

[380] Schmitt, *Political Theology* (n 359) 32; Hofmann (n 375) 52.

[381] See the discussion concerning the difference between sovereign and groundless choices in Part III.A.2.

[382] Schmitt, *Political Theology* (n 359) 12. See also Strong (n 370) xliii.

[383] Note the similarity between Schmitt's sovereign and Kierkegaard's Abraham with respect to Kierkegaard's concept of the 'suspension of the ethical' in this regard. See Kierkegaard (n 69) 59–60.

[384] Schmitt, *Political Theology* (n 359) 7. See also Agamben (n 43) 35.

[385] Gross and Aoláin (n 374) 169.

[386] Agamben observes that, in a state of exception, the 'the norm is in force without any reference to reality'. See Agamben (n 43) 36, 37.

state of exception is certainly not illegal,[387] and that the sovereign is, at least to that extent, immune from any subsequent legal proceedings.

The situation with respect to legal dilemmas is very different, as the legal order is at no time suspended. In none of the scenarios referred to throughout this book do the dilemmatic norm conflicts as such lead to the overall impairment of the legal order itself. In each scenario, the acknowledgement of a legal dilemma entails no more than the recognition of a confined legal question with respect to which law is unable to establish a normative hierarchy or compromise between a specific number of equally valid and applicable legal norms. The acknowledgment of such a dilemmatic state is of no consequence to the legal status of the conflicting conduct norms. The mere existence of a legal dilemma does not alter the applicable legal sanctions. To this extent, the actor facing a dilemma is not 'standing outside' the legal order and is much closer in character to Kierkegaard's 'tragic hero' Agamemnon. The choices of the tragic hero are tragic exactly because he is still within the ethical—within the ordinarily applicable normative order[388]—such that he 'must shirk no argument "from outside". His justification must be tried in face of the strongest objections, the objections of those directly affected'.[389] This insistence on the continued application of sanctions, the resistance to arguments of necessity, and the deliberate subjection of a sovereign actor to 'arguments from outside' may be one of the most controversial aspects of legal dilemmas. It is this feature, however, that makes the contrast between conventional states of exception and legal dilemmas most apparent.

Overall, it should now be apparent that the risk that sovereign actors could abuse legal dilemmas is relatively low. Sovereign actors facing a legal dilemma are not at liberty to choose what to do in dilemmatic circumstances in an unrestricted manner and they are in any event not immune from legal sanctions. This last aspect, in particular, might appear to be especially controversial, unfair, or unreasonable. Arguments of this nature will be addressed in the next sub-section.

3. Unfairness

This section considers the argument that the proposal to hold an actor accountable for the undue impairment of a norm in dilemmatic circumstances is unfair in the sense that there is a discrepancy between what the law requires and an actor's legal and natural ability to meet these requirements. Indeed, the proposal's refusal to accept dilemmatic circumstances as an excuse or justification for unduly impairing

[387] As many have acknowledged, the Schmittian state of exception is paradoxical, in the sense that the exception 'represents the inclusion and capture of a space that is neither outside nor inside' of the legal order (see Agamben (n 43) 35). Thus, an unqualified statement to the effect that anything a sovereign does in a state of exception would be legal or illegal overlooks this underlying complexity of Schmitt's state of exception.

[388] Kierkegaard (n 69) 59.

[389] Mason (n 49) 221–2. Kierkegaard argues the sacrificed Iphigenia 'ought to be permitted ... to weep for two months, not in solitude but at her father's feet, and to use all her art, "which is tears alone," and to entwine herself ... around his knees.' See Kierkegaard (n 69) 87.

a norm holds sovereigns accountable for acts whose commission they could not have avoided. The argument will be rejected for two reasons. First, the proposal is not unfair to the extent that the actors are themselves responsible for the existence of the dilemma. Second, even if an actor is not responsible for the existence of a legal dilemma, the perceived shortcomings of the unfairness of the enforcement of the unduly impaired norm are outweighed by the benefits of the proposed procedure for dealing with legal dilemmas.

With respect to the first argument, legal dilemmas are not unfair to the extent that the actors facing dilemmas are responsible for the occurrence of a particular dilemma. While it was argued above that some dilemmatic norm conflicts are triggered by fundamental metaphysical disagreements[390] and that they are, as such, a contingency of international law, some dilemmas are caused by an actor's prior fault[391] or by a legally imperfect regulation of a specific legal question.[392] For example, there is evidence to suggest that the parties in the *Submarine Warfare* scenario were acutely aware of the contradictory nature of the agreement they concluded. Similarly, in the *Canal Treaties* scenario, Nicaragua assumed treaty obligations towards the United States being fully aware of the otherwise existing obligations Nicaragua owed to Costa Rica. In such situations, and against the background of the largely consensual foundation of international law, it is sovereign decision-makers who are themselves responsible for the state of international law and consequently for the emergence of legal dilemmas. Legal dilemmas arise in response to clearly identified norm conflicts, whose occurrence is often (though certainly not always) predictable based on a transparent legal mechanism. That does not mean that predictable dilemmas are necessarily always avoidable or curable (at least *ex post facto*) but it does mean that decision-makers can take steps to prepare for their occurrence or try to prevent their occurrence.[393] Indeed, where it can be said, 'you should have (ought), because you could have',[394] it is not unfair to hold decision-makers accountable for the decisions they made. This situation is notably different from domestic law, where legal subjects have, normally, considerably less freedom to consent, object to, or modify specific laws and where, consequently, a legislator's intentional creation of legal dilemmas may cloak a 'lawless unlimited power',[395] undermining the rule of law. Thus, at least those dilemmas that are curable to the extent that they respond to epistemic undecidability and/or could have been avoided do not confront sovereign legal actors with any unfair burden.

Second, even if legal dilemmas were perceived to be unfair, the mere unfairness of legal dilemmas is not sufficiently severe to call into question the merits of the proposed procedure for dealing with legal dilemmas. Law in general and international law in particular could be interpreted to be unfair in many respects. Strict

[390] See Part I.C. [391] See Part I.B.1. [392] See Part I.B.2.

[393] See Part III.C.3. [394] Timmermann (n 244) 115.

[395] John Lilburne, 'On the 150th Page: An Untitled Broad-Sheet of August 1645' in Andrew Sharp (ed), *The English Levellers* (CUP 2002) 7; Fuller (n 238) 70–1. This situation is also markedly different from the examples considered by medieval theologians concerning moral agents who faced dilemmatic conflicts emerging from divine law, which they had no power to control. See generally Dougherty (n 20).

liability in domestic law, or the limited, if not non-existent, standing for individuals in the international legal context are examples of apparently unfair circumstances. However, on balance, unfair provisions may be justified by supervening, competing considerations. Collective interests concerning product safety, for example, might at times outweigh the potential unfairness of strict liability. Similarly, the need to safeguard sovereign interests in the international context may justify limiting the standing of individual complainants. Legal provisions frequently and consciously sever the link between the blameworthiness of a legal actor and the legal quality of certain acts.[396] In other words, an act a legal actor did not do can be legally desirable, even though an actor may not be (morally) blamed for not doing it.[397] The normative content of a given legal provision is unaffected by a consideration of the blameworthiness of an actor.[398] Even if, for example, one thinks it unfair to hold the US accountable for failing to prevent the execution of the LaGrand brothers, although the US lacked the domestic legal authority to do so, the potential unfairness of holding the US accountable is trumped by the necessity of ensuring that sovereigns cannot rely on domestic legal norms in defence of violations of international law. Additionally, the perceived unfairness may motivate actors to ensure that their domestic competences are in line with their international legal obligations.

Similarly, the potentially perceived unfairness of legal dilemmas, related to withholding a lawful escape route from legal actors, is outweighed by the benefits of the proposed procedure for dealing with legal dilemmas concerning, for example, the safeguarding of international law's conceptual coherence and the facilitation of competent and accountable decision-making processes. Indeed, legal dilemmas can be distinctly fair because they empower more stakeholders to influence the decision of a dilemmatic norm conflict than judicial processes do. Further, by protecting the normative interests of both conflicting norms, those international legal actors, who are wronged as a result of the decision of a dilemma, can claim compensation for the loss they incurred. Legal dilemmas are fair, because they balance the interests that each norm protects to the best possible extent.

In response to the final research question, this part outlined and defended a novel procedure for addressing irresolvable norm conflicts. It was proposed that judicial actors should acknowledge the existence of an irresolvable norm conflict once a rigorous and transparent application of all available norm conflict resolution devices and accommodation mechanisms, including those discussed in the second part, has proved unable to establish a hierarchy or a compromise between the conflicting norms. Such an acknowledgement was deemed to further the interests of methodological and conceptual clarity. Subsequently, it was argued that the sovereign who confronts the dilemma thus identified, should decide which norm to comply with and which to impair. Compared to the proposal's first element, this second step is likely to attract more criticism. Ultimately, it should be remembered, however, that a sovereign's discretion in dilemmatic circumstances is limited to deciding between

[396] See also Part III.B.2. A similar distinction is drawn by those defending dilemmas in moral philosophy. See Sinnott-Armstrong (n 245) 250; Stern (n 244) 47.

[397] Timmermann (n 244) 113.

[398] Stern (n 244) 47.

impairing or complying with one of two options that law is unable to rank, that are, from a legal point of view equally important. Choices of this kind, choices that necessarily exceed an otherwise tolerable degree of a judicial decision's subjectivity, should not be made by judicial actors who are bound to uphold distinct legal virtues lest respect for those virtues is to suffer. In other words, the outright subjectivity of a sovereign's decision is easier to accept than the outright subjectivity of a judicial actor's decision. The proposal's final element suggested that sovereigns should be held accountable for the undue impairment of any norm as a result of a sovereign's decision of a dilemma. This is a necessary consequence of insisting on the irresolvability of a given norm conflict and, consequently, of denying any precedential value to the sovereign's decision of a dilemma. In order to account for particular circumstances that warrant a dispensation of mercy, the proposal then acknowledged the possibility that wronged States may forego their right to enforce any unduly impaired norms on a casuistic basis. Beyond the outline of the proposal, this part also addressed in great detail various possible objections to the suggested procedure for dealing with legal dilemmas. Nonetheless, it is likely that various misgivings concerning the proposed strategy of legal dilemmas will remain. It could not be otherwise since the very unavailability of a satisfying solution is one of the key features of the concept of a dilemma. However, it is hoped that this final part managed to illustrate that the proposed procedure is the best, though still suboptimal, possible response to a legal dilemma.

Conclusion

This final part offers some concluding thoughts and attempts to distil the book's core findings and arguments. The conclusions will be presented in two sections. The first section focuses on the implications of the concept of a legal dilemma on the international legal order itself. Specifically, it will be considered how the acknowledgement of the concept of a legal dilemma influences the operation and character of the contemporary international legal order. In the second section the focus shifts to a consideration of the implications of the concept of a legal dilemma on the legal discourse in principle and on law's relationship with other normative orders.

A. A Theory of Irresolvable Norm Conflicts

One of the central aims of this book was to show that there are certain norm conflicts which contemporary international law cannot resolve satisfactorily. In response to the question 'What is a legal dilemma?' the book's first part sought to offer a stipulative definition of these norm conflicts and assigned to them the name 'legal dilemma'. It also considered four factors that facilitate the emergence of such legal dilemmas and enquired into the character of the uncertainty that gives rise to the irresolvability of dilemmatic norm conflicts. The second part then sought to validate this stipulative definition by establishing the limits of international law's norm conflict resolution and accommodation devices. It showed that international law's norm conflict resolution and accommodation devices, individually and taken together, are not omnipotent and that, consequently, the second question 'Can legal dilemmas exist in contemporary international law?' should be answered in the affirmative.

At this stage the question becomes: how should international law address norm conflicts that international legal mechanisms cannot resolve? Conventionally, there are two options: First, judicial actors can attempt to conceal situations of this kind by means of outright judicial lawmaking, or, more implicitly, by using and applying international law's norm conflict resolution and accommodation devices in a liberal manner. As a result, a given legal state of affairs is either characterized as legal or illegal. Conversely, the second option is to refrain from any further engagement with an irresolvable conflict and to issue a *non liquet* declaration. Depending on the nature of the interaction between *non liquet* declarations and the *Lotus* Principle a declaration of this kind may result in the characterization of a given legal state of affairs as being neutral or legal.

In contradistinction to these conventional options, the book has argued that irresolvable norm conflicts trigger dilemmatic legal superpositions where states of affairs are both legal and illegal. The book's final part has argued that judicial actors should respond to undecided dilemmatic conflicts by issuing dilemmatic declarations and that dilemmas should then be decided by sovereigns. Subsequently, judicial actors should enforce any norm that the sovereign impaired unduly. The potential objections to this proposal are numerous. They concern theoretical aspects related to logic's law of non-contradiction, the 'ought implies can' maxim, and international law's regulatory monopoly of violence. They also concern the proposal's practical implications concerning questions of jurisdiction, sovereign decisionism, and the potential unfairness of enforcing norms whose impairment legal subjects could not have avoided. While the third part attempted to address and to refute these arguments, the proposed solution certainly remains troubling. Given that the function, operation, and value of international law is conventionally predicated on its ability to distinguish the legal from the illegal, and, perhaps to a lesser extent, to distinguish the regulated from the unregulated, it is not inconsequential to argue that international law is unable to resolve some of law's most intricate problems in this binary fashion. In light of international law's mission to restrain or at least to regulate sovereign power, it may also be problematic to place the responsibility to decide these norm conflicts in the hands of sovereigns. Finally, many will find the enforcement of impaired norms under dilemmatic conditions difficult to accept. The space the book dedicated to the discussion of these concerns shows that these objections are not taken lightly. Indeed, the book takes these objections very seriously. But the book also takes the phenomenon of irresolvable norm conflicts very seriously. That is why it is argued that it is important to address and deal with irresolvable norm conflicts in a manner that is conceptually accurate. That is, in a manner that ensures that an irresolvable norm conflict is acknowledged as what it is.

The accurate legal representation of a legal state of affairs is desirable on jurisprudential grounds alone. At least if one accepts that the study of law aims to shed light on, to disentangle, and then to pronounce upon the relationship between legal norms. Legal pronouncements that cohere with underlying normative states of affairs contribute to legal certainty and to the respect for the rule of law. Most importantly, however, compared to the conventional approaches to irresolvable norm conflicts, making the irresolvability of dilemmatic norm conflicts apparent and delegating the decision-making competence to sovereigns has two interdependent effects.

First, it provides an opportunity and an incentive to develop and to reflect upon the current state of international law. It provides an opportunity for further development and reflection because a genuine understanding of normative relationship between conflicting norms is a precondition for critical engagement and evaluation of the norms in question. By acknowledging rather than concealing the existence of a legal dilemma, the book's proposal provides sovereigns with the opportunity to consider the causes of a dilemma. It opens 'the way for a debate on illegality and legality'[1] of a particular dilemmatic situation. Indeed, in the *Nuclear Weapons Advisory Opinion* the ICJ explicitly encouraged[2] States to reconsider the contemporary legal framework governing nuclear weapons in light of the Court's difficulties to decide the question in an unequivocal manner. Such a conscientious engagement with the matter presupposes, however, that the existence of an irresolvable norm conflict is being communicated to States. The proposed way of dealing with dilemmas also provides an incentive, 'a new stimulus',[3] for States to engage with international law's current approach to a particular norm conflict. The decision of a dilemma will not prevent its future reoccurrence and dilemmatic circumstances are not accepted as an excuse or justification to impair any norm. Thus, the responsibility of a sovereign facing a legal dilemma will inevitably be engaged for as long as a given dilemma remains unaddressed.

Second, by delegating the decision-making responsibility to sovereigns, the proposal politicizes the decision of a given dilemma and facilitates the involvement of other affected stakeholders. Currently, it is for highly skilled lawyers to decide how to approach an irresolvable norm conflict. If in doubt, potentially irresolvable conflicts will be patched up by means of legal techniques. The proposal makes the irresolvability of certain conflicts a concern not only for lawyers, but also for international law's lawmakers and its legal subjects. In an international legal world where 'ideas about political justice are constantly shifting'[4] and where 'imagination[s]' of ideal 'governance arrangements ... keep changing',[5] the concept of a legal dilemma can enfranchise those who have an interest in the design of these governance structures. In some cases, when the stakes are low, the benefit of involving lawmakers and legal subjects may not be apparent. In some circumstances, however, including the scenarios concerning the *Military Alliances* or *Nuclear Weapons*, for example, the stakes will be extremely high. The decisions of these dilemmas may have earth-shattering consequences. In situations of this kind, the proposal aims to ensure that decisions are made by accountable actors and by legitimate means.

Ultimately, and irrespective of the particulars of specific arguments, the book is informed by the conviction that it is preferable to confront the challenge of irresolvable norm conflicts head-on and that it is desirable to make the consideration of the potential promise and the potential dangers of irresolvable norm conflicts a joint exercise that includes all participants of the international legal order: its lawmakers, its subjects, and its judicial guardians.

[1] *Legality of the Threat or Use of Nuclear Weapons (Advisory Opinion)* [1996] ICJ Rep 226 ('*Nuclear Weapons Advisory Opinion*'), Separate Opinion of Judge Ranjeva, 303. See also, more generally, Richard Nobles and David Schiff, 'Review of Paradoxes and Inconsistencies in the Law by Oren Perez; Gunther Teubner' (2007) 70 MLR 505, 510–11; Edward J Lemmon, 'Deontic Logic and the Logic of Imperatives' (1965) 8 Logique Et Analyse 39, 39–61.

[2] *Nuclear Weapons Advisory Opinion* (n 1) [98].

[3] *Nuclear Weapons Advisory Opinion* (n 1), Dissenting Opinion of Judge Weeramantry, 440.

[4] Nico Krisch, *Beyond Constitutionalism: The Pluralist Structure of Postnational Law* (OUP 2010) 79.

[5] Krisch (n 4) 79.

B. The Concept of a Legal Dilemma

Beyond the implications of the book's argument on international law itself, there are two more fundamental insights that the recognition of the concept of a legal dilemma entails. The first insight relates to the relationship of law with other normative orders. The second relates to the nature of a legal discourse that allows for dilemmatic conflicts and narratives.

Conventionally, law's binary logic divides the world into *either* legal *or* illegal states. In accordance with this binary logic, law maps and calibrates the entire realm of human action. Law maintains order, stabilizes relationships, resolves coordination problems, and introduces a sense of clarity to the otherwise apparently disordered social cosmos. Paradoxically, however, the excellent clarity of legal technique simultaneously obscures that system onto which law is projected. Just like maps provide a sense of orientation only by means of manipulated, scaled, and simplified representations of physical space, so can law bring order to the world only by creating and imposing a surreal matrix of legal terms and concepts upon that reality to which it relates. Law blanks out anything that does not fit into law's binary matrix. Thus, the pristine clarity of legal analysis is the result of exiling from the legal matrix all potentially disruptive, troubling factors, factors that transcend law's either-or approach.

Within this legal matrix, the concept of a legal dilemma is an interference, a flicker of the non-legal world. By making it partially and punctually impossible to settle on the one right legal answer, interpretation, understanding, the concept of a dilemma temporarily unveils the structure of the legal matrix. But by exposing the matrix as the matrix, as a normative structure that is imposed upon the world, the concept also briefly uncovers the non-legal realm. The concept of a legal dilemma creates a gateway to the non-legal realm while simultaneously confirming law's detachment from it. The destabilizing potential which this acknowledgement of the non-legal entails is immediately offset by the stabilizing effect of assigning a name, and thereby a conceptual place, to the phenomenon of irresolvable conflicts. In an unprecedented manner, the concept of a dilemma enables judicial actors to acknowledge, confirm, and communicate the existence of an irresolvable norm conflict. In this sense, the concept of a legal dilemma as an interference in the legal matrix allows law to know what it cannot know.

Ultimately, the concept of a legal dilemma is a meaningful reminder that law is a projection, a formal system. Like any formal system,[6] the legal system is necessarily incomplete and prone to generate irresolvable conflicts. This means that it is not

[6] This insight is based on Gödel's incompleteness theorems described in Kurt Gödel, 'Über formal unentscheidbare Sätze der Principia Mathematica und verwandter Systeme I' (1931) 38 Monatshefte für Mathematik und Physik 173. See also Douglas R Hofstadter, *Gödel, Escher, Bach: An Eternal Golden Braid* (20 Anv edition, Basic Books 1999) 15–21, 468–73; Roland Hagenbüchle, 'Was heißt "paradox"? Eine Standortbestimmung' in Roland Hagenbüchle and Paul Geyer (eds), *Das Paradox: eine Herausforderung des abendländischen Denkens* (2nd edn, Königshausen & Neumann 2002) 33.

a deficiency, but an inevitable feature of the (international) legal system that the system's characteristic binary logic can explain and order the social facts to which the system relates only to a limited extent. It is inevitable that there are certain legal questions that law will not be able to answer in a non-dilemmatic manner. The architects of the formal legal system can, of course, systematically preclude the possibility or outright prohibit dilemmas based on a desire to create a well-ordered, dilemma-free legal order. However, it is problematic if such an understanding of the (legal) world becomes an end in itself. The insistence on approaching social realty in this 'symmetrical fashion'[7] can lead to the construction of the legal edifice on non-existent social foundations. Insisting on law's absolute internal consistency is achievable only by risking inconsistency between law and the non-legal, social realm to which it relates.

The recognition of the concept of a legal dilemma, however, equips legal systems with the ability to tolerate not only legal contradictions, but more fundamentally, also different, even mutually exclusive, narratives within the international legal discourse. The concept thus shifts the focus from conventional attempts to establish the one right answer at all costs, the one entitlement or right that trumps another, to more productive, concerted efforts to find creative solutions for extremely difficult problems. The binary nature of traditional legal enquiry is reframed to an analysis of the causes of a given dilemma, its desirability, and whether its future occurrence can be prevented. With respect to sovereign actors, this means that the concept of a dilemma precludes the possibility of sheltering behind the legal armour of allegedly absolute and unquestionable legal entitlements in disregard of another actor's interest. Legal actors are more likely to engage in open-ended negotiations if all negotiating parties know that their legal claims are equally strong. This function of a legal dilemma is particularly important in the context of the contemporary international legal order which consists of an increasingly diverse (and ever changing) group of legal actors and substantive regimes each with distinct and often conflicting visions of the world. With respect to academic contexts, the acceptance of the possibility of legal dilemmas can facilitate the 'adoption of an attitude that acknowledges the incompleteness of the results of one's inquiry'.[8] This may encourage international legal academics, attempting to identify novel solutions to irresolvable norm conflicts, to be 'both more willing and more able to learn from the insights reached by others'.[9]

Overall, the concept of a legal dilemma is a tool to resist the synchronization, the hegemonic streamlining of legal orders and their corresponding narratives. Thus, the key benefit of legal dilemmas is perhaps that dilemmatic thinking counsels against easy and, in any event, one-sided answers in difficult situations. No doubt,

[7] See Isaiah Berlin, 'On Political Judgment' [1996] *The New York Review of Books* 30 <http://www.nybooks.com/articles/archives/1996/oct/03/on-political-judgment> accessed 1 June 2017.

[8] Maksymilian Del Mar, *Jurisprudential Inquiries between Discourse and Tradition: Towards the Incompleteness of Theoretical Pictures* (PhD Thesis, University of Edinburgh 2009) 13.

[9] Del Mar (n 8) 13. See also Julie Dickson, 'Ours Is a Broad Church: Indirectly Evaluative Legal Philosophy as a Facet of Jurisprudential Inquiry' (2015) 6 Jurisprudence 207, 214–15, 230.

it would have been of cold comfort to the Russian president to know that he faced a legal dilemma had there been a real nuclear attack on the morning of 25 January 1995. The book's core thesis would not have made his decision any easier. However, dilemmas as a concept of law are not designed to make decisions easier. Legal dilemmas are designed to make the decision of norm conflicts as difficult as they can possibly be, by forcing the flip-side of every legal decision into view. In this sense, the argument for accepting the concept of a legal dilemma is an anti-fundamentalist plea in a world that frequently witnesses violent battles between actors who are quick to claim that theirs is the only truth.

Bibliography

Adorno T, *Negative Dialektik* (Suhrkamp 1966)

Agamben G, *State of Exception* (University of Chicago Press 2008)

Akande D, 'Nuclear Weapons, Unclear Law? Deciphering the Nuclear Weapons Advisory Opinion of the International Court' (1998) 68 British Yearbook of International Law 165

Akehurst M, 'The Hierarchy of the Sources of International Law' (1974) 47 British Yearbook of International Law 273

Alchurrón CE, 'On Law and Logic' (1996) 9 Ratio Juris 331

Aleinikoff TA, 'Constitutional Law in the Age of Balancing' (1986) 96 Yale Law Journal 943

Alexy R, *A Theory of Constitutional Rights* (Oxford University Press 2002)

Alexy R, 'Constitutional Rights, Balancing, and Rationality' (2003) 16 Ratio Juris 131

Aljaghoub MM, *The Advisory Function of the International Court of Justice 1946–2005* (Springer 2007)

Allott P, 'Interpretation—an Exact Art' in Andrea Bianchi, Daniel Peat, and Matthew Windsor (eds), *Interpretation in International Law* (Oxford University Press 2015)

Amerasinghe CF, 'The Legality of the Use of or Threat to Use Nuclear Weapons' (1999) X Finnish Yearbook of International Law 5

Amr MSM, *The Role of the International Court of Justice as the Principal Judicial Organ of the United Nations* (Martinus Nijhoff 2003)

Andenas M and Zleptnig S, 'Proportionality and Balancing in WTO Law: A Comparative Perspective' (2007) 42 Texas International Law Journal 371

Anzilotti D, *Cours de Droit International*, vol 1 (Gilbert Gidel tr, Sirey 1929)

Asad T, 'Thinking about Terrorism and Just War' (2010) 23 Cambridge Review of International Affairs 3

Barak A, *Proportionality: Constitutional Rights and Their Limitations* (Cambridge University Press 2012)

Bederman DJ, *The Spirit of International Law* (University of Georgia Press 2002)

Beltrán JF and Ratti GB, 'Defeasibility and Legality: A Survey' in Jordi Ferrer Beltrán and Giovanni Battista Ratti (eds), *The Logic of Legal Requirements* (Oxford University Press 2012)

Bendersky JJ, *Carl Schmitt: Theorist for the Reich* (Princeton University Press 2014)

Bentham J, *The Limits of Jurisprudence Defined, Being Part Two of an Introduction to the Principles of Morals and Legislation* (Columbia University Press 1945)

Benvenisti E and Downs GW, 'The Empire's New Clothes: Political Economy and the Fragmentation of International Law' (2007) 60 Stanford Law Review 595

Berlin I, *Liberty* (Oxford University Press 2002)

Berlin I, 'On Political Judgment' [1996] *The New York Review of Books* 30 <http://www.nybooks.com/articles/archives/1996/oct/03/on-political-judgment> accessed 1 June 2017

Berman F, 'The International Court of Justice as an "Agent" of Legal Development?' in Christian J Tams and James Sloan (eds), *The Development of International Law by the International Court of Justice* (Oxford University Press 2013)

Berman F, 'The Uses and Abuses of Advisory Opinions' in Nisuke Ando, Edward McWhinney, and Rüdiger Wolfrum (eds), *Liber Amicorum—Judge Shigeru Oda* (Kluwer Law International 2002)

Bernhardt R, 'Article 103' in Bruno Simma, Daniel-Erasmus Khan, Georg Nolte, Andreas Paulus, and Nikolai Wessendorf (eds), *The Charter of the United Nations: A Commentary*, vol 2 (2nd edn, Oxford University Press 2002)

Besson S, *The Morality of Conflict: Reasonable Disagreement and the Law* (Hart 2005)

Bianchi A, 'Gazing at the Crystal Ball (again): State Immunity and Jus Cogens beyond Germany v Italy' (2013) 4 Journal of International Dispute Settlement 457

Bianchi A, Peat D, and Windsor M, *Interpretation in International Law* (Oxford University Press 2015)

Binder C, *Die Grenzen der Vertragstreue im Völkerrecht: am Beispiel der nachträglichen Änderung der Umstände* (Springer-Verlag 2013)

Binder G, 'The Dialectic of Duplicity: Treaty Conflict and Political Contradiction' (1985) 34 Buffalo Law Review 329

Bleckmann A, 'Zur Feststellung und Auslegung von Völkergewohnheitsrecht' (1977) 37 Zeitschrift für ausländisches öffentliches Recht und Völkerrecht 504

Bodansky D, 'Non Liquet and the Incompleteness of International Law' in Laurence Boisson de Chazournes and Philippe Sands (eds), *International Law, the International Court of Justice and Nuclear Weapons* (Cambridge University Press 1999)

Bodansky D, 'Non Liquet' in Rüdiger Wolfrum (ed), *Max Planck Encyclopedia of Public International Law* (Online edn, Max Planck Institute for Comparative Public Law and International Law 2006)

Bodeau-Livinec P and Morgan-Foster J, 'Article 61' in Olivier Corten and Pierre Klein (eds), *The Vienna Conventions on the Law of Treaties* (Oxford University Press 2011)

Bohlander M, 'Of Shipwrecked Sailors, Unborn Children, Conjoined Twins and Hijacked Airplanes—Taking Human Life and the Defence of Necessity' (2006) 70 The Journal of Criminal Law 147

Bohr N, *Atomic Theory and the Description of Nature* (Cambridge University Press 1934)

Bohr N, 'Discussion with Einstein on Epistemological Problems in Atomic Physics' in J Kalckar (ed), *Foundations of Quantum Physics II (1933-1958)* (Elsevier 1969)

Boldt H and others, 'Staat und Souveränität' in Otto Brunner, Werner Conze, and Reinhart Koselleck (eds), *Geschichtliche Grundbegriffe*, vol 6 (Klett-Cotta 1990)

Bonhoeffer D, *Ethik* (Eberhard Bethge ed, 2nd edn, Christian Kaiser Verlag 1953)

Borgen CJ, 'Resolving Treaty Conflicts' (2005) 37 George Washington International Law Review 573

Borgen CJ, 'Treaty Conflicts and Normative Fragmentation' in Duncan Hollis (ed), *The Oxford Guide to Treaties* (Oxford University Press 2012)

Borges JL, 'The Garden of Forking Paths' in Anthony Kerrigan (ed), *Ficciones* (Grove Press 1994)

Boudreault F, 'Identifying Conflicts of Norms: The ICJ Approach in the Case of the Jurisdictional Immunities of the State (Germany v. Italy: Greece Intervening)' (2012) 25 Leiden Journal of International Law 1003

Brest P, 'Interpretation and Interest' (1982) 34 Stanford Law Review 765

Briggs A, *The Conflict of Laws* (3rd edn, Oxford University Press 2013)

Brown P, 'Bonhoeffer, Schmitt, and the State of Exception' (2013) 26 Pacifica: Australasian Theological Studies 246

Brown PM, 'Costa Rica v. Nicaragua' (1917) 11 American Journal of International Law 156

Brownlie I, 'Some Legal Aspects of the Use of Nuclear Weapons' (1965) 14 International & Comparative Law Quarterly 437

Brownlie I, 'Why Do States Take Disputes to the International Court?' in Nisuke Ando, Edward McWhinney, and Rüdiger Wolfrum (eds), *Liber Amicorum—Judge Shigeru Oda* (Kluwer Law International 2002)

Bulygin E, 'On Norms of Competence' (1992) 11 Law and Philosophy 201

Bumke C, *Relative Rechtswidrigkeit: Systembildung und Binnendifferenzierungen im Öffentlichen Recht* (Mohr Siebeck 2004)

Calabresi G and Melamed AD, 'Property Rules, Liability Rules, and Inalienability: One View of the Cathedral' (1972) 85 Harvard Law Review 1089

Canaris CW, *Die Feststellung von Lücken im Gesetz: eine methodologische Studie über Voraussetzungen und Grenzen der richterlichen Rechtsfortbildung praeter legem* (Duncker & Humblot 1964)

Canaris CW, *Systemdenken und Systembegriff in der Jurisprudenz: Entwickelt am Beispiel des deutschen Privatrechts* (Duncker & Humblot 1969)

Carr EH, *The Twenty Years' Crisis 1919–1939: An Introduction to the Study of International Relations* (2nd edn, Macmillan 1946)

Cassimatis AE, 'International Humanitarian Law, International Human Rights Law, and Fragmentation of International Law' (2007) 56 International & Comparative Law Quarterly 623

Chamberlain A, 'Contribution to a Parliamentary Debate on International Peace and Disarmament' HC Deb 24 November 1927

Christófolo JE, *Solving Antinomies between Peremptory Norms in Public International Law* (Schulthess 2016)

Conway G, 'Conflicts of Competence Norms in EU Law and the Legal Reasoning of the ECJ' (2010) 11 German Law Journal 966

Cornides T, *Ordinale Deontik: Zusammenhänge zwischen Präferenztheorie, Normlogik und Rechtstheorie* (Springer-Verlag 1974)

Crawford E, 'Proportionality' in Rüdiger Wolfrum (ed), *Max Planck Encyclopedia of Public International Law* (Online edn, Max Planck Institute for Comparative Public Law and International Law 2010)

Crawford J, *Brownlie's Principles of Public International Law* (8th edn, Oxford University Press 2012)

Crawford J, *Chance, Order, Change: The Course of International Law, General Course on Public International Law* (Brill-Nijhoff 2014)

Crawford J, *State Responsibility: The General Part* (Cambridge University Press 2013)

Currie C, 'Note on Methods and Objectives in the Conflict of Laws' (1959) 8 Duke Law Journal 171

Czapliński W and Danilenko GM, 'Conflicts of Norms in International Law' (1990) 21 Netherlands Yearbook of International Law 3

d'Aspremont J, 'Articulating International Human Rights and International Humanitarian Law: Conciliatory Interpretation under the Guise of Conflict of Norms-Resolution' in Malgosia Fitzmaurice and Panos Merkouris (eds), *The Interpretation and Application of the European Convention of Human Rights* (Martinus Nijhoff 2013)

da Silva VA, 'Comparing the Incommensurable: Constitutional Principles, Balancing and Rational Decision' (2011) 31 Oxford Journal of Legal Studies 273

de Zayas AM, 'Amnesty Clause' in Rudolf Bernhardt (ed), *Encyclopedia of Public International Law* (Max Planck Institute for Comparative Public Law and International Law 1981)

Del Mar M, *Jurisprudential Inquiries between Discourse and Tradition: Towards the Incompleteness of Theoretical Pictures* (PhD Thesis, University of Edinburgh 2009)

Del Mar M, 'System Values and Understanding Legal Language' (2008) 21 Leiden Journal of International Law 29

Delmas-Marty M, *Global Law: A Triple Challenge* (Transnational Publishers 2003)

Derrida J, 'Force De Loi: Le Fondement Mystique De L'Autorité' (1989) 11 Cardozo Law Review 920

Desierto DA, *Necessity and National Emergency Clauses: Sovereignty in Modern Treaty Interpretation* (Martinus Nijhoff 2012)

Devyanin N, 'All That Has Happened, Alas, Had To Happen' *Moskovskiye Novosti* (Moscow, 31 January 1995)

Dicey AV, *An Introduction to the Law of the Constitution* (8th edn, Macmillan 1915)

Dickson J, 'Ours Is a Broad Church: Indirectly Evaluative Legal Philosophy as a Facet of Jurisprudential Inquiry' (2015) 6 Jurisprudence 207

Dougherty MV, *Moral Dilemmas in Medieval Thought: From Gratian to Aquinas* (Cambridge University Press 2011)

Dubislav W, *Die Definition* (3rd edn, Felix Meiner 1931)

Dunn FS, *The Diplomatic Protection of Americans in Mexico* (Columbia University Press 1933)

Duxbury N, *Random Justice: On Lotteries and Legal Decision-Making* (Oxford University Press 1999)

Dworkin R, 'Hard Cases' (1975) 88 Harvard Law Review 1057

Dworkin R, 'No Right Answer?' in PMS Hacker and Joseph Raz (eds), *Law, Morality and Society—Essays in Honour of H.L.A. Hart* (Clarendon Press 1977)

Dworkin R, *Taking Rights Seriously* (A&C Black 2013)

Dyzenhaus D, *Hard Cases in Wicked Legal Systems: Pathologies of Legality* (2nd edn, Oxford University Press 2010)

Einstein A, 'Physik und Realität' (1936) 221 Journal of the Franklin Institute 313

Einstein A, Born M, and Born H, *Briefwechsel 1916–1955* (Rowohlt 1972)

Einstein A, Podolsky B, and Rosen N, 'Can Quantum-Mechanical Description of Physical Reality Be Considered Complete?' (1935) 47 Physical Review 777

Eleftheriadis P, *Legal Rights* (Oxford University Press 2008)

Endicott TAO, *Vagueness in Law* (Oxford University Press 2000)

Engisch K, *Die Einheit der Rechtsordnung* (Winter 1935)

Engisch K, *Die Idee der Konkretisierung in Recht und Rechtswissenschaft unserer Zeit* (Winter 1953)

Engisch K, *Einführung in das juristische Denken* (9th edn, Kohlhammer 1997)

Engisch K, 'Logische Überlegungen zur Verbrechensdefinition' in Paul Bockelmann, Arthur Kaufmann, and Ulrich Klug (eds), *Beiträge zur Rechtstheorie* (Vittorio Klostermann 1984)

Falichev O, '"Iron Cucumbers" in Dangerous Orbits. Necessary Postscript to Norwegian Missile Incident (Interview with Lieutenant General Anatoliy Sokolov)' *Krasnaya Zvezda* (Moscow, 7 February 1995)

Falk RA, 'Nuclear Weapons, International Law and the World Court: A Historic Encounter' (1997) 91 American Journal of International Law 64

Fastenrath U, *Lücken im Völkerrecht: zu Rechtscharakter, Quellen, Systemzusammenhang, Methodenlehre und Funktionen des Völkerrechts* (Duncker & Humblot 1991)

Febbrajo A, 'The Rules of the Game in the Welfare State' in Gunther Teubner (ed), *Dilemmas of Law in the Welfare State* (De Gruyter 1988)

Feldbrugge FJM, 'Good and Bad Samaritans: A Comparative Survey of Criminal Law Provisions Concerning Failure to Rescue' (1965) 14 American Journal of Comparative Law 630

Ferguson RA, 'The Place of Mercy in Legal Discourse' in Austin Sarat (ed), *Merciful Judgments and Contemporary Society* (Cambridge University Press 2011)

Finnis J, 'Natural Law and Legal Reasoning' in Robert P George (ed), *Natural Law Theory: Contemporary Essays* (Clarendon Press 1992) 146

Finnis J, *Nuclear Deterrence, Morality and Realism* (Clarendon Press 1987)

Fischer-Lescano A and Teubner G, 'Fragmentierung des Weltrechts: Vernetzung Globaler Regimes statt etatistischer Rechtseinheit' in Mathias Albert and Rudolf Stichweh (eds), *Weltstaat und Weltstaatlichkeit: Beobachtungen globaler politischer Strukturbildung* (Verlag für Sozialwissenschaft 2007)

Fischer-Lescano A and Teubner G, 'Regime-Collisions: The Vain Search for Legal Unity in the Fragmentation of Global Law' (2004) 25 Michigan Journal of International Law 999

Fitzmaurice G, 'The Law and Procedure of the International Court of Justice 1951–4: Treaty Interpretation and Other Treaty Points' (1957) 33 British Year Book of International Law 203

Fitzmaurice G, 'The Problem of Non-Liquet: Prolegomena To a Restatement' *Mélanges offerts à Charles Rousseau: la communauté internationale* (A Pedone 1974)

Fitzmaurice M, 'Exceptional Circumstances and Treaty Commitments' in Duncan Hollis (ed), *The Oxford Guide to Treaties* (Oxford University Press 2012)

Fletcher GP, 'Paradoxes in Legal Thought' (1985) 85 Columbia Law Review 1263

Foot P, 'The Problem of Abortion and the Doctrine of the Double Effect' (1967) 5 Oxford Review 1

Franck TM 'On Proportionality of Countermeasures in International Law' (2008) 102 American Journal of International Law 715

From L, 'Ambassadør Advarer: Missilskjold Vil Koste Dyrt Og Give Mindre Sikkerhed' *Jyllands-Posten* (Viby, 20 March 2015)

Fuller LL, 'Positivism and Fidelity to Law: A Reply to Professor Hart' (1958) 71 Harvard Law Review 630

Fuller LL, 'The Case of the Speluncean Explorers' (1949) 62 Harvard Law Review 616

Fuller LL, *The Morality of Law* (rev edn, Yale University Press 1969)

Gadamer HG, *Wahrheit und Methode: Grundzüge einer philosophischen Hermeneutik* (Mohr 1960)

Gaja G, *Jus Cogens Beyond the Vienna Convention* (Brill 1981)

García-Salmones Rovira M, *The Project of Positivism in International Law* (Oxford University Press 2013)

Gardam JG, 'Proportionality and Force in International Law' (1993) 87 American Journal of International Law 391

Gardam JG, *Necessity, Proportionality and the Use of Force by States* (Cambridge University Press 2004)

Gardner J, 'Hart and Feinberg on Responsibility' in Matthew Kramer and others (eds), *The Legacy of H.L.A. Hart: Legal, Political and Moral Philosophy* (Oxford University Press 2008)

Gaus G, Interview with Hannah Arendt (28 October 1964) <http://www.rbb-online.de/zurperson/interview_archiv/arendt_hannah.html> accessed 27 January 2016

Geyer P, 'Historisch-systematische Grundlegung' in Roland Hagenbüchle and Paul Geyer (eds), *Das Paradox: eine Herausforderung des abendländischen Denkens* (2nd edn, Königshausen & Neumann 2002)

Giegerich T, 'Article 61' in Oliver Dörr and Kirsten Schmalenbach (eds), *Vienna Convention on the Law of Treaties: A Commentary* (Springer 2012)

Gillon R, 'Jodie and Mary, Conjoined Twins: A Case of Judicial Moral Hubris?' (2004) 72 Medico-Legal Journal 3

Gödel K, 'Über formal unentscheidbare Sätze der Principia Mathematica und verwandter Systeme I' (1931) 38 Monatshefte für Mathematik und Physik 173

Goldie LFE, 'Legal Pluralism and "No-Law" Sectors' (1958) 32 Australian Law Journal 220

Gomula J, 'Responsibility and the World Trade Organization' in James Crawford, Alain Pellet, and Simon Olleson (eds), *The Law of International Responsibility* (Oxford University Press 2010)

Gordon RW, 'Critical Legal Histories' (1984) 36 Stanford Law Review 57

Gottlieb P, 'Aristotle on Non-Contradiction' in Edward N Zalta (ed), *The Stanford Encyclopedia of Philosophy* (Summer edn, 2015) <http://plato.stanford.edu/archives/sum2015/entries/aristotle-noncontradiction/> accessed 24 May 2017

Gowlland-Debbas V, 'Responsibility and the United Nations Charter' in James Crawford, Alain Pellet, and Simon Olleson (eds), *The Law of International Responsibility* (Oxford University Press 2010)

Gray J, *Isaiah Berlin* (Princeton University Press 1996)

Green J, *The International Court of Justice and Self-Defence in International Law* (Hart 2009)

Greenspan PS, 'Moral Dilemmas and Guilt' (1983) 43 Philosophical Studies 117

Griffin J, 'The Human Good and the Ambitions of Consequentialism' (1992) 9 Social Philosophy and Policy 118

Grigoleit HC and Neuner J, *Claus-Wilhelm Canaris, Gesammelte Schriften* (Walter de Gruyter 2012)

Gross O and Ní Aoláin F, *Law in Times of Crisis: Emergency Powers in Theory and Practice* (Cambridge University Press 2006)

Grosse Ruse-Khan H, 'A Conflict-of-Laws Approach to Competing Rationalities in International Law: The Case of Plain Packaging between Intellectual Property, Trade, Investment and Health' (2013) 9 Journal of Private International Law 309

Grotius H, *The Rights of War and Peace* (first published 1625, Liberty Fund 2005)

Habermas J, *Between Facts and Norms: Contributions to a Discourse Theory of Law and Democracy* (William Rehg tr, Polity 1996)

Hafner G, 'Pros and Cons Ensuing from Fragmentation of International Law' (2003) 25 Michigan Journal of International Law 849

Hagenbüchle R, 'Was heißt "paradox"? Eine Standortbestimmung' in Roland Hagenbüchle and Paul Geyer (eds), *Das Paradox: eine Herausforderung des abendländischen Denkens* (2nd edn, Königshausen & Neumann 2002)

Hallaq WB, *The Impossible State: Islam, Politics, and Modernity's Moral Predicament* (Columbia University Press 2012)

Hamblin CL, 'Quandaries and the Logic of Rules' (1972) 1 Journal of Philosophical Logic 74

Harris JW, 'Kelsen and Normative Consistency' in Richard Tur and William L Twining (eds), *Essays on Kelsen* (Clarendon Press 1986)

Hart HLA, 'Kelsen's Doctrine of the Unity of Law' in Howard E Kiefer and Milton K Munitz (eds), *Ethics and Social Justice* (State University of New York Press 1968)

Hart HLA, 'Positivism and the Separation of Law and Morals' (1957) 71 Harvard Law Review 593

Hart HLA, *Punishment and Responsibility* (2nd edn, Oxford University Press 2008)

Hart HLA, *The Concept of Law* (2nd edn, Clarendon Press 1994)

Hawking S, 'Does God Play Dice?' <http://www.hawking.org.uk/does-god-play-dice.html> accessed 25 January 2017

Herdegen M, 'Interpretation in International Law' in Rüdiger Wolfrum (ed), *Max Planck Encyclopedia of Public International Law* (Max Planck Institute for Comparative Public Law and International Law 2013)

Hernandez G, *The International Court of Justice and the Judicial Function* (Oxford University Press 2014)

Hesse K, *Grundzüge des Verfassungsrechts der Bundesrepublik Deutschland* (20th edn, CF Müller Verlag 1999)

Higgins R, 'Derogations under Human Rights Treaties' (1977) 48 British Yearbook of International Law 281

Higgins R, *Problems and Process: International Law and How We Use It* (Clarendon Press 1995)

Hill HH, 'A Functional Taxonomy of Normative Conflict' (1987) 6 Law and Philosophy 227

Hofmann H, *Legitimität gegen Legalität: Der Weg der politischen Philosophie Carl Schmitts* (Duncker & Humblot 2010)

Hofstadter DR, *Gödel, Escher, Bach: An Eternal Golden Braid* (20 anniversary edn, Basic Books 1999)

af Holberg L, *Einleitung in das Natur- und Völkerrecht* (Wentzel 1748)

Holwitt JI, *'Execute against Japan': The U.S. Decision to Conduct Unrestricted Submarine Warfare* (Texas A&M University Press 2009)

Home JP and others, 'Complete Methods Set for Scalable Ion Trap Quantum Information Processing' (2009) 325 Science 1227

Howse RL, Langille J, and Sykes K, 'Pluralism in Practice: Moral Legislation and the Law of the WTO After *Seal Products*' (2015) 48 The George Washington International Law Review 81

Hruschka J, *Das deontologische Sechseck bei Gottfried Achenwall im Jahre 1767* (Vandenhoeck & Ruprecht 1997)

Hruschka J and Joerden JC, 'Supererogation: Vom deontologischen Sechseck zum deontologischen Zehneck: Zugleich ein Beitrag zur strafrechtlichen Grundlagenforschung' (1987) 73 Archiv für Rechts- und Sozialphilosophie 93

Hurd I, 'Is Humanitarian Intervention Legal? The Rule of Law in an Incoherent World' (2011) 25 Ethics & International Affairs 293

Isaacs T, *Moral Responsibility in Collective Contexts* (Oxford University Press 2011)

Jaspers K, *The Question of German Guilt* (EB Ashton tr, Oxford University Press 1947)

Jaspers K, *Die Atombombe und die Zukunft des Menschen. Politisches Bewußtsein in unserer Zeit* (Piper 1960)

Jenks CW, 'The Conflict of Law-Making Treaties' (1953) 30 British Year Book of International Law 401

Jennings RY, 'The Proliferation of Adjudicatory Bodies: Dangers and Possible Answers' in *Implications of the Proliferation of International Adjudicatory Bodies for Dispute Resolution* (1995) 9 ASIL Bulletin 2

Jennings RY, 'Treaties as "Legislation"' in Gabriel M Wilner (ed), *Jus et Societas: Essays in Tribute to Wolfgang Friedmann* (Martinus Nijhoff 1979)

Jennings RY, 'The Judiciary, International and National, and the Development of International Law' (1996) 45 International & Comparative Law Quarterly 1

Jennings RY and Watts A, *Oppenheim's International Law*, vol 1 (9th edn, Longman 1992)

Jeutner V, 'A Critique of the EU Commission's Proposal Concerning Intergovernmental Energy Agreements' (2016) 9 International Energy Law Review 181

Jeutner V, 'Aporia' (1 April 2015) <https://www.youtube.com/watch?v=B9D6LP8wvL0> accessed 16 November 2016

Jeutner V, 'Water Claims of an Independent Palestine in Practice: Reconciling Conflicting Water Claims in the Region' in Mutaz Qafisheh (ed), *Palestine Membership in the United Nations: Legal and Practical Implications* (Cambridge Scholars Publishing 2013)

Jochnick C and Normand R, 'The Legitimation of Violence: A Critical History of the Laws of War' (1994) 35 Harvard International Law Journal 49

Jonas H, *Das Prinzip der Verantwortung—Versuch einer Ethik für die technologische Zivilisation* (Suhrkamp 1984)

Joseph S and Castan M, *The International Covenant on Civil and Political Rights: Cases, Materials, and Commentary* (3rd edn, Oxford University Press 2013)

Justinian, *Digesta* (Theodor Mommsen and Paul Krüger eds, Weidmann 1954)

Kahan DM, 'The Supreme Court 2010 Term—Foreword: Neutral Principles, Motivated Cognition, and Some Problems for Constitutional Law' (2011) 125 Harvard Law Review 1

Kammerhofer J, *Uncertainty in International Law: A Kelsenian Perspective* (Taylor & Francis 2010)

Kammerhofer J, 'Unearthing Structural Uncertainty through Neo-Kelsenian Consistency: Conflicts of Norms in International Law' 3 <http://www.esil-sedi.eu/sites/default/files/Kammerhofer.pdf> accessed 23 January 2017

Kant I, *Die Religion innerhalb der Grenzen der bloßen Vernunft* (Gesammelte Schriften, Preußische Akademie der Wissenschaften 1900)

Kant I, *Grundlegung zur Metaphysik der Sitten* (Gesammelte Schriften, Preußische Akademie der Wissenschaften 1900)

Kant I, *Kritik der praktischen Vernunft* (Gesammelte Schriften, Preußische Akademie der Wissenschaften 1900)

Kant I, *Kritik der reinen Vernunft* (Gesammelte Schriften, Preußische Akademie der Wissenschaften 1900)

Karl W, 'Conflicts between Treaties' in Rudolf Bernhardt (ed), *Encyclopedia of Public International Law*, vol 7 (North-Holland 1984)

Kedar N, 'The Political Origins of the Modern Legal Paradoxes' in Oren Perez and Gunther Teubner (eds), *Paradoxes and Inconsistencies in the Law* (Hart 2006)

Keith KJ, 'The Advisory Jurisdiction of the International Court of Justice: Some Comparative Reflections' (1996) 16 Australian Yearbook of International Law 39

Keith KJ, *The Extent of the Advisory Jurisdiction of the International Court of Justice* (Sijthoff 1971)

Kelsen H, *General Theory of Law and State* (Harvard University Press 1945)

Kelsen H, *General Theory of Norms* (Clarendon Press 1991)

Kelsen H, *Principles of International Law* (Robert W Tucker ed, 2nd edn, Holt, Rinehart and Winston 1966)

Kelsen H, *Reine Rechtslehre* (Deuticke 1960)

Kelsen H, 'Was ist ein Rechtsakt?' in Hans R Klecatsky (ed), *Die Wiener Rechtstheoretische Schule* (Franz Steiner 2010)

Khosla M, 'Proportionality: An Assault on Human Rights?: A Reply' (2010) 8 International Journal of Constitutional Law 298

Kierkegaard S, *Fear and Trembling/Repetition* (Howard Vincent Hong and Edna Hatlestad Hong trs, Princeton University Press 1983)

Klabbers J, *International Law* (Cambridge University Press 2013)

Klabbers J, 'Setting the Scene' in Jan Klabbers, Anne Peters, and Geir Ulfstein (eds), *The Constitutionalization of International Law* (Oxford University Press 2009)

Klabbers J, *Treaty Conflict and the European Union* (Cambridge University Press 2009)

Klabbers J, 'Virtuous Interpretation' in Malgosia Fitzmaurice, Olufemi Elias, and Panos Merkouris (eds), *Treaty Interpretation and the Vienna Convention on the Law of Treaties 30 Years On* (Martinus Nijhoff 2010)

Klatt M and Meister M, *The Constitutional Structure of Proportionality* (Oxford University Press 2012)

Klein F, 'Vertragskonkurrenz' in Karl Strupp and H-J Schlochauer (eds), *Wörterbuch des Völkerrechts* (De Gruyter 1962)

Klug U, 'Der Handlungsbegriff des Finalismus als methodologisches Problem' in Ulrich Klug (ed), *Philosophie und Recht—Festschrift zum 70. Geburtstag von Carl August Emge* (Franz Steiner 1960)

Klug U, *Juristische Logik* (Springer-Verlag 1982)

Kobusch T, 'Paradoxon und Religiöse Existenz' in Roland Hagenbüchle and Paul Geyer (eds), *Das Paradox: Eine Herausforderung des abendländischen Denkens* (2nd edn, Königshausen & Neumann 2002)

Kohen MG, 'The Notion of "State Survival" in International Law' in Laurence Boisson de Chazournes and Philippe Sands (eds), *International Law, the International Court of Justice and Nuclear Weapons* (Cambridge University Press 1999)

Kokott J, *The Burden of Proof in Comparative and International Human Rights Law: Civil and Common Law Approaches with Special Reference to the American and German Legal Systems* (Martinus Nijhoff 1998)

Kolb R, 'Conflits Entre Normes de Jus Cogens' in Nicolas Angelet and others (eds), *Droit du Pouvoir, Pouvoir du Droit: Mélanges offerts à Jean Salmon* (Bruylant 2007)

Kononenko V, 'Yeltsin Leaves Chechnya Behind in Lipetsk, But Takes the "Black Attache Case" With Him' *Moscow Izvestiya* (Moscow, 27 January 1995)

Koskenniemi M, 'Case Analysis: Faith, Identity, and the Killing of the Innocent: International Lawyers and Nuclear Weapons' (1997) 10 Leiden Journal of International Law 137

Koskenniemi M, *From Apology to Utopia: The Structure of International Legal Argument* (Cambridge University Press 2005)

Koskenniemi M, 'Hegemonic Regimes' in Margaret A Young (ed), *Regime Interaction in International Law* (Cambridge University Press 2012)

Koskenniemi M, 'The Fate of Public International Law: Between Technique and Politics' (2007) 70 The Modern Law Review 1

Koskenniemi M, 'The Lady Doth Protest Too Much—Kosovo, and the Turn to Ethics in International Law' (2002) 65 Modern Law Review 159

Kramer MH, 'Moral Rights and the Limits of the Ought-Implies-Can Principle: Why Impeccable Precautions Are No Excuse' (2005) 48 Inquiry 307

Kramer MH, 'When Is There Not One Right Answer?' (2008) 53 American Journal of Jurisprudence 49

Kratochwil FV, *Rules, Norms, and Decisions: On the Conditions of Practical and Legal Reasoning in International Relations and Domestic Affairs* (Cambridge University Press 1989)

Krimphove D, 'Grenzen der Logik' (2013) 44 Rechtstheorie 315

Krisch N, *Beyond Constitutionalism: The Pluralist Structure of Postnational Law* (Oxford University Press 2010)

Kulick A, *Global Public Interest in International Investment Law* (Cambridge University Press 2012)

Kumm M, 'What Do You Have in Virtue of Having a Constitutional Right? On the Place and Limits of the Proportionality Requirement' (2006) Paper 46 New York University Public Law and Legal Theory Working Papers

Kutz CL, 'Just Disagreement: Indeterminacy and Rationality in the Rule of Law' (1994) 103 Yale Law Journal 997

Lachs M, 'Some Reflections on the Contribution of the International Court of Justice to the Development of International Law' (1983) 10 Syracuse Journal of International Law and Commerce 239

Ladiges M, *Die Bekämpfung nicht-staatlicher Angreifer im Luftraum: Unter besonderer Berücksichtigung des § 14 Abs. 3 LuftSiG und der strafrechtlichen Beurteilung der Tötung von Unbeteiligten* (Duncker & Humblot 2013)

Laplace PS, *A Philosophical Essay on Probabilities* (Frederick Wilson Truscott and Frederick Lincoln Emory trs, Chapman & Hall 1902)

Lauterpacht H, 'Some Observations on the Prohibition of "Non Liquet" and the Completeness of the Law' in Elihu Lauterpacht (ed), *International Law—Collected Papers*, vol 2 (Cambridge University Press 1975)

Lauterpacht H, 'The Covenant as the "Higher Law"' (1936) 17 British Year Book of International Law 54

Lauterpacht H, *The Development of International Law by the International Court* (Cambridge University Press 1982)

Lauterpacht H, *The Function of Law in the International Community* (Clarendon Press 1933)

Leibniz GW, 'Meditation on the Common Concept of Justice' in Patrick Riley (ed), *Political Writings* (2nd edn, Cambridge University Press 1988)

Leibniz GW, 'Inaugural Dissertation on Perplexing Cases in the Law' in Alberto Artosi, Bernardo Pieri, and Giovanni Sartor (eds), *Leibniz: Logico-Philosophical Puzzles in the Law* (Springer 2013)

Leiss JR and Paulus A, 'Article 103' in Bruno Simma and others (eds), *The Charter of the United Nations: A Commentary*, vol 2 (3rd edn, Oxford University Press 2012)

Lemmon EJ, 'Deontic Logic and the Logic of Imperatives' (1965) 8 Logique Et Analyse 39

Lenk H, 'Konträrbeziehungen und Operatorengleichungen im deontologischen Sechseck' in Hans Lenk (ed), *Normenlogik. Grundprobleme der deontischen Logik* (Verlag Dokumentation 1974)

Ley I, *Opposition im Völkerrecht—Ein Beitrag zur Legitimation internationaler Rechtserzeugung* (Springer 2015)

Lilburne J, 'On the 150th Page: An Untitled Broad-Sheet of August 1645' in Andrew Sharp (ed), *The English Levellers* (Cambridge University Press 2002)

Linderfalk U, 'The Effect of Jus Cogens Norms: Whoever Opened Pandora's Box, Did You Ever Think About the Consequences?' (2007) 18 European Journal of International Law 853

Linderfalk U, 'The Principle of Rational Decision-Making—As Applied to the Identification of Normative Conflicts in International Law' [2013] Zeitschrift für ausländisches öffentliches Recht und Völkerrecht 591

Lindroos A, 'Addressing Norm Conflicts in a Fragmented Legal System: The Doctrine of Lex Specialis' (2005) 74 Nordic Journal of International Law 27

Loui RP, 'Alchurrón and von Wright on Conflict among Norms' in Donald Nute (ed), *Defeasible Deontic Logic* (Kluwer 1997)

Lowe V, 'Shock Verdict: Nuclear War May or May Not Be Unlawful' (1996) 55 The Cambridge Law Journal 415

Luhmann N, *Das Recht der Gesellschaft* (Suhrkamp 1995)

Luhmann N, *Die Religion der Gesellschaft* (André Kieserling ed, Suhrkamp 2000)
Luhmann M, *Law as a Social System* (Fatima Kastner and others eds, Klaus A Ziegert tr, Oxford University Press 2004)
MacCormick N, 'Risking Constitutional Collision in Europe?' (1998) 18 Oxford Journal of Legal Studies 517
MacIntyre A, 'Moral Dilemmas' (1990) 50 Philosophy and Phenomenological Research 367
MacIntyre A, *Whose Justice? Which Rationality?* (Duckworth Gerald 1988)
Mann FA, 'The Proper Law in the Conflict of Laws' (1987) 36 The International & Comparative Law Quarterly 437
Marceau G, 'Conflicts of Norms and Conflicts of Jurisdictions—The Relationship between the WTO Agreement and MEAs and Other Treaties' (2001) 35 Journal of World Trade 1081
Marcus RB, 'Moral Dilemmas and Consistency' (1980) 77 The Journal of Philosophy 121
Marcus RB, 'More about Moral Dilemmas' in HE Mason (ed), *Moral Dilemmas and Moral Theory* (Oxford University Press 1996)
Marks P, 'Ditching Binary Will Make Quantum Computers More Powerful' *NewScientist* (10 August 2009)
Mason HE, 'Responsibilities and Principles: Reflections on the Sources of Moral Dilemmas' in HE Mason (ed), *Moral Dilemmas and Moral Theory* (Oxford University Press 1996)
McConnell T, 'Moral Dilemmas' in Edward N Zalta (ed), *The Stanford Encyclopedia of Philosophy* (Fall edn, 2014) <http://plato.stanford.edu/archives/fall2014/entries/moral-dilemmas/> accessed 27 January 2017
McCormick JP, 'The Dilemmas of Dictatorship: Carl Schmitt and Constitutional Emergency Powers' in David Dyzenhaus (ed), *Law as Politics* (Duke University Press 1998)
McGoldrick D, 'The Interface between Public Emergency Powers and International Law' (2004) 2 International Journal of Constitutional Law 380
McKenna M and Coates DJ, 'Compatibilism' in Edward N Zalta (ed), *The Stanford Encyclopedia of Philosophy* (Summer edn, 2015) <http://plato.stanford.edu/archives/sum2015/entries/compatibilism/> accessed 4 November 2016
Merkel R, '§14 Abs. 3 Luftsicherheitsgesetz: Wann und warum darf der Staat töten?' (2007) 62 JuristenZeitung 373
Merkl A, 'Die Rechtseinheit des österreichischen Staates. Eine staatsrechtliche Untersuchung auf Grund der Lehre von der lex posterior' (1918) 37 Archiv des öffentlichen Rechts 56
Michaels R and Pauwelyn J, 'Conflict of Norms or Conflict of Laws?: Different Techniques in the Fragmentation of Public International Law' (2012) 22 Duke Journal of Comparative & International Law 349
Mik C, 'Jus Cogens in Contemporary International Law' (2013) 33 Polish Yearbook of International Law 27
Milanovic M, 'Norm Conflicts, International Humanitarian Law and Human Rights Law' in Orna Ben-Naftali (ed), *International Humanitarian Law and International Human Rights Law* (Oxford University Press 2011)
Milanovic M, 'The Lost Origins of *Lex Specialis*: Rethinking the Relationship between Human Rights and International Humanitarian Law' in Jens David Ohlin (ed), *Theoretical Boundaries of Armed Conflict and Human Rights* (Cambridge University Press 2016)
Minow M, *Between Vengeance and Forgiveness: Facing History After Genocide and Mass Violence* (Beacon Press 1998)
Möller K, 'Balancing and the Structure of Constitutional Rights' (2007) 5 International Journal of Constitutional Law 453
Möller K, *The Global Model of Constitutional Rights* (Oxford University Press 2012)

Möllers C, *Möglichkeit der Normen: Über eine Praxis jenseits von Moralität und Kausalität* (Suhrkamp 2015)

Morris JHC, 'The Proper Law of Tort' (1951) 64 Harvard Law Review 881

Mothersill M, 'The Moral Dilemmas Debate' in HE Mason (ed), *Moral Dilemmas and Moral Theory* (Oxford University Press 1996)

Nagel T, *Mortal Questions* (Cambridge University Press 1979)

Nagel T, 'War and Massacre' (1972) 1 Philosophy & Public Affairs 123

Navarro PE and Rodríguez JL, *Deontic Logic and Legal Systems* (Cambridge University Press 2014)

Newton M and May L, *Proportionality in International Law* (Oxford University Press 2014)

Nobles R and Schiff D, 'Introduction' in Fatima Kastner and others (eds), Klaus A Ziegert (tr), *Law as a Social System* (Oxford Socio-Legal Studies 2004)

Nobles R and Schiff D, 'Review of Paradoxes and Inconsistencies in the Law by Oren Perez; Gunther Teubner' (2007) 70 The Modern Law Review 505

Nollkaemper A, *National Courts and the International Rule of Law* (Oxford University Press 2012)

Nolte G, 'Thin or Thick? The Principle of Proportionality and International Humanitarian Law' (2010) 4 Law & Ethics of Human Rights 245

Nori F, 'Quantum Football' (2009) 325 Science 689

Nussbaum MC, *The Fragility of Goodness: Luck and Ethics in Greek Tragedy and Philosophy* (Cambridge University Press 2001)

OED Online, OUP (December 2016) <http://www.oed.com>

Orakhelashvili A, *Peremptory Norms in International Law* (Oxford University Press 2006)

Orakhelashvili A, *The Interpretation of Acts and Rules in Public International Law* (Oxford University Press 2008)

Parsons T, 'The Traditional Square of Opposition' in Edward N Zalta (ed), *The Stanford Encyclopedia of Philosophy* (Spring edn, 2014) <http://plato.stanford.edu/archives/spr2014/entries/square/> accessed 24 May 2017

Pasqualucci JM, *The Practice and Procedure of the Inter-American Court of Human Rights* (Cambridge University Press 2012)

Pauwelyn J, 'Bridging Fragmentation and Unity: International Law as a Universe of Inter-Connected Islands' (2003) 25 Michigan Journal of International Law 903

Pauwelyn J, *Conflict of Norms in Public International Law* (Cambridge University Press 2003)

Pauwelyn J, 'Fragmentation' in Rüdiger Wolfrum (ed), *Max Planck Encyclopedia of Public International Law* (Online edn, Max Planck Institute for Comparative Public Law and International Law 2006)

Pauwelyn J, 'The Rule of Law without the Rule of Lawyers? Why Investment Arbitrators Are from Mars, Trade Adjudicators from Venus' (2015) 109 American Journal of International Law 761

Pellet A, 'Article 38' in Andreas Zimmermann and others (eds), *The Statute of the International Court of Justice: A Commentary* (Oxford University Press 2012)

Perez O, 'Law in the Air: A Prologue to the World of Legal Paradoxes' in Oren Perez and Gunther Teubner (eds), *Paradoxes and Inconsistencies in the Law* (Hart 2005)

Peters A, 'Verhältnismäßigkeit als Globales Verfassungsprinzip (Proportionality as a Global Constitutional Principle)' in Björnstern Baade and others (eds), *Verhältnismäßigkeit im Völkerrecht* (Mohr Siebeck 2015)

Popitz H, 'Soziale Normen' (1961) 2 European Journal of Sociology/Archives Européennes de Sociologie 185

Posner EA, *The Perils of Global Legalism* (University of Chicago Press 2009)

Priest G, 'What's So Bad about Contradictions?' in Graham Priest, JC Beall, and Bradley Armour-Garb (eds), *The Law of Non-Contradiction* (Oxford University Press 2004)

Priest G, *In Contradiction* (Oxford University Press 2006)

Priest G, Koji Tanaka, and Zach Weber, 'Paraconsistent Logic' in Edward N Zalta (ed), *The Stanford Encyclopedia of Philosophy* (Winter edn, 2016) <http://plato.stanford.edu/archives/fall2013/entries/logic-paraconsistent/> accessed 17 January 2017

Prud'homme N, 'Lex Specialis: Oversimplifying a More Complex and Multifaceted Relationship' (2007) 40 Israel Law Review 356

Pry PV, *War Scare: Russia and America on the Nuclear Brink* (Greenwood Publishing Group 1999)

Pufendorf S, *The Political Writings of Samuel Pufendorf* (Craig L Carr ed, Michael J Seidler tr, Oxford University Press 1994)

Pulkowski D, *The Law and Politics of International Regime Conflict* (Oxford University Press 2014)

Quane H, 'Silence in International Law' (2014) 84 British Yearbook of International Law 243

Rabello AM, 'Non Liquet: From Modern Law to Roman Law' (2004) 10 Annual Survey of International & Comparative Law 1

Radbruch G, 'Gesetzliches Unrecht und übergesetzliches Recht' (1946) 1(5) Süddeutsche Juristenzeitung 105

Ranganathan S, *Strategically Created Treaty Conflicts and the Politics of International Law* (Cambridge University Press 2014)

Raz J, *Between Authority and Interpretation: On the Theory of Law and Practical Reason* (Oxford University Press 2009)

Raz J, *The Authority of Law: Essays on Law and Morality* (2nd edn, Oxford University Press 2009)

Raz J, *The Morality of Freedom* (Clarendon Press 1986)

Rescher N, *Paradoxes: Their Roots, Range, and Resolution* (Open Court 2001)

Rhodes R, *The Making of the Atomic Bomb* (Simon & Schuster 1986)

Rivers J, 'Proportionality and Discretion in International and European Law' in Nicholas Tsagourias (ed), *Transnational Constitutionalism* (Cambridge University Press 2007)

Robinson D, 'Inescapable Dyads: Why the International Criminal Court Cannot Win' (2015) 28 Leiden Journal of International Law 323

Robinson R, *Definition* (Clarendon Press 1950)

Rödig J, *Die Denkform der Alternative in der Jurisprudenz* (Springer-Verlag 1969)

Romano CPR, 'The Project on International Courts and Tribunals: The International Judiciary in Context (A Synoptic Chart)' <http://www.pict-pcti.org/publications/synoptic_chart/synop_c4.pdf> accessed 27 January 2017

Rosenne S, *Rosenne's the World Court: What It Is and How It Works* (Terry D Gill ed, 6th edn, Martinus Nijhoff 2003)

Rosenne S, *The Law and Practice of the International Court, 1920-2005* (4th edn, Martinus Nijhoff 2006)

Rousseau C, 'De la Compatibilité des Normes Juridiques Contradictoires dans l'Ordre International' (1932) 39 Revue Générale de Droit International Public 133

Salmon J, *Dictionnaire de Droit International Public* (Bruylant 2001)

Sarat A, 'When Can or Should Legal Judgment Be Merciful? An Introduction' in Austin Sarat (ed), *Merciful Judgments and Contemporary Society* (Cambridge University Press 2011)

Schachter O, 'Invisible College of International Lawyers' (1977) 72 Northwestern University Law Review 217

Schauer F, 'Instrumental Commensurability' (1998) 146 University of Pennsylvania Law Review 1215

Scheuerman WE, *Carl Schmitt: The End of Law* (Rowman & Littlefield 1999)

Schill SW, 'Cross-Regime Harmonization through Proportionality Analysis: The Case of International Investment Law, the Law of State Immunity and Human Rights' (2012) 27 ICSID Review 87

Schill SW and Kingsbury B, 'Public Law Concepts to Balance Investors' Rights with State Regulatory Actions in the Public Interest—the Concept of Proportionality' in Stephan W Schill (ed), *International Investment Law and Comparative Public Law* (Oxford University Press 2010)

Schmalenbach K, 'Article 53' in Oliver Dörr and Kirsten Schmalenbach (eds), *Vienna Convention on the Law of Treaties: A Commentary* (Springer 2012)

Schmitt C, *Political Theology: Four Chapters on the Concept of Sovereignty* (University of Chicago Press 1985)

Schmitt MN, 'Fault Lines in the Law of Attack' in Susan C Breau and Agnieszka Jachec-Neale (eds), *Testing the Boundaries of International Humanitarian Law* (British Institute of International & Comparative Law 2006)

Schmitt-Dorotić C, *Die Diktatur: von den Anfängen des modernen Souveränitätsgedankens bis zum proletarischen Klassenkampf* (Duncker & Humblot 1921)

Schneider E, *Logik für Juristen: die Grundlagen der Denklehre und der Rechtsanwendung* (Vahlen 2006)

Schrijver N, 'The Changing Nature of State Sovereignty' (1999) 70 British Yearbook of International Law 65

Schrödinger E, 'Die gegenwärtige Situation in der Quantenmechanik' (1935) 23 Die Naturwissenschaften 807

Schulz H and Basler O, *Deutsches Fremdwörterbuch* (De Gruyter 2004)

Schwarzenberger G, *International Law as Applied by International Courts and Tribunals*, vol 1 (3rd edn, Stevens 1957)

'Scialabba v Cuellar de Osorio' (2014) 128 Harvard Law Review 341

Scott RD, 'Kansas v. Colorado Revisited' (1958) 52 American Journal of International Law 432

Scott T, *Foure Paradoxes of Art. Of Law. Of Warre. Of Service.* (Thomas Snodham 1611)

Shapiro SJ, 'The "Hart-Dworkin" Debate: A Short Guide for the Perplexed' (2007) Working Paper No. 77 Public Law and Legal Theory Working Paper Series

Shaw MA, *International Law* (7th edn, Cambridge University Press 2014)

Shaw MN and Fournet C, 'Article 62' in Olivier Corten and Pierre Klein (eds), *The Vienna Conventions on the Law of Treaties* (Oxford University Press 2011)

Shelton D, 'Normative Hierarchy in International Law' (2006) 100 American Journal of International Law 291

Simma B and Pulkowski D, 'Of Planets and the Universe: Self-Contained Regimes in International Law' (2006) 17 European Journal of International Law 483

Singer JW, *Entitlement: The Paradoxes of Property* (Yale University Press 2000)

Sinnott-Armstrong W, '"Ought" Conversationally Implies "Can"' (1984) XCIII The Philosophical Review 249

Sinnott-Armstrong W, *Moral Dilemmas* (Blackwell 1988)

Siorat L, *Le problème des lacunes en droit international: Contribution à l'étude des sources du droit et de la fonction judiciaire* (Pichon & Durant-Auzias 1958)

Slye RC, 'The Legitimacy of Amnesties under International Law and General Principles of Anglo-American Law: Is a Legitimate Amnesty Possible' (2002) 43 Virginia Journal of International Law 173

Sorensen R, 'Epistemic Paradoxes' in Edward N Zalta (ed), *The Stanford Encyclopedia of Philosophy* (Spring edn, 2014) <http://plato.stanford.edu/archives/spr2014/entries/epistemic-paradoxes/> accessed 24 May 2017

Spiermann O, 'Lotus and the Double Structure of International Legal Argument' in Laurence Boisson de Chazournes and Philippe Sands (eds), *International Law, the International Court of Justice and Nuclear Weapons* (Cambridge University Press 1999)

Statman D, *Moral Dilemmas* (Rodopi 1995)

Stern R, 'Does "Ought" Imply "Can"? And did Kant Think it Does?' (2004) 16 Utilitas 42

Stockholm International Peace Research Institute, *SIPRI Yearbook 2016: Armaments, Disarmament and International Security* (SIPRI Yearbook Series, Oxford University Press 2016)

Stone J, 'Non Liquet and the Function of Law in the International Community' (1959) 35 British Year Book of International Law 124

Stone J, *Legal System and Lawyers' Reasonings* (Stanford University Press 1964)

Stone J, 'Non Liquet and the International Judicial Function' in Chaim Perelman (ed), *Le problème des lacunes en droit* (Bruylant 1968)

Strong TB, 'Foreword' in Carl Schmitt, *Political Theology* (n 359) *Four Chapters on the Concept of Sovereignty* (George Schwab tr, University of Chicago Press 2005)

Styron W, *Sophie's Choice* (Random House 1979)

Sugarman D, 'A Hatred of Disorder: Legal Science, Liberalism and Imperialism' in Peter Fitzpatrick (ed), *Dangerous Supplements: Resistance and Renewal in Jurisprudence* (Pluto Press 1991)

Sylvest C, 'International Law in Nineteenth-Century Britain' (2005) 75 British Yearbook of International Law 9

Szurek S, 'The Notion of Circumstances Precluding Wrongfulness' in James Crawford and others (eds), *The Law of International Responsibility* (Oxford University Press 2010)

Tadros V, *The Ends of Harm: The Moral Foundations of Criminal Law* (Oxford University Press 2011)

Tammelo I, 'On the Logical Openness of Legal Orders: A Modal Analysis of Law with Special Reference to the Logical Status of Non Liquet in International Law' (1959) 8 American Journal of Comparative Law 187

Tammelo I, 'The Test of Inconsistency Between Commonwealth and State Laws' (1957) 30 Australian Law Journal 496

Tams CJ and Sloan J, *The Development of International Law by the International Court of Justice* (Oxford University Press 2013)

Tavernier P, 'Relevance of the Intertemporal Law' in James Crawford and others (eds), *The Law of International Responsibility* (Oxford University Press 2010)

Teubner G (ed), *Dilemmas of Law in the Welfare State* (Walter de Gruyter 1986)

Teubner G, 'Dealing with Paradoxes of Law: Derrida, Luhmann, Wiethölter' in Oren Perez and Gunther Teubner (eds), Ian L Fraser (tr), *Paradoxes and Inconsistencies in the Law* (Hart 2006)

Thirlway H, 'The Nuclear Weapons Advisory Opinions: The Declarations and Separate and Dissenting Opinions' in Laurence Boisson de Chazournes and Philippe Sands (eds), *International Law, the International Court of Justice and Nuclear Weapons* (Cambridge University Press 1999)

Timmermann J, 'Kant und die Lüge aus Pflicht: Zur Auflösung moralischer Dilemmata in einer kantischen Ethik' (2000) 107 Philosophisches Jahrbuch 267

Timmermann J, 'Sollen und Können. "Du kannst, denn du Sollst" und "Sollen impliziert Können" im Vergleich' (2003) 6 Logical Analysis and History of Philosophy 113

Tobler A and Lommatzsch E, 'Soveraineté', *Altfranzösisches Wörterbuch*, vol 9 (Steiner 1973)

Tomuschat C, *International Law: Ensuring the Survival of Mankind on the Eve of a New Century* (Brill 1999)

Tsakyrakis S, 'Proportionality: An Assault on Human Rights?' (2009) 7 International Journal of Constitutional Law 468

Tzanakopoulos A, 'Collective Security and Human Rights' in Erika de Wet and Jure Vidmar (eds), *Hierarchy in International Law: The Place of Human Rights* (Oxford University Press 2012)

Vattel, E de *The Law of Nations* (Luke White 1792)

Veel PEN, 'Incommensurability, Proportionality, and Rational Legal Decision-Making' (2010) 4 Law & Ethics of Human Rights 178

Venzke I, *How Interpretation Makes International Law: On Semantic Change and Normative Twists* (Oxford University Press 2012) 60

Verdross A, 'Eine Antinomie der Rechtstheorie' in Hans R Klecatsky (ed), *Die Wiener Rechtstheoretische Schule* (Franz Steiner 2010)

Verdross A, *Völkerrecht* (5th edn, Springer 1964)

Verdross A and Koeck HF, 'Natural Law: The Tradition of Universal Reason and Authority' in Ronald St John MacDonald and Douglas M Johnston (eds), *The Structure and Process of International Law: Essays in Legal Philosophy, Doctrine, and Theory* (Brill 1986)

Vereshchetin V, 'Is "Deceptive Clarity" Better than "Apparent Indecision" in an Advisory Opinion?' in Emile Yakpo and Tahar Boumedra (eds), *Liber Amicorum—Mohammed Bedjaoui* (Kluwer Law International 1999)

Verhoeven J, 'The Law of Responsibility and the Law of Treaties' in James Crawford, Alain Pellet, and Simon Olleson (eds), *The Law of International Responsibility* (Oxford University Press 2010)

Vermeule A, *Law and the Limits of Reason* (Oxford University Press 2009)

Vidmar J, 'Norm Conflicts and Hierarchy in International Law' in Erika de Wet and Jure Vidmar (eds), *Hierarchy in International Law: The Place of Human Rights* (Oxford University Press 2012)

Villiger ME, *Commentary on the 1969 Vienna Convention on the Law of Treaties* (Brill 2009)

Villiger ME, *Customary International Law and Treaties: A Study of their Interactions and Interrelations, with Special Consideration of the 1969 Vienna Convention on the Law of Treaties* (Brill 1985)

Viñuales JE, *Foreign Investment and the Environment in International Law* (Cambridge University Press 2012)

Vinx L, 'Carl Schmitt' in Edward N Zalta (ed), *The Stanford Encyclopedia of Philosophy* (Spring edn, 2016) <https://plato.stanford.edu/archives/spr2016/entries/schmitt/> accessed 26 January 2017

von Bernstorff J , 'Hans Kelsen on Judicial Law-Making by International Courts and Tribunals: A Theory of Global Judicial Imperialism?' (2015) 14 The Law and Practice of International Courts and Tribunals 35

von Bogdandy A and Venzke I, *In Whose Name? A Public Law Theory of International Adjudication* (Oxford University Press 2014)

von Jhering R, *Geist des römischen Rechts auf den verschiedenen Stufen seiner Entwicklung* (Breitkopf & Härtel 1858)

von Wright GH, *An Essay in Modal Logic* (North-Holland 1951)

von Wright GH, 'Deontic Logic' (1951) 60 Mind 1

von Wright GH, *Norm and Action: A Logical Enquiry* (Routledge & Kegan Paul 1963) 144

von Wright GH, 'Norms, Truth and Logic' in AA Martino (ed), *Deontic Logic, Computational Linguistics, and Legal Information Systems* (North-Holland 1982)

von Wright GH, 'Deontic Logic: A Personal View' (1999) 12 Ratio Juris 26

Vos JA, *The Function of Public International Law* (Springer 2013)

Vranes E, 'Lex Superior, Lex Specialis, Lex Posterior—Zur Rechtsnatur der "Konfliktlösungsregeln"' (2005) 65 Zeitschrift für ausländisches öffentliches Recht und Völkerrecht 391

Vranes E, 'The Definition of "Norm Conflict" in International Law and Legal Theory' (2006) 17 European Journal of International Law 395

Waibel M, 'Interpretive Communities in International Law' in Andrea Bianchi, Daniel Peat, and Matthew Windsor (eds), *Interpretation in International Law* (Oxford University Press 2015)

Waldron J, *Law and Disagreement* (Oxford University Press 1999)

Webber GCN, 'Proportionality, Balancing, and the Cult of Constitutional Rights Scholarship' (2010) 23 Canadian Journal of Law and Jurisprudence 179

Weber M, 'Der Sinn der "Wertfreiheit" der soziologischen und ökonomischen Wissenschaften' *Gesammelte Aufsätze zur Wissenschaftslehre* (Mohr Siebeck 1922)

Weber M, *Wirtschaft und Gesellschaft. Grundriß einer verstehenden Soziologie* (Mohr 1980)

Weber V, *Tugendethik und Kommunitarismus: Individualität, Universalisierung, moralische Dilemmata* (Königshausen & Neumann 2002)

Weeramantry CG, 'Cultural and Ideological Pluralism in Public International Law' in Nisuke Ando, Edward McWhinney and Rüdiger Wolfrum (eds), *Liber Amicorum—Judge Shigeru Oda* (Kluwer Law International 2002)

Weil P, 'Towards Relative Normativity in International Law?' (1983) 77 American Journal of International Law 413

Weil P, '"The Court Cannot Conclude Definitively ..." *Non Liquet* Revisited' (1998) 36 Columbia Journal of Transnational Law 109

Weinberger O, *Rechtslogik* (Duncker & Humblot 1989)

Welzel H, 'Zum Notstandsproblem' (1951) 63 Zeitschrift für die gesamte Strafrechtswissenschaft 47

Wetzel RG and Rauschning D, *The Vienna Convention on the Law of Treaties: Travaux Préparatoires* (Metzner 1978)

Wiederin E, 'Was ist und welche Konsequenzen hat ein Normenkonflikt?' (1990) 21 Rechtstheorie 311

Wiethölter R, 'Begriffs- oder Interessenjurisprudenz—Falsche Fronten im IPR und Wirtschaftsverfassungsrecht: Bemerkungen zur Selbstgerechten Kollisionsnorm' in Alexander Lüderitz and Jochen Schröder (eds), *Festschrift für Gerhard Kegel* (1977)

Williams B, *Problems of the Self: Philosophical Papers 1956-1972* (Cambridge University Press 1976)

Williams S, 'A Feminist View of Mercy, Judgment and the "Exception" in the Context of Transitional Justice' in Austin Sarat (ed), *Merciful Judgments and Contemporary Society* (Cambridge University Press 2011)

Winter F, Heiko Rauhut, and Dirk Helbig, 'How Norms Can Generate Conflict: An Experiment on the Failure of Cooperative Micro-Motives on the Macro-Level' (2012) 90 Social Forces 919

Wolfrum R, 'Sources of International Law' in Rüdiger Wolfrum (ed), *Max Planck Encyclopedia of Public International Law* (Online edn, Max Planck Institute for Comparative Public Law and International Law 2011)

Wolfrum R and Matz N, *Conflicts in International Environmental Law* (Springer 2003)

Wolitz D, 'Indeterminacy, Value Pluralism, and Tragic Cases' (2014) 62 Buffalo Law Review 529

Wyrozumska A, 'Poland' in Dinah Shelton (ed), *International Law and Domestic Legal Systems* (Oxford University Press 2011)

Zarmanian T, 'Carl Schmitt and the Problem of Legal Order: From Domestic to International' (2006) 19 Leiden Journal of International Law 41

Zuleeg M, 'Vertragskonkurrenz im Völkerrecht. Teil I: Verträge zwischen souveränen Staaten' (1977) 20 German Yearbook of International Law 246

Index

Previously Published in the Oxford Monographs in International Law Series

1987

1. **The Exclusive Economic Zone in International Law**
   David Joseph Attard
2. **Judicial Remedies in International Law**
   Christine Gray
3. **Occupation, Resistance, and Law**
   International Law on Military Occupations and on Resistance
   Adam Roberts

1988

4. **The Juridical Bay**
   Gayl Shaw Westerman
5. **The Legality of Non-Forcible Counter-Measures in International Law**
   Omer Yousif Elagab
6. **State Responsibility and the Marine Environment**
   The Rules of Decision
   Brian D. Smith
7. **The Shatt-Al-Arab Boundary Question**
   A Legal Reappraisal
   Kaiyan Homi Kaikobad

1989

8. **Relevant Circumstances and Maritime Delimitation**
   Malcolm D. Evans

1990

9. **Land-Locked and Geographically Disadvantaged State in the International Law of the Sea**
   Stephen C. Vasciannie

1991

10. **Surrender, Occupation, and Private Property in International Law**
    An Evaluation of US Practice in Japan
    Nisuke Ando

1992

11. **Human Rights in States of Emergency in International Law**
Jaime Oraá

12. **China's Practice in the Law of the Sea**
Jeanette Greenfield

1993

13. **Third Parties in International Law**
C. M. Chinkin

14. **The International Law of Maritime Boundaries and the Practice of States in the Mediterranean Sea**
Faraj Abdullah Ahnish

15. **Human Rights in the Private Sphere**
Andrew Clapham

1994

16. **The Human Rights Committee**
Its Role in the Development of the International Covenant on Civil and Political Rights
Dominic McGoldrick

17. **The New International Law of Fisheries**
UNCLOS 1982 and Beyond
William T. Burke

1995

18. **The Termination and Revision of Treaties in the Light of New Customary International Law**
Nancy Kontou

19. **The International Covenant on Economic, Social, and Cultural Rights**
A Perspective on its Development
Matthew C. R. Craven

20. **International Management of Hazardous Wastes**
The Basel Convention and Related Legal Rules
Katharina Kummer

1996

21. **Land and Maritime Zones of Peace in International Law**
Surya P. Subedi

1997

22. **Self Determination and National Minorities**
Thomas D. Musgrave

1998

23. **Recognition of Governments in International Law**
With Particular Reference to Governments in Exile
Stefan Talmon

24. **Naval Weapons Systems and the Contemporary Law of War**
James J. Busuttil

1999

25. **The United Nations and the Development of Collective Security**
The Delegation by the UN Security Council and its Chapter VII Powers
Danesh Sarooshi

26. **International Law and Infectious Diseases**
David P. Fidler

2000

27. **Human Rights Standards and the Movement of People Within States**
Chaloka Beyani

28. **The Responsibility of States for International Crimes**
Nina H. B. Jørgensen

29. **State Responsibility for Transboundary Air Pollution in International Law**
Phoebe N. Okowa

2001

30. **Just War or Just Peace?**
International Law and Humanitarian Intervention
Simon Chesterman

31. **Towards an International Criminal Procedure**
Christoph J. M. Safferling

32. **The Law of International Watercourses**
Non-Navigational Uses
Stephen McCaffrey

2003

33. **International Criminal Justice and the International Criminal Court**
Between Sovereignty and the Rule of Law
Bruce Broomhall

34. **Human Rights in International Criminal Proceedings**
Salvatore Zappalà

35. **Universal Jurisdiction**
International and Municipal Legal Perspectives
Luc Reydams

36. **International Human Rights and Islamic Law**
Mashood A. Baderin

2005

37. **International Organizations and their Exercise of Sovereign Powers**
Dan Sarooshi

2006

38. **Differential Treatment in International Environmental Law**
Lavanya Rajamani

39. **Peremptory Norms in International Law**
Alexander Orakhelashvili

40. **Defining Terrorism in International Law**
Ben Saul

2007

41. **Complementary Protection in International Refugee Law**
Jane McAdam

42. **Investment Treaty Arbitration and Public Law**
Gus Van Harten

43. **The Decolonization of International Law**
State Succession and the Law of Treaties
Matthew Craven

2008

44. **Human Rights and Non-Discrimination in the 'War on Terror'**
Daniel Moeckli

45. **Diplomatic Protection**
Chittharanjan F. Amerasinghe

46. **The Immunity of States and their Officials in International Criminal Law and International Human Rights Law**
Rosanne van Alebeek

47. **The Fair and Equitable Treatment Standard in the International Law of Foreign Investment**
Ioana Tudor

48. **Targeted Killing in International Law**
Nils Melzer

49. **The Interpretation of Acts and the Rules in Public International Law**
Alexander Orakhelashvili

50. **Jurisdiction in International Law**
Cedric Ryngaert

2009

51. **The Collective Responsibility of States to Protect Refugees**
Agnès Hurwitz

2010

52. **Extraterritorial Use of Force Against Non-State Actors**
Noam Lubell

2011

53. **Maritime Security and the Law of the Sea**
Natalie Klein

54. **Disobeying the Security Council**
Countermeasures Against Wrongful Sanctions
Antonios Tzanakopoulos

55. **State Responsibility for International Terrorism**
Problems and Prospects
Kimberley N. Trapp

56. **Extraterritorial Application of Human Rights Treaties**
Law, Principles, and Policy
Marko Milanovic

57. **Formalism and the Source of International Law**
A Theory of the Ascertainment of Legal Rules
Jean d'Aspremont

2012

58. **Individual Criminal Responsibility in International Law**
Elies van Sliedregt

59. **The Margin of Appreciation in International Human Rights Law**
Deference and Proportionality
Andrew Legg

2013

60. **The International Minimum Standard and Fair and Equitable Treatment**
Martins Paparinskis

61. **Applicable Law in Investor-State Arbitration**
The Interplay Between National and International Law
Hege Elisabeth Kjos

62. **A Contemporary Concept of Monetary Sovereignty**
Claus D. Zimmermann

63. **Corporate Obligations Under International Law**
Markos Karavias

2014

64. Economic, Social, and Cultural Rights in Armed Conflict
Gilles Giacca

2015

65. Complicity in International Law
Miles Jackson

66. Treaties on Transit of Energy via Pipelines and Countermeasures
Danae Azaria

67. Jurisdiction in International Law
Second Edition
Cedric Ryngaert

2016

68. The Power of Process
The Value of Due Process in Security Council Sanctions Decision-Making
Devika Hovell

69. Institutionalizing State Responsibility
Global Security and UN Organs
Vincent-Joël Proulx